'Undetermined' Ukrainians

NATIONALISMS ACROSS THE GLOBE

VOL. 11

PETER LANG
Oxford · Bern · Berlin · Bruxelles · Frankfurt am Main · New York · Wien

Olesya Khromeychuk

'Undetermined' Ukrainians

Post-War Narratives of the Waffen SS 'Galicia' Division

PETER LANG
Oxford · Bern · Berlin · Bruxelles · Frankfurt am Main · New York · Wien

Bibliographic information published by Die Deutsche Nationalbibliothek.
Die Deutsche Nationalbibliothek lists this publication in the Deutsche Nationalbibliografie; detailed bibliographic data is available on the Internet at http://dnb.d-nb.de.

A catalogue record for this book is available from the British Library.

Library of Congress Cataloging-in-Publication Data:

Khromeychuk, Olesya, 1983-
"Undetermined" Ukrainians : postwar narratives of the Waffen SS "Galicia" Division / Olesya Khromeychuk.
pages cm. -- (Nationalisms across the globe ; 11)
Includes bibliographical references and index.
ISBN 978-3-0343-0874-8 (alk. paper)
1. Waffen-SS. Grenadier-Division, 14--History. 2. Ukraïns'ka natsional'na armiia. Ukraïns'ka dyviziia "Halychyna"--History. 3. Ukraine--History--German occupation, 1941-1944. 4. Ukrainians--Canada--Ethnic identity. 5. Ukraine--Emigration and immigration--History--20th century. 6. Collective memory--Ukraine. 7. Nationalism and collective memory--Ukraine. 8. World War, 1939-1945--Regimental histories--Germany. 9. World War, 1939-1945--Regimental histories--Ukraine. I. Title.
D757.85.K46 2013
940.54'134770922--dc23

2013004830

Cover image © NASA/Goddard Space Flight Center Scientific Visualization Studio

ISSN 1662-9116
ISBN 978-3-0343-0874-8

Hochfeldstrasse 32, CH-3012 Bern, Switzerland
info@peterlang.com, www.peterlang.com, www.peterlang.net

Printed in Germany

Contents

Acknowledgements

It is a great pleasure to thank everyone who made this book possible. First of all, I would like to express my sincere gratitude to Dennis Deletant and Catherine Andreyev for offering their guidance and support in every step of my research. I would also like to thank Peter Duncan and Marko Bojcun for their insightful comments. I am indebted to all interviewees who contributed to this study. I wish to thank Alti Rodal for permission to cite her work. I am indebted to my colleagues and friends Alisa Voznaya and Oleksandr Mel'nyk, whose suggestions and ideas were used to improve the book. I sincerely thank Michael James Melnyk for the time he took to comment on the earlier draft of the book. I am grateful to David Marples for contributing the foreword to this monograph and setting the subject of the Waffen SS 'Galicia' Division in a larger context. Particular thanks to Rory Finnin for his encouragement, inspiration and support. The publication of this book was made possible thanks to the support of Cambridge Ukrainian Studies to whom I am most grateful. My very special thanks go to Uilleam Blacker for his patience, priceless ideas and most helpful comments on the many drafts of the book. I am most grateful to all my colleagues for their comments and for providing stimulating discussions on many aspects of war and memory as well as other issues inseparable from historical research. Last but not least, I would like to thank my family, my parents, Olha and Yuriy, for providing a supportive environment for me.

Acronyms and Abbreviations

1st UD UNA	1-a Ukraïns'ka Dyviziia Ukraïns'koï Natsional'noï Armiï, 1st Ukrainian Division of the Ukrainian National Army.
AUGB	Association of Ukrainians in Great Britain.
CROWCASS	Central Registry of War Criminals and Security Suspects.
CURB	Central Ukrainian Relief Bureau.
DP	Displaced Person.
DUN	Druzhyny ukraïns'kykh natsionalistiv, Legion of Ukrainian Nationalists.
EVW	European Voluntary Workers.
HIAG	Hilfsorganisation auf Gegenseitigkeit der ehemaligen Angehörigen der Waffen-SS, Mutual Support Organization of Former Members of the Waffen SS.
Hiwi	Hilfswillige, voluntary assistant.
IGCR	Intergovernmental Committee on Refugees.
IRO	International Refugee Organization.
NA	National Archives, UK.
NKVD	Narodnyi komissariat vnutrennikh del, People's Commissariat for Interior Affairs.
OKW	Oberkommando der Wehrmacht, German Supreme Command of the Armed Forces.
Orpo	Ordnungspolizei or Order Police, regular uniformed German police.
OUN	Orhanizatsiia ukraïns'kykh natsionalistiv, Organization of Ukrainian Nationalists. (OUN-B: Stepan Bandera's branch; OUN-M: Andrii Mel'nyk's branch).

POW	Prisoner of War.
ROA	Russkaia osvoboditel'naia armiia, Russian Liberation Army.
RONA	Russkaia osvoboditel'naia narodnaia armiia, Russian Liberation People's Army.
SA	Sturmabteilung, 'Storm Detachment' or assault division.
SEP	Surrendered Enemy Personnel.
SS	Schutzstaffel, 'Protection Squadron' or defence corps.
UNDO	Ukraïns'ke natsional'no-demokratychne ob'iednannia, Ukrainian National-Democratic Alliance.
UNR	Ukraïns'ka Narodna Respublika, Ukrainian People's Republic.
UNWCC	United Nations War Crimes Commission also known as United Nations Commission for the Investigation of War Crimes.
UPA	Ukraïns'ka povstans'ka armiia, Ukrainian Insurgent Army.
UTsK	Ukraïns'kyi tsentral'nyi komitet, Ukrainischen Hauptausschuß, Ukrainian Central Committee.
UVO	Ukraïns'ka viis'kova orhanizatsiia, Ukrainian Military Organization.
UVV	Ukraïns'ke Vyzvol'ne Viis'ko, Ukrainische Befreiungsarmee, Ukrainian Liberation Army.
ZUNR	Zakhidnoukraïns'ka Narodna Respublika, Western Ukrainian People's Republic.

List of Illustrations

Foreword

Olesya Khromeychuk has written a very important book. At first glance, that statement might not be immediately obvious to the reader. The topic is not one with which many people will be deeply familiar. The formation of the Galicia Division occurred in central Europe in the latter part of the Second World War, at a time when the German army was on the retreat, and the return of the Red Army to lands that were contested between Poles and Ukrainians was all but inevitable. The volunteers – and she makes clear there were many of them – were essentially expressing their willingness to sign up for a unit that would serve a notorious military organization, the Waffen SS. Most of them died subsequently at the Battle of Brody. Why then would an author focus on this ostensibly peripheral army unit, which failed to make a serious impact on the war, even after its eventual reformation and use for other duties by the German authorities, and which today is identified by many with collaborationism and war crimes? And why would a young author write her first major academic publication on this subject?

A few years ago when writing my book *Heroes and Villains: Creating National History in Contemporary Ukraine*,[1] I discussed the competing narratives about Ukraine's past, and particularly in the Second World War (or Great Patriotic War to use the former Soviet term). That book appeared five years ago, but subsequently the tempo of the debate increased sharply. And it did so on a number of levels. One can divide these into the following: debates between scholars; debates at the state level as the Ukrainian leadership sought to define its *raison d'etre* and the part played by 'freedom fighters' for an independent Ukraine during the Second World War; and at what might be termed the popular level, meaning, largely, the Ukrainian

1 David R. Marples, *Heroes and Villains: Creating National History in Contemporary Ukraine* (Budapest: Central European University Press, 2008).

diaspora in a number of countries in Europe and North America using the media or public lectures. These discussions have been partly useful and partly destructive. I will take some space here to comment on them further because they form the backdrop to this monograph.

Usually when scholars begin to discuss what one might term 'the Battle for Memory' in Ukraine, they begin with former president Viktor Yushchenko (2005–10), who was instrumental in designating two national figures of the western regions, Roman Shukhevych and Stepan Bandera, as 'heroes of Ukraine.' But this is an error. The conflict predates Yushchenko and posed a problem for Ukraine's earlier leaders as well. The first difficulty was the role of Soviet historiography and propaganda in determining that such figures were traitors to their nation and, equally important, collaborators with the German occupation forces at various times. The term 'Banderite' after all was one of the most frequent terms of abuse directed at enemies of the USSR, alongside the equally virulent 'bourgeois nationalist'. The USSR also not only demanded the return after the war of displaced persons who were members of nationalist units, but also pursued a protracted campaign to bring war criminals to justice, providing evidence for those agencies in the West and Israel that were embarked on such campaigns.

The Soviet quest instantly created polemics from recent history and polarized public opinion. That many war criminals were at large in Western countries is well established. But it was also evident that the Soviets were not averse to taking irrational steps to find and convict them, including at one point, assembling entire villages of Ukraine to hear information about their alleged crimes – partly in the expectation that before long investigators would arrive in these villages to ask questions about the collaborators in question. In short, the issue was openly politicized. With the collapse of the Soviet Union in December 1991, the Ukrainian leadership, which included many of those prominent in the late Soviet period, faced a dilemma: how to approach the past, what to teach schoolchildren, and what should be included in school textbooks and those approved for the higher educational system? There were discussions, conferences, official commissions of historians, not only on the war years, but also, most notably, on the Famine of 1932–3. But few definitive conclusions were reached.

Thus when Yushchenko became president following the Orange Revolution, Ukraine was a confused nation, divided in opinion and torn politically between those who wished to promote a version of the war that continued to highlight the triumphs of the Red Army and those who preferred to laud the small bands who resisted it, such as the Ukrainian Insurgent Army and its mentor and founder, the Bandera wing of the Organization of Ukrainian Nationalists. At that time, there was little mention of the Waffen SS Division Galicia. Even Yushchenko could not bring himself to go so far as to include this group in his acts of rehabilitation. The president's motivations in making first Shukhevych and later Bandera 'Heroes of Ukraine' were unclear. The title was a Soviet device, which linked modern Ukraine to the past. Not surprisingly some of Ukraine's reputable historians wondered why the president would see fit to use it in the modern 'post-Orange' era when such ties were seemingly being severed. Most likely, there were both ideological and political reasons for him to do so. The elevation of Bandera in particular appeared to be an attempt to revive Yushchenko's fading popularity in the western regions of Ukraine.

But such an action could no longer be taken in isolation, as in Soviet times. Ukraine's neighbor Poland (along with Jewish organizations worldwide) was the most vocal critic, citing the massacres in Volhynia carried out in the spring and summer of 1943 by members of UPA, initiated by followers of Bandera.[2] Poland duly persuaded the European Union, which it had joined just six years earlier, to condemn the designation. At that point, Ukraine's nationalist past became globalized. Olesya Khromeychuk cites the ensuing debates in this book because they form the background to her decision to reopen the question of the Galicia Division. I would

2 Jeffrey Burds has commented that 'One of the greatest obstacles to understanding the history of Galicia during the Second World War has been that the memory of the events themselves have been constructed ethnically – which is to say, each ethnic group has recorded their own versions of the tragic devastation of that era.' Jeffrey Burds, 'Comments on Timothy Snyder's article "To Resolve the Ukrainian Question Once and for All: The Ethnic Cleansing of Ukrainians in Poland, 1943–1947", *Journal of Cold War Studies*, Vol. 1. No. 2 (Spring 1999)', <www.fas.harvard.edu/~hpcws/comment13.htm> accessed 30 January 2013.

like to take advantage of my privileged position here to add some personal comments, which also help to explain why I think her book is so important. Three years ago, my local city newspaper asked me to write an article about Yushchenko's decision to make Bandera a Hero of Ukraine. Since I wrote regularly for this outlet, the request was not exceptional but for the fact that rarely before had it suggested the subject matter of my topics. It transpired that it had received another editorial on the same topic that it considered 'too extreme' to publish.

I attempted, naively perhaps, to write an objective account of the life of Bandera in an 800-word format. The response was so rapid, virulent, and spontaneous that it shocked me. One writer wrote that I had maligned Ukrainians, which was the furthest thing from my mind. The then director of the Canadian Institute of Ukrainian Studies wrote a letter to the paper condemning my article. Another colleague defended me.[3] That article followed me all the way to Australia, where a member of the audience raised it during a talk on the Ukrainian presidential elections in Adelaide. Obviously the topic raised extreme emotions. It was not possible to detach Bandera from those who admired him any more than it would have been feasible to suggest to the former Soviet authorities that they had adopted a one-sided stance on the issue of Ukrainian nationalism. I later compared this perspective of Bandera to the reverence with which Winston Churchill, the British wartime leader, is held in Britain and several other countries. It is not a fair comparison, however, because Ukraine in this period was not a nation and the regions from which Bandera came had fought a quasi-war with the Polish authorities for about a decade before the Second World War broke out.

In January 2010, Viktor Yanukovych became the new president of Ukraine. He appointed as Minister of Education and Science, Youth and

3 John-Paul Himka described the exchanges in a 2010 article in *Ab Imperio*. See John-Paul Himka, 'The Organization of Ukrainian Nationalists and the Ukrainian Insurgent Army: Unwelcome Elements of an Identity Project', *Ab Imperio*, 4 (2010), 83–101 <http://www.academia.edu/499198/The_Organization_of_Ukrainian_Nationalists_and_the_Ukrainian_Insurgent_Army_Unwelcome_Elements_of_an_Identity_Project> accessed 30 January 2013.

Sports, Dmytro Tabachnyk, a man with a doctorate in history who had derided overtly Western Ukrainians, mocked the Ukrainian language, and vindicated some of the worst excesses of the Stalin regime in Ukraine. Although his outlook proved extreme even to the leaders of the ruling Party of Regions, the appointment signified at least a partial reversal of the positions adopted by Yushchenko on nationalist heroes. Official Soviet commemorations such as Victory Day were restored, leading to skirmishes in cities like L'viv, where monuments had been raised to Bandera, and streets named after him. But while the emergent nation wrestled with its past, the conflicts in Ukraine spilled over into the academic world, as well as to the diaspora, which rigorously defended its traditional heroes, and argued that the new interpretations of the war in their ancestral home was simply a reinstatement of the former Soviet views, i.e. the scholars in question were no better than agents of the former KGB. Further, there was hostile interaction between some of the defenders of wartime nationalists prominent in the Yushchenko period and Western scholars, who derided and deplored their writings.

Retrospectively, I have concluded that these heated debates have been too divisive, despite some advances in delineating the 'truth' about war crimes and concerning the role of Ukrainian nationalists in the Jewish Holocaust, and how one should regard events in modern Ukraine such as the rise of the Svoboda Party in the 2012 parliamentary elections. One of my brightest former graduate students has commented to me that he has been dissuaded from a career in academia precisely because he has no wish to enter the minefield of his thesis topic, which pertains to Ukraine in the Second World War. This has been a rather lengthy digression. But I wanted to explain from my own perspective the incendiary background to the general area of the study of Ukrainian wartime nationalism. In other words, and sometimes from the best of motives, recent scholarship has approached the debate on wartime nationalism less from a detached standpoint and more frequently with the sort of frenzied righteousness with which their opponents have defended figures like Bandera, or the Soviet authorities used to seek out former Nazi collaborators who had fought against them in the latter part of the war. Ultimately, such an approach is self-negating because of the inflammatory language applied. Perhaps then we have reached a point of no return, at which accusatory language becomes so familiar that it is no longer startling or helpful to the general reader. Ultimately, it reaches the stage at which it ceases to be useful.

The present study, in my view, adopts a new and refreshing approach to a topic that I considered quite recently to be 'beyond the pale'. When I met Olesya recently in Cambridge, I told her that the topic of her book was 'courageous', reminiscent of the phrase of the fictitious civil servant Sir Humphrey Appleby in the BBC series, *Yes Minister*, when he considers a policy to be particularly ill-advised. Having read the book, I am persuaded that it is not only courageous, but also very much needed, an antidote to the current debates and one that demonstrates that a new approach to Ukrainian wartime nationalism is possible. Without minimizing the crimes of some of its members (indeed they are expressly stated), the author has forged a new path by looking at the subject differently and in a contextual manner that deserves to be applied more widely. The book highlights the diversity of reasons why Ukrainians volunteered to join the unit in the spring of 1943, and how its membership changed over time. Through interviews in Ukrainian, she has ascertained such motives. She has also examined why and how the members of the Division were able to find their way into the UK after the war. At one point, she notes, the British had no designation of what constituted a *Ukrainian*. She also shows the limited nature of investigations of the background of individual soldiers by the Deschênes Commission in Canada in the 1980s, as well as others.

Ultimately, perhaps the overriding lesson to be learned here is that one needs to discover the motives behind actions that later appear to be cynical or political. Why in Galicia in 1943 would young men be willing to swear allegiance to Adolf Hitler? Why would such a formation receive support from the Ukrainian Catholic Metropolitan Andriy Sheptyts'kyi? It may not be possible to find out definitive answers to every question, but one can be persuaded at least that not all those who volunteered to join a new army did so because of base motives or because they wanted to defend Hitler's Germany. It would have been evident to most of them that the Nazi Empire was crumbling and that the Red Army would reappear in these lands before long. The very term 'nationalism' is in some circles derisory today and it is not one that I would ever wish to apply to myself.

But it was the defining motive of much of late nineteenth- and twentieth-century history, it lay behind brutal conflicts, and it was the rationale for Hitler to establish a German empire on Slavic lands from the outset of the war. It had become more popular in Galicia following the failure of the Paris peace treaties to recognize independence or even autonomy for one of the largest ethnic groups in post-First World War Europe, the Ukrainians. And ultimately an extreme form was embraced after other methods and political affiliations had been tried and failed – the short-lived Ukrainian People's Republic of 1918 (UNR), Communism, the parliamentary system of the Polish Sejm, etc.

Thus from my perspective, Olesya has achieved something I didn't think possible until very recently. She has found a third mode of inquiry between two antithetical standpoints, and one that manages to conduct an investigation without adopting a strong political stance or particular viewpoint. And she has done so without denying her own Ukrainian background – she could hardly have conducted the interviews otherwise – or the crimes committed by some Division members. Though this book has been published in the West, its approach would be especially beneficial to those in Ukraine who have struggled to deal with the wartime past for the past twenty-one years without reaching any kind of consensus. One cannot sweep war crimes under the carpet; but little is to be achieved by blanket condemnations either. Scholarship should not be, or at least should not exclusively be, a war by diction. During warfare, people do not act the same way as in peacetime. Some commit gross crimes, others are persuaded to do likewise, others try to defend what they believe is right, others – perhaps the majority – have no strong opinions and are caught between powers that threaten them and force them to reach a decision. The complexity of their situation is well represented here, in the first book by a new scholar who has opted to circumvent current debates and offer something new.

— DAVID R. MARPLES
University of Alberta, Edmonton, Canada

Introduction

Collaboration with the Third Reich during the Second World War continues to provoke debate throughout the world. The topic is especially emotionally charged in those societies that had to readdress their national identities after the collapse of the Soviet Union. For much of Eastern and Central Europe, memory of the Second World War is not only about coming to terms with the trauma of the Holocaust, large-scale destruction and mass civilian and military casualties; it is also about dealing with the legacy of complex, brutal ethnic conflicts and cleansings, and histories of failed attempts to secure political sovereignty. The history of the Second World War in the region that Timothy Snyder has called the 'bloodlands'[1] is further complicated by the collaboration of the local population with the Nazis.

During the Second World War a large number of Eastern Europeans joined the German Armed Forces. Among them were Russians, Croatians, Bosnians, Slovenes, Serbs, Bulgarians and others.[2] Around 200,000 Ukrainians served in the Wehrmacht, the Waffen SS, the Luftwaffe and other formations within the German Armed Forces.[3] However, the best-known German formations that consisted of self-identified Ukrainians

1 Timothy Snyder, *Bloodlands. Europe between Hitler and Stalin* (London: Bodley Head, 2010).

2 Wolfdieter Bihl, 'Ukrainians in the Armed Forces of the Reich: the 14th *Waffen* Grenadier Division of the SS', in Hans-Joachim Torke and John-Paul Himka (eds), *German-Ukrainian Relations in Historical Perspective* (Edmonton: Canadian Institute of Ukrainian Studies Press, 1994), pp. 138–62 (p. 138). The Eastern Troops commander General Ernst Köstring in October 1944 estimated that there were over 800,000 Eastern volunteers in the German Army, and 100,000 in the Luftwaffe and Navy. See Andrii Bolianovskyi, *Ukraïns'ki viis'kovi formuvannia v zbroinykh sylakh Nimechchyny (1939–1945)* (L'viv: LNU im. Ivana Franka, 2003), p. 583.

3 See Bolianovskyi, *Ukraïns'ki viis'kovi formuvannia*, p. 583.

were the relatively small Wehrmacht battalions, *Nachtigall* and *Roland*, totalling about 800 men, and the Waffen SS 'Galicia' Division,[4] which throughout its existence consisted of on average 11,000 men.[5] While some Ukrainians joined the German Armed Forces as Soviet prisoners of war with little choice before them, others enlisted in German formations voluntarily, arguably because of their Ukrainian nationalist and anti-Soviet motivations. The Waffen SS 'Galicia' Division, which is the focus of this book, belongs to the latter group.

The controversy around the Waffen SS 'Galicia' Division lies largely in its post-war history; and particularly in the decision of the British authorities not to repatriate the Division to the USSR in the aftermath of the Second World War. Although there are still disagreements as to the exact activities of the 'Galicia' with regard to its alleged participation in war crimes, the involvement of the Division in action has been described in detail both by those who served in the formation and those who have researched its history. This book seeks to address the unresolved controversy of the Division's post-war history by examining why 8,000 Ukrainian men who fought in the Waffen SS were allowed to settle in the West as civilians.

4 The original name of the Division was *14 Waffen-Grenadier-Division der SS (galizische Nr 1)*. In Ukrainian, it is usually referred to as *Dyviziia* (the Division) or *Dyviziia 'Halychyna'* (the 'Galicia' Division) and sometimes as *SS Strilets'ka Dyviziia Halychyna* (the SS Riflemen Division Galicia). This monograph will refer to it as the 'Galicia' Division or the Waffen SS 'Galicia'. The official name of the Division underwent a number of changes, which played an important role in post-war narrative creation; they will be discussed later in the book. Here and elsewhere in the monograph, the Library of Congress transliteration system is used for Cyrillic text, including Russian and Ukrainian languages (apart from some proper names where a different spelling is conventional). Unless otherwise indicated, all translations from Ukrainian, Russian or Polish are mine.

5 Wolf-Dietrich Heike estimates that in the autumn of 1944 the 'Galicia' accounted for 22,000 men, including the reserve regiment. (See Wolf-Dietrich Heike, *Ukraïns'ka Dyviziia Halychyna: Istoriia formuvannia i boiovykh dii u 1943–45* (Toronto: Zapysky/Naukove tovarystvo im. Shevchenka, 1970), p. 124). The number of 'Galicians' who found themselves in the Surrendered Enemy Personnel camp in 1947 was 8,272 men. (See UK National Archives (NA) HO/213/1851, Screening Commission Report, 21 February 1947. Original reference LACAB/18/RSC/RIC.)

Unsurprisingly, the story of the 'Galicia' has fascinated a great number of authors, both historians and members of the Division. Some based their accounts on individual testimonies, while others relied on archival material, each writing their own vision of the truth about the Waffen SS 'Galicia'. The second task of this monograph is to analyse how the numerous, often conflicting narratives about the Division came to exist and evolve and what influence they had on the members of the Division, those who came in contact with them and those who took interest in the Division after the war and continue to do so to the present day. It is inevitable that, by analysing the existing narratives, this book will form a narrative of its own; yet instead of following the well-trodden paths of attempting to justify or condemn the Division's actions, this study will employ a microhistorical approach to the analysis of narratives, relating them to the lived experience of the narrators as well as the larger contexts in which their stories are set. This approach will be used to examine memoirs, interview testimonies, secondary data as well as the archival reports, in order to address the complexity of the 'Galician' phenomenon.

Historical and Historiographical Background

The Waffen SS 'Galicia' was founded by the governor of the Galicia district, Otto Gustav von Wächter[6] in April 1943 as a front-line division and originally recruited residents of the Galicia district (part of the *Generalgouvernement*).[7] The main body of the Waffen SS 'Galicia' Division

6 Otto Gustav von Wächter (1901–49) was an Austrian lawyer who later became an SS officer and the governor of the Kraków administrative district in 1939 and the Galicia district in 1942. After the war, Wächter lived in Rome under a false name and thus escaped the Nuremberg Trials.

7 The *Generalgouvernement* was an administrative region of the Third Reich. It included much of central and southern Poland. The region of eastern Galicia was incorporated into the *Generalgouvernement* in 1941.

entered combat in July 1944 in what has become known as the Battle of Brody. Following the battle, the 'Galicia' Division suffered great losses and had to be reformed using around 3,000 survivors, as well as reserve personnel and recruits from other military formations.[8] Once reformed, the 'Galicia' was deployed in Slovakia fighting a military revolt.[9] It was later moved to Slovenia to participate in anti-partisan operations. The Division then returned to the frontline to fight against the Red Army on the Austro-Slovenian border.[10] In May 1945 the 'Galicia' surrendered to the Western Allies.

The 'Galicia' was one of thirty-eight Waffen SS divisions. Similar formations consisted of Croats, Bosnians, Latvians, Estonians, Belarusians and others and existed all over Europe. The 'Galicia' membership accounts for around ten per cent of all ethnic Ukrainians who served in the German Armed Forces during the Second World War.[11] Although the Division presented itself as fighting for Ukrainian independence, its place in the nationalist state-building mythology is of far less significance than that of the Ukrainian Insurgent Army.[12] Nevertheless, the history of the Division forms one of the most controversial and the least studied pages of Ukrainian

8 See Michael James Melnyk, *To Battle. The Formation and History of the 14th Galician Waffen-SS Division* (Solihull: Helion & Company, 2002), pp. 149–95.

9 See Andrii Bolianovs'kyi, *Dyviziia 'Halychyna'. Istoria* (L'viv: IU, 2000), pp. 270–81.

10 See Marc J. Rikmenspoel, *Waffen-SS Encyclopaedia* (Bedford, PA: The Aberjona Press, 2004), pp. 35–6. For more information on these military engagements of the 'Galicia', see Melnyk, *To Battle*, Bolianovs'kyi, *Dyviziia 'Halychyna'* and Heike, *Ukraïns'ka Dyviziia Halychyna*.

11 See Bolianovskyi, *Ukraïns'ki viis'kovi formuvannia*.

12 The Ukrainian Insurgent Army (*Ukraïns'ka Povstans'ka Armiia*, UPA) was the largest Ukrainian nationalist paramilitary resistance group during the Second World War. The question of the Organization of Ukrainian Nationalists (OUN) and the Ukrainian Insurgent Army has received much attention in recent years in both academic and public debates. While the OUN, UPA and the 'Galicia' Division are part of the larger discussion on the collaboration of Ukrainians during the Second World War, each formation merits a separate study and entails rather different questions. This study alone cannot address all aspects of such complex organizations as the UPA and OUN and will thus limit its reference to them only when it is relevant to the question of the Waffen SS 'Galicia' Division.

participation in the Second World War. Its uniqueness lies in a number of factors. The 'Galicia' is different from other Ukrainian nationalist organizations because throughout its existence it was part of the German Army. It stands out among the formations of the German Armed Forces which recruited Ukrainians because the majority of its members joined voluntarily.[13] Unlike most Waffen SS divisions, the Waffen SS 'Galicia' was formed to fight exclusively on the Eastern Front. And, most importantly, its men were not repatriated to their countries of origin after the war, but allowed to settle in the West.

At present, there is no balanced account of the civilianization process of the 'Galicia' Division men.[14] On the one hand, the ex-members of the Division are portrayed as traitors, opportunists who did not care for their motherland, or as war criminals. On the other hand, the ex-'Galicians' are seen as having arguably chosen 'the lesser of two evils' and joined the German Army in order to defend their motherland against the Soviet invasion and attempt to build a nucleus for a Ukrainian army that would serve the future independent Ukrainian state. Both of these strands of historiography tend to focus on the war-time accounts of the Division; the discussion of the 'Galicia' members' post-war history is usually passed over or avoided. Yet the period between 1945 and 1950 is crucial in the Division's story. The narratives which came to exist in that period help to clarify the reasons why some see the 'Galicia' as a division of freedom fighters and others regard it as a group of war criminals. They also shed light on the possible explanations as to why the 'Galician' men avoided repatriation.

13 During the occupation, the German administration in the region of Galicia issued a list of categories for those who were due for compulsory registration. This included men who were born in the years 1920 to 1925; non-commissioned officers up to the age of forty, who had served in any army; officers and cadets who had graduated from military academies but had not yet obtained a commission, as well as military officials up to the age of forty-five. It also included doctors and veterinary surgeons up to the age of forty-five. Thus a number of those who volunteered to join the Division would have been obliged to register anyway (Melnyk, *To Battle*, p. 31).

14 The term civilianization refers to the processes through which the members of the 'Galicia' Division gained their civilian status in post-war Britain.

Focusing on the details of the immediate post-war situation in which the 'Galicians' found themselves contributes to a better understanding of the Division's history and its contemporary relevance.

A number of aspects of the history of the Division, as well as the political ideology of its members, remain a dilemma for historians and a contentious question for the Ukrainian nation. These issues require a thorough scholarly analysis, yet little impartial academic research has been carried out on these topics. Instead, there has been a historiographical war of dichotomous stances with regard to the Division's history, offering strongly politicized narratives, lacking in evidence and independent analysis.

The pro-'Galician' strand of historiography was initially developed by those who lobbied against the Division members' repatriation to the USSR[15] and by the ex-members of the 'Galicia' Division themselves. This position is often supported by the nationalist fractions of the émigré community[16] as well as nationalist groups in contemporary Ukraine. Memoirs were crucial in constructing the image of the Division among the Ukrainian diaspora and in post-Soviet Ukraine, especially its western regions.[17] While

15 Here, I mean organizations like the Canadian Relief Mission for Ukrainian Refugees and its director Gordon Richard Bohdan Panchuk, whose contribution to a particular presentation of the 'Galicia' Division will be discussed throughout the book.

16 The Ukrainian diaspora of the Second World War period consists of a number of groups, many of which were of a nationalistic nature. The 'Galicians' form a small percentage of the émigré community. Other nationalist groups include supporters of political leaders of the Organization of Ukrainian Nationalists (OUN), such as Andrii Mel'nyk (1890–1964) and Stepan Bandera (1909–59).

17 Memoirs or works authored and/or edited by the 'Galicians' came out at different periods, including some that were published only recently. Earlier works had an influence on the perception of the 'Galicia' within the diaspora, and were not available in Soviet Ukraine, while the intended readership of texts published more recently includes contemporary Ukrainians who live in Ukraine, and so these works are not limited to the diaspora audience. See Leonid Mukha, *Z Avstrii̇̈ na Kolymu* (L'viv: Liha-Pres, 2010); Roman Kolisnyk, Bohdan Matsiv and Leonid Mukha (eds), *Dyviziia 'Halychyna' v zapytanniakh i vidpovidiakh veteraniv* (L'viv: Halyts'ka vydavnycha spilka, 2009); Michael Hrycyszyn, *God Save Me From My Friends. A Ukrainian Memoir* (Cambridge: Pegasus Elliot Mackenzie Publishers, 2006); Vasyl' [Wasyl] Veryha, *Slidamy bat'kiv: narys istorii̇̈ 30 polku Dyvizii̇̈ 'Halychyna' 1-oï dyvizii̇̈*

these works hold a great deal of detailed information on the formation, training, military actions and surrender of the Waffen SS 'Galicia', their main drawback is that they are based on the emotional testimonies of the members who participated directly in the Division's activities.[18] Naturally, their accounts are subjective and of a justificatory nature.

The authors of the memoirs are usually former Division members who settled in the UK, Canada or elsewhere in the West and went on to

---

Ukraïns'koï Natsional'noï Armiï (L'viv: Bratstvo kol. Voiakiv 1-oï UD UNA, 2002); Ievhen Pobihushchyi, *Mozaïka moïkh spomyniv* (Ivano-Frankivs'k: Lileia-NV, 2002) (1st edn, Munich–London 1982); Lev Stetkevych, *Iak z Berezhan do Kadry* (Ternopil': Dzhura, 1998); Roman Kolisnyk, *Viis'kova Uprava ta ukraïns'ka Dyviziia Halychyna* (Kyiv: Iaroslaviv Val, 2009); Roman Lazurko, *Na shliakhakh Ievropy* (Chicago: Vydavnytstvo Bratstva Kolyshnikh Voiakiv 1 UD UNA, 1971); Pavlo Hrytsak, *Vezhi i kulemety, spohady z dyvizii i bol'shevyts'koho polonu* (Munich: Vydannia bratstva kolyshnikh Voiakiv 1-oï Dyvizii UNA, 1959); Pavlo Shandruk, *Arms of Valor* (New York: Robert Speller, 1959); Ivan Nahaievs'kyi, *Spohady pol'ovoho dukhivnyka* (Toronto: Ukraïns'ka Knyzhka, 1955); Iurii Tys-Krokhmaliuk, *Shchodennyk Natsional'noho heroia Selepka Lavochky* (Buenos Aires: YU. Serediak, 1954); Volodymyr Kubiiovych, 'Pochatky Ukraïns'koï Dyvizii "Halychyna"', *Visti Bratstva Kol. Voiakiv 1 UD UNA*, 3–4 (1954) <http://www.google.com/gwt/n?u=http%3A%2F%2Flib.galiciadivision.com%2Farticles%2Fkubijovich.html > accessed 7 February 2013; Oleh Lysiak, *Za strilets'kyi zvychai* (Munich: Vydannia Bratstva kol. Voiakiv 1-oï UD UNA, 1953); Ievstakhii Zahachevs'kyi, *Spohady frontovyka. Odiseia siroho 'koliaboranta'* (Munich: Vydannia Bratstva Kol. Voiakiv 1-oï Ukraïns'koï Dyvizii UNA, 1952).

18 These autobiographical articles focus specifically on the experience of training and on the Division's main battle – the Battle of Brody (13–22 July 1944). See Dmytro Ferkuniak, *Uryvky z shchodennyka* (Drohobych: Vidrodzhennia, 2003); Feliks Korduba, *Dyvizion tiazhkoï artylerii pid Brodamy* (Drohobych: Vidrodzhennia, 2003); Ivan Poliuliakh, *Nazustrich tankam* (Drohobych: Vidrodzhennia, 2003); Roman Ts'olko, 'Heneral Pavlo Shandruk v Dyvizii', *Visti kombatanta*, 4 (2002), 65–71; Oleksa Midzhak, *Pomsta komunistam. Poryv: Pravda pro Pershu Ukraïns'ku Dyviziiu (UNA) 'Halychyna' (Statti, narysy, spohady)* (L'viv: Osnova, 1994); Liubomyr Ortyns'kyyi, *Vylim z Brids'koho kitla/Uryvky z spomyniv* (L'viv: Osnova, 1994); Pavlo Shandruk, *Faktychnyi stan i taktychne polozhennya 1 UD UNA pid Brodamy* (L'viv: Osnova, 1994). These articles are available online and can be downloaded at *Ukraïns'ka Dyviziia 'Halychyna'*, <http://www.galiciadivision.com/library/> accessed 17 January 2011.

live in the same diaspora communities and often communicated with each other, especially during the times of the official inquiries into their alleged participation in war crimes. Thus, their picture of the 'Galicia' is created through the process of consolidation of a shared history. That is not to say that the narratives presented by the direct participants of the Waffen SS 'Galicia' are to be dismissed by researchers. They are extremely rich in detail of individual experiences. Moreover, unintentionally, they also tell us how the 'Galician' narrative was formed. Interesting examples of this are the collections of articles authored by the former 'Galicians' in the 1950s and 1960s and by Ukrainian political dissidents and activists of the 1990s and 2000s.[19] Although the pieces have been written by a great variety of authors at different points in time, they tell the same story, almost as if composed by one person. Not only do all authors of this collection agree on the 'main facts'[20] of the 'Galicia's' story, they also use the same arguments, often quoting the same sources to support their claims. In addition, the authors refer to each other's works, which helps trace the creation of the pro-'Galician' narrative. These processes result in a self-referential, closed historical narrative.

The autobiographical work which created the 'blueprint' for the military history of the Division was in fact written by a German officer.[21] The Division's chief of staff from January 1944 until its surrender in May 1945, Wolf-Dietrich Heike, addresses various aspects of Ukrainian involvement in the war. Unlike most other memoirs, Heike's work does not offer a sentimental view of the events, but mainly gives factual information. Heike

19 Mykhailo Slaboshpyts'kyi and Valerii Stetsenko (eds) *Ukraïns'ka dyviziia 'Halychyna.' Istoryko-publitsystychnyi zbirnyk* (Kyiv and Toronto: Bratstvo kolyshnikh voiakiv 1-oï UD UNA, 1994) and Mykhailo Slaboshpyts'kyi (ed.) *Ukraïns'ka dyviziia 'Halychyna.' Istoryko-publitsystychnyi zbirnyk*, 3rd edn (Kyiv: Iaroslaviv Val, 2008).

20 Here, by 'main facts' I mean what microhistorian István Szijárto calls 'little facts', i.e. dates or locations of battles, or other milestones in the history of the unit. See István Szijárto, 'Four Arguments for Microhistory', *Rethinking History* 6/2 (2002), 209–15, p. 209.

21 Wolf-Dietrich Heike, *Sie Wollten Die Freiheit. Die Geschichte der Ukrainischen Division 1943–1945* (Dorheim: Podzun, 1973).

is critical of some German personnel for not recognizing the Division's political position and its full potential. He depicts the Division members as brave soldiers who were hoping to form their own independent army, and in doing this helps to reinforce the state-building narrative of the 'Galicia'. Heike's work is thus held in high regard by members of the Ukrainian diaspora.[22]

Another important memoir was written by Pavlo Shandruk, the last General of the Division, who was firmly convinced of the Division's intended role as a foundation for a Ukrainian national army and lobbied against its repatriation. In his *Arms of Valor*,[23] Shandruk gives an account of the Division's life leading up to its surrender. He supervised the symbolic transformation of the Waffen SS 'Galicia' into the 1st Ukrainian Division of the Ukrainian National Army (1st UD UNA) in March 1945 as well as the creation of the 2nd Ukrainian Division (the anti-tank brigade 'Free Ukraine' (*Vil'na Ukraïna*)) in April 1945.[24]

Although most of the memoirs of the 'Galicians' have a very similar structure and focus on almost the same 'milestones', each of them has a slightly different angle. Lev Stetkevych[25] offers a detailed description of the prisoner-of-war camps in Austria near Tamsweg and Spittal and in Italy near Bellaria and Rimini, where the Division members were held after the end of the Second World War, and the witnessing of the Cossacks' repatriation in Austria: an event of huge importance in the British authorities' decision-making process with regard to the Division members' repatriation. During the Second World War, the Cossacks fought in the ranks of the Wehrmacht and the Waffen SS against the Soviet Union with the hope of establishing their own sovereign state. In May 1945, they surrendered

22 There are Ukrainian, English and the original German language editions of Heike's memoir. The most recent edition was published in 2012 by the Mandrivets' publishing house in Ukraine (see bibliography for full details).

23 Pavlo Shandruk, *Arms of Valor* (New York: Robert Speller, 1959).

24 The historiography of the 2nd Division is very scarce. For more information see Ivan Burtyk, *Ternystyi shliakh Druhoï Dyvizii UNA: stvorennia UNK i Druhoï Dyvizii UNA* (New York: Ob'iednannia Voiakiv i Pryiateliv Druhoï Dyvizii UNA, 1994).

25 Stetkevych, *Iak z Berezhan*.

to the British in Austria and later that month they and their dependants were transported across the Mur River, toward the town of Judenburg (Austria), where the Soviet forces were based, and faced forced repatriation. A number of the Cossacks committed suicide before they reached the Soviet side in order to escape the repressions which they would have suffered once in the USSR.[26] Among those forcefully repatriated in May 1945 was a small number of Ukrainian 'Galicians' who were mistaken for Cossacks.[27] Witnessing this forceful repatriation had a profound impact on the Ukrainians, who began to realize that a similar fate might await their division. They subsequently made every effort to avoid repatriation to the USSR by presenting themselves to the British as a group of Ukrainian freedom fighters, both anti-Bolshevik and anti-Nazi.

All memoirs give an insight into the lives of those who participated in the 'Galicia' Division and shed light on what the Second World War and Ukrainian nationalism meant for them. These works also give us a flavour of the self-perception of the former Ukrainian Waffen SS men: some viewed their choices with regret, but most stood by them as necessary in the context of the Second World War and the struggle for Ukraine's independence. Predictably, they do not discuss the accusations of the 'Galicia's' involvement in war crimes, and when they mention the question of collaboration, they at once attempt to justify their actions through nationalistic motivations.

26 A large body of literature has been written on the event widely known as the 'betrayal of the Cossacks'. These include Samuel J. Newland, *Cossacks in the German Army 1941–1945* (London: Frank Cass, 1991); Catherine Andreyev, *Vlasov and the Russian Liberation Movement: Soviet Reality and Emigré Theories* (Cambridge: Cambridge University Press, 1987); Nikolai Tolstoy, *The Minister and the Massacres* (London: Century Hutchinson, 1986); Nikolai Tolstoy, *The Victims of Yalta* (London: Corgi Book, 1986, original Hodder & Stoughton edition, 1977); Nikolai Tolstoy, *Stalin's Secret War* (London: Jonathan Cape, 1981); Nikolai Tolstoy, *The Secret Betrayal* (New York: Charles Scribner's Sons, 1978); Józef Mackiewicz, *Kontra* (London: Kontra, 1993; 1st edn, 1957). See also Andrew Roberts, 'Blood on Our Hands; They Surrendered in Good Faith Only to Be Sent to Certain Torture and Death; the Betrayal of the Cossacks 60 Years Ago Was Not the Work of the Nazis or the Red Army, but of British Politicians', *The Daily Mail*, 4 June 2005.

27 See Leonid Mukha, *Z Avstriï na Kolymu* (L'viv: Liha-Pres, 2010).

The literature which sets itself the task of condemning the Division is not as vast as that which justifies its creation. Works that criticize the 'Galicia' do so mostly because of the Division's belonging to the Waffen SS. In this context, the collaboration is not seen as a necessary action in order to bring about Ukraine's independence, as the pro-'Galicians' would have it, but as ideologically driven support for Nazi Germany. Unlike the memoirs and other works that are of a justificatory nature, these accounts discuss the Division's alleged involvement in war crimes. They also pose the question of why the former 'Galicians' were allowed to settle in the West despite having served in the army of the enemy. Yet, in spite of raising the important questions that the pro-'Galician' literature fails to address, the anti-'Galician' works tend to be equally coloured by emotional involvement.

The best-known critical text on the question of the 'Galicia' Division is Sol Littman's *Pure Soldiers or Sinister Legion*[28] which portrays the 'Galicia' as war criminals whose civilianization and history was 'fudged for Cold War purposes'.[29] Littman's book is one of the few published works on the Division that refers to the archival material of the post-war period, but does so very selectively. Similarly to Littman, an earlier work by David Cesarani[30] tries to provide an explanation as to how the former Waffen SS soldiers succeed in settling in the West with the consent of the governments which accepted them. While raising this question, Littman and Cesarani offer highly emotional accounts of the 'Galicia's' history, which lack balance and neutral analysis.[31]

The historiography of the Waffen SS 'Galicia' is dominated by authors who have a direct interest in the telling of the 'Galicia's' history, such as its

28 Sol Littman, *Pure Soldiers or Sinister Legion, The Ukrainian 14th Waffen-SS Division* (London: Black Rose Books, 2003).

29 *Ibid.*, p. xiii.

30 David Cesarani, *Justice Delayed: How Britain Became a Refuge for Nazi War Criminals* (London: Heinemann, 1992).

31 Other authors who criticize the 'Galicia' include Eliyahu Yones, *Smoke in the Sand: the Jews of Lvov in the War Years 1939–1944* (Jerusalem: Gefen Publishing House, 2004), and Edward Prus, *SS-Galizien. Patrioci czy zbrodniarze?* (Wrocław: Nortom, 2001).

members or those who see the Division men as war criminals and lobby for the investigation of the alleged war crimes. Other studies that take on the subject of the 'Galicia' vary in the degree of politicization of their findings with some of the authors falling into the trap of taking sides on the question of the 'Galicia', and others succeeding in offering a more impartial account of the Division's history.[32] Michael James Melnyk's work on the 'Galicia' stands out among the books written about the Division.[33] Melnyk provides extensive factual information on the Division's formation and military activity. This book does not try to justify or condemn the 'Galicia', and does address the question of the alleged war crimes. Although it mentions the 'Galicia's' success in avoiding repatriation to the USSR, the book does not explain why the Division was civilianized. On the whole, Melnyk's work marks a step towards a neutral presentation of the 'Galicia' Division. The book is, however, dominated by detailed factual accounts of the Division's wartime actions and pays little attention to the analysis of how the history of the Division changes over time. The situating of the 'Galicia's' portrayal in the contemporary public and academic debate is what the present study aims to accomplish.

The lack of impartial analysis and polarization in debates on the Second World War are harmful to the endeavour to understand the complex events of the period. This situation is not unique to the Ukrainian case. When examining other Waffen SS divisions formed in Eastern Europe, it is clear

32 See Per Anders Rudling, '"They Defended Ukraine": The 14. Waffen-Grenadier-Division der SS (Galizische Nr. 1) Revisited', *The Journal of Slavic Military Studies* 25/3 (2012), 329–68; David Marples, 'Beyond the Pale?: Conceptions and Reflections in Contemporary Ukraine about the Division Galizien', *Journal of Ukrainian Studies*, 33–4 (2008–9), 337–50; Andrii Bolianovs'kyi, *Ukraïns'ki viis'kovi formuvannia v zbroinykh sylakh Nimechchyny (1939–1945)* (L'viv: LNU im. Ivana Franka, 2003) and *Dyviziia 'Halychyna'. Istoria* (L'viv: IU, 2000); Taras Hunczak, *On the Horns of a Dilemma* (New York: University Press of America, 2000); Michael O. Logusz, *Galicia Division: The Waffen-SS 14th Grenadier Division, 1943–1945* (Altglen, PA: Schiffer Military History, 1997). There is also a *kandydats'ka* dissertation (equivalent to the PhD) being written by Oksana Tovarians'ka at the Kyiv-Mohyla University in Ukraine, focusing on the history of the 'Galicia' Division veteran organizations in Ukraine.

33 Melnyk, *To Battle*.

that their portrayals suffer from similarly polarized presentations.[34] The so-called Latvian Legion (*15 Waffen-Grenadier Division der SS (lettische Nr. 1)* and *19 Waffen-Grenadier Division der SS (lettische Nr. 2)*) has been at the centre of both Latvian and international discussions, especially after the official establishment of the Legion's anniversary day in 1998. Similarly to the Ukrainian 'Galicians', those who served in the Latvian Legion emphasized that the formation was established in 1943, towards the end of the war and thus participated in no campaigns against the Jewish population. Indeed, British officials did not see Latvians who belonged to the Legion as 'war criminals or traitors', as they fought predominantly 'against the Soviet armed forces'.[35] The veterans of the Latvian Legion celebrate their formation as first and foremost anti-Soviet and even hold public commemorative events.[36] In 2004, however, the Russian Federation issued a statement about the alleged involvement of the Legion in war crimes.[37]

34 For a variety of views on the non-German formations within the German Armed Forces, see Viktor Chernov and Andrei Shliakhtunov, *Pribaltiiskie Waffen-SS. Geroi ili palachi* (Moscow: Lin – Inter, 2004); Marc J. Rikmenspoel, *Waffen-SS Encyclopaedia*; George Stein, *The Waffen SS: Hitler's Elite Guard at War, 1939–1945* (Ithaca, NY: Cornell University Press, 1984); Carlos Caballero Jurado, *Foreign Volunteers of the Wehrmacht, 1941–45* (London: Osprey, 1983); and Peter Abbott and Nigel Thomas, *Germany's Eastern Front Allies, 1941–45* (London: Osprey, 1982).

35 Letter from the Foreign Office to the Political Adviser to Commander-in-Chief, Germany (Berlin), 4 February 1946; (NA) Foreign Office (FO) 817/252/59 cited in Visvaldis Lācis, *The Latvian Legion According to Independent Observers* (Riga: Jumava, 2006), p. 8.

36 See *The Volunteer SS Legion in Latvia* in the 'Information on the History of Latvia' page of the Ministry of Foreign Affairs of the Republic of Latvia website <http://www.am.gov.lv/en/policy/history/legion> accessed 6 September 2012.

37 See 'Permanent Mission of the Russian Federation to the United Nations. Involvement of the Lettish SS Legion in War Crimes in 1941–1945 and the Attempts to Revise the Verdict of the Nuremberg Tribunal in Latvia' <http://www.un.int/russia/other/latv1941.htm#russian> accessed 6 September 2012. For more details on the Latvian case, see Pascal Bonnard, 'Pam'iat' pro radians'ke mynule ta ievropeis'ki normy vyznannia rozmaïttia kul'tur: superechlyvi modeli etnichnoï klasyfikatsiï u Latviï', *Ukraïna Moderna* 4 (2009), 219–37; Karsten Brüggemann and Andres Kasekamp, 'The Politics of History and the "War of Monuments" in Estonia', *Nationalities Papers* 26/3 (2008) 425–48; Mintauts Blosfelds, *Stormtrooper on the Eastern Front. Fighting*

The debate about the history of the Latvian Legion and what it means for the population of contemporary Latvia highlights the same problems as exist in the case of the 'Galicia' Division. In countries with strong political, ethnic and linguistic divisions such as Latvia and Ukraine, the discussion of the Second World War memory is dominated by those who wish to commemorate their anti-Soviet formations, including those within the Waffen SS, as such that fought for independence, on the one hand, and those who see these acts as celebrations of the country's collaboration with the Nazis, on the other. It is clear that, in countries like Latvia and Ukraine, which are still in the process of rediscovering and rewriting their wartime histories after decades of distortion under Soviet rule, heated debates over a difficult history are inevitable. It is, however, precisely the way these debates are conducted that indicates the level of political and social 'maturity' of these societies in the eyes of the world.

This study offers an analysis of the political framing of history in contemporary Ukraine and discusses the challenges that Ukrainian society faces with regard to the question of the Second World War. First, however, it will address the period preceding the Second World War, which is vital in understanding why it was possible for the Waffen SS 'Galicia' to be formed. This chapter will provide the foundation for the later analyses of the narratives which developed after the Second World War. It will argue that the 'Galicia' Division was formed as a result of the existing anti-Soviet tendencies and as part of the tradition of nationalist military resistance which already existed in Ukraine before the war. Chapter 2 addresses the most controversial aspect of the 'Galicia's' story: the Division's association with the Waffen SS. Examining war-crime allegations made after the Second World War against the Division members, the chapter does not aim to establish whether the 'Galicians' were war criminals or not; instead, it will analyse how alleged participation in war crimes affected the general narrative about the 'Galicia' Division and the specific narratives related to their repatriation and settlement.

---

with Hitler's Latvian SS (Barnsley: Pen & Sword, 2008); Chernov and Shliakhtunov, *Pribaltiiskie Waffen-SS*..

The central questions of this study are the following: how did the Division members manage to escape repatriation to the USSR, and how was the UK Screening Commission persuaded to allow them to be moved to the UK? These are examined in Chapter 3. In order to address these questions, the chapter explains how confusion about the nationality question and repatriation policies affected the Division's specific experience of the end of the Second World War. The Division's journey to civilianization in the UK and its members' move to Canada are detailed in Chapter 4, which will analyse the public reaction to the arrival of the 'Galicia' men in the UK and what influence this had on their gaining civilian status.

In order to construct a new and balanced way of approaching the 'Galicia' Division, this book uses a number of primary sources.[38] It does not necessarily treat primary documents as having a higher validity than interview testimonies or the secondary data. Instead, it tries to establish the significance the documents had in the creation of various narratives and in contributing to the Division's successful civilianization. The study approaches the examined archival documents bearing in mind the contextual setting in which they were written. It also uses interview testimonies when working with primary sources.[39] The narratives about the former 'Galicia' members offered by the archival records, interviews and secondary literature form a great number of 'truths', equally valid for their authors and some intended readers. This study will, therefore, resist constructing another 'truth'. Instead, it will try to get closer to the contextualized reality of the events and the narratives which describe them.

38 UK National Archives (NA). Also 'Admission of "Surrendered Enemy Personnel" – Ukrainian Refugees from England' stored at the Library and Archives Canada.

39 All interviews referred to in the book were conducted by me, in Ukrainian, during 2007–12 in London, L'viv, Ternopil', Kyiv and Toronto. The names of the former members of the 'Galicia', who were interviewed for this research have been changed on request of the interviewees to protect their anonymity. Inevitably, similarly to memoir works, interviews present problems, particularly when they are gathered several decades after the event. While the reliability of the 'Galicians'' interview testimonies can be questioned, their individual take on the wartime and post-war events is very useful for this research in giving insight into continuing narratives and self-perceptions.

Memory and Identity

This study uses the microhistorical approach to history, in that it attempts to move away from trying to develop general historical explanations of events.[40] Instead, it focuses on a specific set of concerns and incidents and uses these as a lens through which the history of the 'Galicia' Division can be analysed. According to Georg Iggers, this 'conceptual and methodological approach to history [...] sees history no longer as a unified process, a grand narrative in which the many individuals are submerged, but as a multifaceted flow with many individual centres.'[41] And so when dealing with 'the individual lives of the many, we need an epistemology geared to the experiences of these many that permits knowledge of the concrete rather than abstract.'[42] At the same time, the 'abstract' is not rejected by this study. Recognizing that the story of the 'Galicia' unfolds in several contexts at once (i.e., Ukrainian nationalism, collaboration, the state-building process), the monograph attempts to assess the Division in each of these contexts. In this way, the complex individual story can be merged with the general history of the period without losing sight of either. In the 'Galicia's' case, the more generalized historiographical approach does tell us much about the issues arising with regard to collaboration in Eastern Europe or repatriation in the aftermath of the Second World War. However, the very attempt to fit the Division into a pre-existing historiographical scheme has led precisely to their being viewed simply as either 'collaborators' or

40 See Georg G. Iggers, *Historiography in the Twentieth Century: from Scientific Objectivity to the Postmodern Challenge* (Hanover, NH: Wesleyan University Press, 1997); Sigurdur Gylfi Magnusson, 'The Singularization of History: Social History and Microhistory within the Postmodern State of Knowledge', *Journal of Social History* 36 (Spring 2003), 701–35; Carlo Ginzburg and Carlo Poni, 'The Name and the Game: Unequal Exchange and the Historical Marketplace', in Edward Muir and Guido Ruggiero, eds, *Microhistory and the Lost People of Europe*, trans. Eren Branch (Baltimore, MD: Johns Hopkins University Press, 1991), 1–10; Giovanni Levi, 'On Microhistory', in Peter Burke, ed., *New Perspectives on Historical Writing* (University Park, PA: Pennsylvania State University Press, 1991).

41 Georg G. Iggers, *Historiography in the Twentieth Century*, p. 103.

42 *Ibid.*

'freedom fighters', depending on the historiographical approach that has already been adopted by the commentator or writer. The recognition of the fact that all knowledge is mediated and that we gain access to it 'by means of various clues, signs and symptoms'[43] enables historians to move away from trying to present reality as objective and allows for subjective narratives to help form the history and understanding of an event. In this way, the analysis of both events and narratives that describe those events forms the basis of the historian's findings.[44]

The notion of narrative is closely linked with questions of collective and individual memory as well as cultural identity. Since the end of the Second World War and until the present day, ex-'Galicians' have been actively seeking to tell their stories. Their narratives have influenced the Ukrainian nationalist discourse over the last seven decades and are used by both nationalist and anti-nationalist political groups in present-day Ukraine. This study will offer a critical analysis of the development of cultural memory of the Division and how this has played out and continues to play out in contemporary Ukraine. Memory, as well as its absence, is central to the creation of national identities. The interrelation between individual and group memory has been analysed by the growing field of memory studies. In his classic text, Maurice Halbwachs[45] argues that 'while the collective memory endures and draws strength from its base in a coherent body of people, it is individuals as group members who remember.'[46] Halbwachs also says that 'the individual remembers by placing himself in the perspective of the group'.[47] Just as Halbwachs describes, it is through the creation and re-creation of memories that the Division members define and re-define both the status of the Division and their role within it. At the same time, these problems are important in wider Ukrainian memory discourse.

43 Giovanni Levi, 'On Microhistory', p. 106, cited in Georg G. Iggers, *Historiography in the Twentieth Century*, p. 109.

44 See Georg G. Iggers, *Historiography in the Twentieth Century*, p. 110.

45 Maurice Halbwachs, *On Collective Memory*, edited by Lewis A. Coser (Chicago, IL: University of Chicago Press, 1992).

46 *Ibid.*, p. 22.

47 *Ibid.*, p. 40.

Developing the concept of collective memory further, Jan Assmann introduces the idea of cultural memory,[48] which 'preserves the store of knowledge from which a group derives an awareness of its unity and peculiarity.'[49] What is even more applicable to the 'Galicia' case is that '[t]he objective manifestations of cultural memory are defined through a kind of identificatory determination in a positive ("We are this") or in a negative ("That's our opposite") sense.'[50] The literature is likely to refer to the Division describing what they are, for example, 'the blossom of Ukrainian intelligentsia',[51] as well as what they 'are not', i.e., anti-Soviet; 'not at heart pro-German'.[52] Identity itself, however, is neither simple nor stable and is always ambivalent.[53] The task of analysing the impact of memory on the identity of a group as complex as the 'Galicia' requires studying the traces of memory in that group's language, its oral tradition, and its relation to history at the time when memory is formed or retrieved.

The name of the Division itself, for example, had a profound effect on both the self-perception of the members of the 'Galicia' as well as those who came in contact with them throughout the Division's history. The Waffen SS 'Galicia' Division's official designation underwent a number of changes. It was known as *Freiwilligen-Division Galizien* between April 1943 and June 1944. Then it was officially called *14. Freiwilligen-Grenadier-Division der SS (galizische Nr. 1)* and *14. Waffen-Grenadier-Division der SS (galizische Nr. 1)* between June 1944 and November 1944. In early 1945 the formation was renamed to *14. Waffen-Grenadier-Division der*

48 See Jan Assmann, *Religion and Cultural Memory: Ten Studies* (Stanford, CA: Stanford University Press, 2006).

49 Jan Assmann and John Czaplicka, 'Collective Memory and Cultural Identity', *New German Critique*, 65 (1995), 125–33.

50 *Ibid.*, p. 130.

51 Protocol of the Military Board meeting on 22 August 1947 in Munich, in Kolisnyk, *Viis'kova Uprava*, p. 253. See also Ihor Arkusha, 'Dyviziia SS "Halychyna". Pravda i vyhadky', *Narodnyi ohliadach* (27 April 2007) <http://sd.org.ua/news.php?id=11849> accessed 12 October 2012.

52 In (NA) HO/213/1851, p. 6. Screening Commission Report dated 21 February 1947.

53 See Stuart Hall, *Ethnicity: Identity and Difference*, 1991 cited in Amritjit Singh, Joseph T. Skerrett and Robert E. Hogan, eds, *Memory Narrative and Identity. New Essays in Ethnic American Literatures* (Boston, MA: Northeastern University Press, 1994).

SS (ukrainische Nr. 1) and, finally, between April 1945 and its surrender in May 1945, the Division came to be known as 1st Ukrainian Division of the Ukrainian Army (*1-a Ukraïns'ka Dyviziia Ukraïns'koï Natsional'noï Armiï* or *1. Ukrainische Division der Ukrainischen National-Armee*. It is also known informally as the *'Galicia' Division* or *Dyviziia Halychyna*.[54]

The fact that the 'Galicia' was renamed several times during its relatively brief existence was used during its members' efforts to be spared forceful repatriation, as well as when the Canadian government was approached to grant the 'Galicians' entry to Canada after the war. Interestingly, the various names of the Division continue to play a part in contemporary studies of the 'Galicia'. Those works which adopt a non-critical approach are likely to avoid the mention of the 'Waffen SS' part in the Division's name. Equally, it is not uncommon to see the formation referred to as the 'SS Galizien', rather than Waffen SS 'Galicia', in works which take a condemnatory tone. What to call the 'Galician' Ukrainians, not only as a military formation, but as a group more generally, has created confusion for most who came to deal with the Division, from Adolf Hitler, who referred to the members of the Waffen SS 'Galicia' as 'Austrian Ruthenians',[55] to the British POW camp officials who classified them as 'undetermined nationals'[56] or as 'doubtful Poles'.[57] In this, the 'Galicia' differs from the Latvian Legion or other non-German Waffen SS formations with clear national belonging. The complex identity of the Division's members can be understood only in relation to the complex history of the region from which they originated.

54 Wolf-Dietrich Heike, *The Ukrainian Division 'Galicia', 1943–45: A Memoir* (Toronto: The Shevchenko Scientific Society, 1988), p. xi. This list is offered by Yury Boshyk, who wrote the Editor's Note to Heike's book. Another source suggests that the 'Galicia' Division was also known as *SS-Schützen-Division Galizien* (between some time in 1943 and October 1943). Axis History Factbook <http://www.axishistory.com/index.php?id=1959> accessed 18 February 2011.

55 'Abendlage von 23. Marz 1945 in Berlin (Fuhrerwohnung)', *Hitlers* Lagebesprechungen, pp. 938ff, cited in Stein, *The Waffen SS*, p. 195.

56 PW & DP Technical Instruction, Subject: Displaced Persons Formerly Living in the Ukraine, (NA) PDWP/58378, 15 March 1947.

57 See Lieut. Colonel G.B. Vaughan-Hughes to Lt. Colonel F.R.C. Bray, Zonal Executive Offices, (NA) PWDP/59808/23, 18 March 1947, p. 2; and Mark Wyman, *DPs: Europe's Displaced Persons, 1945–1950* (Ithaca, NY: Cornell University Press, 1998), pp. 220–5.

Studying the history of the Second World War in Ukraine is complicated from the outset. The territories that comprise contemporary Ukraine before and during the different periods of the war belonged to Poland, Romania, Hungary, Czechoslovakia and the USSR. Each of these territories, thus, has to be examined in its particular political context. It is, however, important to study the situation in the whole of Ukraine, as it is known today, when examining questions of collaboration, the Holocaust, ethnic violence and cleansings, civilian losses, the nationalist struggle and many other issues, which, if excluded, will result in only a partial history of the Second World War. Comprehensive histories of the Shoah in Ukraine are starting to appear, with authors such as Wendy Lower, Ray Brandon, Dieter Pohl, Frank Golczewski and other scholars carefully researching all aspects of the Holocaust on the territory of present-day Ukraine, including the participation of the local administration, police units, nationalist groups and individuals in the implementation of the Holocaust, but also studying the many cases of rescue of Jews and unwillingness of the population to take part in the anti-Jewish campaigns.[58] Unfortunately, studies which adopt such an approach are rare. They do not enjoy much popularity

58 See Frank Golczewski, *Deutsche und Ukrainer 1914–1939* (Paderborn: Ferdinand Schöningh Verlag, 2010); John-Paul Himka, *Ukrainians, Jews and the Holocaust: Divergent Memories* (Saskatoon: Heritage Press, 2009); Ray Brandon and Wendy Lower, eds, *The Shoah in Ukraine. History, Testimony, Memorialization* (Bloomington, IN: Indiana University Press, 2008); Wendy Lower, *Nazi Empire-Building and the Holocaust in Ukraine* (Chapel Hill, NC: University of North Carolina Press in association with the United States Holocaust Memorial Museum, 2005); Dieter Pohl, 'The Murder of Ukraine's Jews under German Military Administration and in the Reich Commissariat Ukraine' in Ray Brandon, and Wendy Lower, eds, *The Shoah in Ukraine*, pp. 23–76; Frank Golczewski, 'Shades of Grey: Reflections on Jewish-Ukrainian and German-Ukrainian Relations in Galicia', in Ray Brandon, and Wendy Lower, eds, *The Shoah in Ukraine*, pp. 114–55; Iaroslav Hrytsak, *Strasti za natsionalizmom, Istorychni eseï* (Kyiv: Krytyka, 2004); Shimon Redlich, *Together and Apart in Brzezany: Poles, Jews, and Ukrainians 1919–1945* (Bloomington, IN: Indiana University Press, 2002); Martin Dean, *Collaboration during the Holocaust: Crimes of the Local Police in Belorussia and Ukraine, 1941–44* (New York: St Martin's Press, published in association with the United States Holocaust Memorial Museum, 2000).

or debate in Ukraine itself where there is still sharp competition between those who simply accuse Ukrainians of collaborating with the Nazis and those who prefer to focus solely on the suffering endured by the Ukrainian population and mention the Holocaust, at most, as a shared tragedy of Jewish and Ukrainian peoples.

In spite of the many difficulties (methodological, practical, political) of researching the Second World War in Ukraine, one thing is clear – this history consists of many pages. Some tell the story of sacrifice and compassion, and others reveal participation in violence which can be hard to admit. Yet all these pages must be included if one is to come closer to understanding what really happened in Ukraine during the war. This book hopes to become one such page in a more complex history of the Second World War and its post-war understanding.

CHAPTER 1

The Development of Ukrainian Nationalist Militarized Resistance

The formation of the Waffen SS 'Galicia', as well as the creation of narratives surrounding its establishment, activities and legacy, are difficult to understand without analysis of the developments that took place in the interwar period. The Division was not purely a consequence of Nazi occupation of western Ukraine; it emerged as a result of the already formed tradition of nationalist militarized resistance on the territory populated by Ukrainians under Polish, Czechoslovak and Soviet rule. This was represented by a number of Ukrainian paramilitary units, namely, the Carpathian Sich – a paramilitary organization in the Carpatho-Ukrainian State; the 'first' Ukrainian Insurgent Army – or the Polissian Sich, organized by Taras Bul'ba-Borovets', the *Nachtigall* and *Roland* battalions which are an earlier example of co-operation between German officials, especially the *Abwehr*,[1] and Ukrainian nationalists; and, finally, the Ukrainian Insurgent Army (*Ukraïns'ka povstans'ka armiia*, UPA) controlled by one branch of the Organization of Ukrainian Nationalists (*Orhanizatsiia ukraïns'kykh natsionalistiv*, OUN). The resentment towards most local regimes by the ethnic Ukrainian population and their subsequent support for nationalist groups rose dramatically in the territories populated by Ukrainians between the wars. The desire to have an independent army was growing too. This increasing nationalism manifested itself through the establishment of a number of military formations, which often fought for popularity among the local population, and each aspired to form a basis for the future army of an independent Ukrainian state. This new trend laid down the foundations for the Waffen SS 'Galicia'.

1 The German military intelligence organization (1921–1944).

The foundations of the struggle to transform lands populated by Ukrainians into an independent state are rooted in the events of the late nineteenth and early twentieth centuries, when these lands formed part of the Russian and Hapsburg empires. In the course of the First World War, western Ukrainians fought in the Austro-Hungarian Army. Soon after the collapse of the Hapsburg Empire (in 1918), up to 25,000 of those Ukrainian men and women who formerly belonged to the Austro-Hungarian Army formed the military unit of the Sich Riflemen (*Sichovi Stril'tsi*), which later became a unit of the Army of the Ukrainian People's Republic (*Ukraïns'ka Narodna Respublika*, UNR). However, just as with the Army of the People's Republic and the People's Republic itself, the activity of the *Sichovi Stril'tsi* only lasted from 1917 until 1919.[2]

Starting from the late 1920s and until the 1940s, Ukrainians received little support from the West which foresaw prospects for Ukraine's autonomous existence only as a republic within the Soviet Union or as part of another state. The militarization of the population in order to gain independence was seen by many Ukrainians as a necessary step. The fact that in the years preceding the Second World War more than 7 million western Ukrainians had no state of their own meant that their militarization involved co-operation with those regimes which posed lesser threats.[3]

The Specificity of Ukrainian Nationalism

Ukrainian nationalist movements had been developing throughout the nineteenth century in what is now contemporary Ukraine. These movements, however, were pursuing a different political programme from

2 The first division of the *Sichovi Stril'tsi*, which was formed in Kyiv in 1917, was commanded by Ievhen Konovalets', who went on to become a leader of the Organization of Ukrainian Nationalists in 1929.

3 See Serhy Yekelchyk, *Ukraine. Birth of a Modern Nation* (Oxford: Oxford University Press, 2007), p. 121.

the ones which appeared in the years before the Second World War. The Ukrainian nationalist movement of the interwar period played a crucial role in the formation of the military groups before and during the Second World War, including the Waffen SS 'Galicia'. John Armstrong characterized the political situation in Ukraine in the years preceding the war in the following way:

> [w]hile there is a tradition of separate political development in the [sic] Ukraine, modern nationalism – the doctrine that persons of a distinctive culture should constitute an independent state – came late to the area.[4]

One of the first to openly declare the colonial status of Ukraine within the Russian Empire, and speak of the right to self-determination for Ukrainian people, was a lawyer from Kharkiv (Kharkov) Mykola Mikhnovs'kyi. In 1900 he presented a speech entitled 'An Independent Ukraine',[5] which was turned into a brochure and published later that year. Mikhnovs'kyi presented the problems of Ukraine-Russia relations from the point of view of the state system. This approach was innovative and received great attention. In spite of not being able to offer a clear solution to the problem, Mikhnovs'kyi raised the question of Ukrainian independence as essential for the survival of the Ukrainian people. Mikhnovs'kyi's ideas found support among Ukrainian nationalist groups in the 1920s in Poland.

The work of Dmytro Dontsov also had a major influence on Ukrainian nationalism of this period. Having once belonged to the Ukrainian Socialist-Democratic Party, he became disillusioned by the ideas of socialism and gradually moved away from his Party comrades. He began to encourage Ukrainians to turn toward the West, which was experiencing a growing popularity of totalitarian regimes, with the rise of Fascism in Italy and Nazism in Germany. In 1926 Dontsov wrote what became his quintessential

4 John Armstrong, *Ukrainian Nationalism* (New York: Columbia University Press, 1963), p. 3.

5 Mykola Mikhnovs'kyi, *Samostiina Ukraïna* (London: Nakladom Viddilu Soiuzu Ukraïntsiv u Velykii Brytanii u Volverhemptoni, 1967 edn).

theoretical work, *Nationalism*.[6] According to Dontsov, nationalism had to be amoral and the movement had to be led by an individual 'aggressive and intolerant towards other views',[7] whose 'truth' would be recognized as a shared truth and would have to be accepted by others. Oleksandr Zaitsev argues that Dontsov's notion of nationalism could be compared to a religion: indeed, in Dontsov's view, in order to be successful in attracting a large number of people, nationalism had to be fanatical.[8] This kind of creation of a 'nationalist faith' was growing stronger in the context of political developments, in the interwar period, especially among Ukrainians in the Polish state.

In the late 1920s and throughout the 1930s, there were several attempts to form legally recognized Ukrainian political parties in Poland. The most prominent of them were the Ukrainian National Democratic Alliance (*Ukraïns'ke Natsional'no-Demokratychne Ob'iednannia*, UNDO), set up in Galicia in 1925. The UNDO was supported by the Ukrainian elites as well as by Metropolitan Andrei Sheptyts'kyi, the head of the Greek Catholic Church and an influential figure in Galicia. As well as political parties, another movement was being created, supporting the ideology of 'integral nationalism'.[9] Originating in France at the turn of the century, this ideology 'never had much appeal in France or other Western European countries, but in modified forms it became a dominant force in the "dissatisfied" countries of Central and Southern Europe'.[10] As pointed out by Alexander Motyl,

6 Dmytro Dontsov, *Natsionalizm* (London and Toronto: Ukraïns'ka vydavnycha spilka, 1966 edn). For more information on Dmytro Dontsov see Alexander J. Motyl, *The Turn to the Right: The Ideological Origins and Development of Ukrainian Nationalism, 1919–1929*. (New York: Boulder, 1980), pp. 61–85.

7 *Ibid.*, p. 263.

8 Oleksandr Zaitsev, 'Natsionalizm iak relihiia: pryklad Dmytra Dontsova'. A paper presented at a seminar: 'Khrystyians'kyi universalizm ta natsionalizm: Hreko-Katolyts'ka tserkva ta ukraïns'kyi natsionalistychnyi rukh', L'viv, Ukraïns'kyi Katolyts'kyi Universytet (27 May 2009) <http://www.ucu.edu.ua/ukr/current/library/article;4215/> accessed 18 May 2010.

9 Armstrong, *Ukrainian Nationalism*, p. 19.

10 *Ibid.*, p. 21.

> [a] comparison of the ideology of the Organization of Ukrainian Nationalists with French integral nationalism, Italian Fascism, and Ukrainian conservatism is warranted because all four ideologies flourished in the same historical period; because the Ukrainian Nationalists were acquainted with, sometimes admiring of, and perhaps even directly influenced by the other three [...].[11]

Armstrong argues that this type of nationalism with totalitarian aspirations was supported by two Ukrainian groups. It appealed to the dissatisfied former *Sichovi Stril'tsi*, who in the 1920s and 1930s were repressed by the Polish authorities, and to radical nationalist groups that arose as a reaction to Communism, which was winning popularity among Ukrainian students, deprived of higher education by the Polish authorities.[12] Armstrong suggests that the students were turned from Communism to nationalism by the formation of groups like the Union of Ukrainian Nationalist Youth (*Soiuz ukraïns'koï natsionalistychnoï molodi*) whose ideology was based on the writings of Dontsov. The combination of the embittered former *Sichovi Stril'tsi*, who had formed the Ukrainian Military Organization (*Ukraïns'ka viis'kova orhanizatsiia*, UVO), and the nationalistic youth gave firm grounds for the establishment of the Organization of Ukrainian Nationalists in 1929,[13] headed by the former leader of the *Sichovi Stril'tsi*, Ievhen Konovalets' until his assassination by the NKVD in May 1938.

The role of Germany and its leaders in the development of Ukrainian nationalism preceding the Second World War must not be underestimated. The way the relationships among the leadership of Ukrainian nationalists unfolded often depended precisely on their relations with the German authorities and often with specific individuals representing the authorities. The policies of the OUN in particular depended to a large extent on their connections with Germany at the time. This dependence was especially evident in 1939, when Ukrainian nationalists and groups who wanted to see Ukraine independent and united realized that such a chance could arise only as a result of fundamental changes in Europe, which could be

11 Motyl, *The Turn to the Right'*, p. 162.
12 See Yekelchyk, *Ukraine*, pp. 126–7.
13 *Ibid.*, p. 127.

brought about by a war. Thus, Ukrainian nationalists, especially the OUN, were ready to support German policies in 1939 in the hope of war first with Poland and then with the Soviet Union, which would offer an opportunity to set up a united independent Ukrainian state. There was, however, one group of Ukrainian nationalists that was less prepared for the forthcoming changes in Europe, and that was the movement led by Pavlo Skoropads'kyi. The Hetmanate,[14] was unable to compete with the OUN in 'numerical strength and youthful vigor';[15] however, they too had close links with the leaders of the Third Reich. The Hetman himself was thought of as being on 'terms of personal friendship with Hermann Göring'.[16] Unlike the OUN, the Hetmanites preferred to avoid violence as a strategy and thus did not win as much support among the Nazi leadership as the OUN did.

At the outbreak of the Second World War, the leadership of the OUN was the same as it had been before the assassination of Konovalets': two members of the *Provid* (the leadership) were generals from the revolutionary period (1917–21), Viktor Kurmanovych and Mykola Kapustians'kyi. They both contributed to the prestige of the organization and added to the creation of the nationalist narrative of brave military struggle for independence. A number of the OUN *Provid* members were from the younger generation, among them Iaroslav Baranovs'kyi and Dmytro Andriievs'kyi. Another interesting member of the *Provid* was Richard Franz Marian Iarii (Riko Jary). Iarii was of Czech and Hungarian-Jewish descent, but, having served in the Austro-Hungarian Army with numerous Ukrainians from the Galicia region, joined the UNR Army and remained in Ukrainian nationalist circles. He was particularly valuable for his connections with the German intelligence. Another link between the Ukrainian nationalists and the *Abwehr* was Roman Sushko, who also served in the Austro-Hungarian

14 The Hetmanate is a form of Ukrainian state, which is ruled by the Hetman, the highest military title in the Cossack Ukraine. This title was revived between 1917 and 1919 in Ukraine by the Ukrainian Central Council (*Ukraïns'ka Tsentral'na Rada*) which was headed by Pavlo Skoropads'kyi.

15 Armstrong, *Ukrainian Nationalism*, p. 27.

16 Joesten Joachim, 'Hitler's Fiasco in the Ukraine', *Foreign Affairs* XXI (January 1943), p. 334, cited in Armstrong, *Ukrainian Nationalism*, p. 28.

Army and in the UNR Army. In the summer of 1939, Sushko was preparing a group of 600 men in Wiener-Neustadt (Austria) to act as an auxiliary to the Wehrmacht in its approaching attack on Poland. This military group was intended to become the nucleus for an armed force which would take part in the uprising, leading to the independence of Ukraine.[17] The theme of creating a nucleus for the independent army is evidently repeated throughout the interwar period and during the years of the Second World War.

The most prominent figure in the Ukrainian nationalist movement of this period was Andrii Mel'nyk. He was nominated as successor to Konovalets'. Mel'nyk was once the chairman of the Catholic youth organization in Galicia, and had good connections with the Greek Catholic Church in general and Metropolitan Sheptyts'kyi in particular.[18] He also maintained a good relationship with Reverend Augustyn Voloshyn, the president of Carpatho-Ukraine.[19] Mel'nyk was the director of the *Provid*, but it was a charismatic and radical person that the young members of the

17 Wilhelm Franz Canaris, who was a head of the *Abwehr*, permitted the group led by Sushko, at the time based in Slovakia, to proceed to the territories on the San River, populated by Ukrainians, but it had to withdraw in the face of the advancing Soviet Army. See Armstrong, *Ukrainian Nationalism*, p. 42 and Wolfdieter Bihl, 'Ukrainians in the Armed Forces', p. 139. Sushko's military group will be discussed later in the chapter.

18 See Armstrong, *Ukrainian Nationalism*, p. 36. It is important to note that Sheptyts'kyi's attitude towards the nationalists changed as the OUN became more radical and focused on more violent practices. A sermon issued by Sheptyts'kyi in 1932 clearly condemned the growing violence and radicalism of the nationalists, accusing them of trying to force their ideas on others, using force and blind terror, and situating them in the larger context of the general radicalisation of youth that produced fascism on the one hand and Bolshevism on the other. Later, Sheptyts'kyi opposed the split in the OUN and tried to use his influence to prevent Ukrainians from joining the German police and from participating in violent activities. See John-Paul Himka, 'Christianity and Radical Nationalism: Metropolitan Andrei Sheptytsky and the Bandera Movement', in Catherine Wanner, ed, *State Secularism and Lived Religion in Soviet Russia and Ukraine* (New York: Oxford University Press, 2012), pp. 93–116 (pp. 97–100).

19 Carpatho-Ukraine will be discussed in more detail later in the chapter.

OUN wished to see as their leader.[20] Stepan Bandera, who had been freed from a Polish prison,[21] was considered by the younger generation of the Ukrainian nationalists as a person more appropriate to lead the OUN in the turbulent times which awaited them.

The start of the Second World War and the Soviet invasion of Poland united Ukrainians under one state, the Soviet Union, for the first time in modern history. The USSR, however, was perceived by the nationalist groups as their biggest threat, which partly led to their radicalization and alignment with Nazi Germany. In spite of the Molotov-Ribbentrop pact,[22] Ukrainian nationalists continued their co-operation with the German authorities in the *Generalgouvernement*, who pursued a policy of *divide et impera* (the phrase was used by Governor Frank to describe the policy towards nationalities in the *Generalgouvernement*).[23] The formation of a number of national political groups was encouraged by the Nazi authorities. There was a certain degree of disagreement among these groups, but they sought to create a body which would unite them all. Volodymyr Kubiiovych (Kubijovyč)[24] was one of those who took on the mission of creating a unifying institution for Ukrainian political nationalists. He too, like his

20 Armstrong, *Ukrainian Nationalism*, p. 39.

21 In 1935–6, Bandera, together with other OUN members stood trials in Warsaw and L'viv (Lwów) for organizing and participating in a number of terrorist activities, organized by the OUN. As a result, Bandera was sentenced to death, but the sentence was commuted to life imprisonment. In 1939 he escaped from a Polish prison to return to L'viv (Lwów) on the OUN matters.

22 The Molotov-Ribbentrop Pact, as it came to be known, was named after the Soviet foreign minister, Viacheslav Molotov, and the German foreign minister, Joachim von Ribbentrop. This agreement's official title was the Treaty of Non-Aggression between Germany and the Soviet Union. It was signed in Moscow on 23 August 1939. The pact remained in effect until 22 June 1941, when Nazi Germany started 'Operation Barbarossa' and invaded the USSR.

23 See Armstrong, *Ukrainian Nationalism*, p. 48.

24 Professor Volodymyr Kubiiovych (1900–85) headed the Ukrainian Central Committee (*Ukraïns'kyi Tsentral'nyi Komitet*), an organization founded in 1940 to serve as a representative body of Ukrainians, whose aim was to provide welfare to the Ukrainian population of the *Generalgouvernement* and to assist the Ukrainian refugees from the USSR.

contemporaries in the OUN, enjoyed good contacts with the Germans, in his case, with German scholars with whom he had worked before the war as a geographer. He spoke fluent German, and according to Armstrong, Kubiiovych was 'able to maintain his initial prestige as a patriot standing above parties because of his tact, moderation, and good judgement, and was also [able] to carry out the difficult task of negotiating with the Germans without losing his – and his fellow Ukrainians' – self-respect.'[25]

Between 13 and 15 April 1940, Ukrainian groups' representatives met in Kraków and set up an organization, formally recognized as the Ukrainian Central Committee (*Ukraïns'kyi tsentral'nyi komitet* (UTsK), *Ukrainischen Hauptausschuß*), with Volodymyr Kubiiovych as its president.[26] Orest Subtelny characterizes the UTsK as 'a Ukrainian social-welfare agency whose mandate was to look after the sick, the aged, and homeless children, to care for public health and education, to help prisoners of war, and to represent the interests of the Ukrainian workers from the General Government who were sent to Germany.'[27] Although the Germans were keen to make sure that the UTsK had no political influence, the Committee grew to become powerful in the nationalist movement arena. In Subtelny's view, Nazi authorities favoured the appointment of Ukrainians to low-level administrative posts and to the police in ethnically mixed communities; and when Ukrainians used their positions against the Poles, 'the Germans were not dismayed by the communal tensions that arose.'[28] Although the UTsK had no official influence on education, through its good relationships with the German authorities, it managed to affect the provision of institutional facilities, recruitment of Ukrainian teachers, and availability of Ukrainian textbooks. It also established a newspaper, *Krakivs'ki Visti* (the Kraków News).[29] By 1943 the UTsK operated 1,366 kitchens, it was

25 Armstrong, *Ukrainian Nationalism*, p. 50.

26 *Ibid.*, p. 51.

27 Orest Subtelny, *Ukraine: A History* (Toronto: University of Toronto Press, 1988), p. 457.

28 *Ibid*, p. 458.

29 The German policy did not allow the use of 'Ukrainian' in the title, hence names of cities or regions (i.e., Kraków, Galician) were used instead.

also able to build student residences for 7,000 individuals, provided scholarships, and organized over 100 youth groups, camps and sports clubs.[30]

The UTsK, and Kubiiovych in particular, suggested the creation of a Ukrainian military force in *Generalgouvernement* on a number of occasions, and in 1943 Kubiiovych worked closely with the Germans on the formation of the 'Galicia' Division. His view of the Ukrainian Division was based on the example of the Ukrainian legion within the Austro-Hungarian Army during the First World War. Kubiiovych and the UTsK leadership believed that the attempt to achieve Ukraine's independence in 1917–20 failed because of the lack of sufficient regular armed force and saw the formation of a Ukrainian military unit within the Waffen SS as an opportunity to establish a basis for a new Ukrainian regular army, which would stand for Ukrainian interests in the aftermath of the possible defeat of Germany and the subsequent chaos on the territory populated by Ukrainians.[31] However, as will be detailed later in the chapter, the UTsK's idea of the 'Galicia' Division and that of the German authorities were quite different.

Nationalism and Anti-Semitism

While the subject of anti-Jewish attitudes of the nationalist groups in Ukraine during the Second World War requires more research, and the current studies disagree as to the degree and the role of anti-Semitism in Ukrainian nationalism of the twentieth century, what is clear is that many nationalist groups engaged in anti-Jewish campaigns even if they did not

30 Myroslav Yurkevich, 'Galician Ukrainians in German Military Formations and in the German Administration', *Ukraine during World War II: History and its Aftermath: a Symposium*, edited by Yuri Boshyk, Roman Waschuk and Andriy Wynnyckyj (Edmonton: University of Alberta, Canadian Institute of Ukrainian Studies Press, 1986), p. 69.

31 Subtelny, *Ukraine: A History*, p. 472.

see the Jewish population as their primary enemy.[32] The discussion of the OUN's position towards the Jews has being widely debated in Ukraine and in the West in recent years. However, these debates, with few exceptions, rarely engage in a constructive dialogue. The pro-nationalist historians continue to argue the innocence of the OUN when it comes to participating in violence against Jews such as the L'viv pogrom of 1941,[33] despite the fact that other scholars offer undeniable evidence of the nationalists' anti-Semitic sentiment, even if its exact details are still under-researched.[34]

As for the 'Galicia' Division, the often cited argument that this formation had no role to play in the violence against Jews because it was formed in 1943 is not convincing. As a division of the Waffen SS, the 'Galicia' was part of a profoundly anti-Semitic structure. Even if the recruits joined the Division in 1943 primarily because of their nationalistic state-building aspirations, they could not have been completely unaware of what had happened to the Jews throughout Europe by the time the 'Galicia' was formed. The recruitment posters called for young Ukrainian men to join the 'SS Riflemen Division Galicia' in order to fight 'shoulder to shoulder with the invincible German Army', and 'destroy the Judeo-Bolshevik monster once and for all'.[35] The posters called for revenge for the 'innocent blood of millions of Our brothers murdered in the NKVD prisons, the Solovki, Siberia, in Kazakhstan.'[36] The wide-spread myth that all Bolsheviks were Jews and all Jews were Bolsheviks combined with the fear and hatred of the Soviet regime equated the Jews with the Soviets and made the anti-Jewish sentiment part of the nationalist struggle.[37] Thus, even though the 'Galicia' might

32 See Frank Golczewski, 'Shades of Grey'.

33 See Volodymyr V'iatrovych, *Stavlennia OUN do ievreïv. Formuvannia pozytsiï na tli katastrofy* (L'viv: Vydavnytstvo Ms., 2006).

34 See John-Paul Himka, 'The Lviv Pogrom of 1941: The Germans, Ukrainian Nationalists, and the Carnival Crowd', *Canadian Slavonic Papers/Revue canadienne des slavistes* LIII/2–4 (June–September–December 2011), 209–43.

35 From the poster published in special issue of the wall newspaper *Novi Visti* (Latest News) for the peasants of the General Government in 1943 in Golczewski, 'Shades of Grey', p. 142.

36 *Ibid.*

37 See Golczewski, 'Shades of Grey', pp. 130–1.

not have taken part in anti-Jewish campaigns directly as a division,[38] being part of the Nazi anti-Semitic structures cannot be downplayed. Some of the German officers of the 'Galicia' had a history of participating in brutal anti-Jewish and counter-insurgency operations before joining the Division. The 'Galicia' served alongside the infamous Dirlewanger Brigade.[39] In addition, the 'Galicia' was joined by the former members of the *Nachtigall* battalion who in 1942 had served in *Schutzmannschaft Bataillon* 201 in Belarus. The exact activities of the battalion require further research but it is known that *Schutzmannschaft* battalions were widely used against the Jewish population and to fight the partisans.[40] Another important aspect that needs to be mentioned in this context is the history of the *Galizische SS-Freiwilligen Regimenter 4–8*.[41] They consisted of Ukrainians who had originally volunteered to join the 'Galicia' when it was being formed but were not accepted into the Division.[42] In the spring of 1944 these police regiments were incorporated into the Division.[43]

38 Dieter Pohl suggests that part of the 'Galicia' Division might have helped to round up Jews in Brody in February 1944. See Dieter Pohl, *Nationalsozialistische Judenverfolgung in Ostgalizien 1941–1944: Organisation und Durchführung eines staatlichen Massenverbrechens* (Munich: R. Oldenbourg Verlag, 1997), p. 365.

39 Both the German officers of the Division and the Dirlewanger Brigade are discussed later in the book.

40 See John-Paul Himka, 'Be Wary of Faulty Nachtigall Lessons' *Kyiv Post* (27 March 2008) <http://www.kyivpost.com/opinion/oped/28686/> accessed 11 February 2013. See also Per Rudling, 'Navuka zabivats'. 201-y batal'ion akhounai palitsyi i hauptman Raman Shukhevich u Belarusi u 1942 hodze', *ARCHEI* (7–8) (2012), 67–87.

41 The 8th Regiment was never fully developed; the other four regiments were trained under the control of *Ordnungspolizei* (*Orpo*). Melnyk states that the *Orpo* exercised complete control over the regiments, which 'facilitated the deployment of two of the regiments, the 4th and 5th for security duties.' (Melnyk, *To Battle*, p. 63). For detailed information on the *Galizische SS-Freiwillige Regimenter 4–8* and their commanders, most of whom were experienced *Polizei* officers, see Melnyk, *To Battle*, pp. 61–3.

42 The *4 Galizische SS-Freiwillige Regiment* was involved in the Huta Pieniacka massacre. The Huta Pieniacka massacre as well as other war crimes in which the 'Galicia' Division allegedly participated are discussed in Chapter 2.

43 See Heike, *The Ukrainian Division*, p. 24.

Ukrainians in Czechoslovakia

In the aftermath of the First World War, around one million Ukrainians living in Bessarabia and Bukovyna regions found themselves in the Kingdom of Romania. The strict policy of assimilation enforced by the Romanian authorities during most of the interwar period weakened Ukrainian civic life in the region.[44] The situation of Ukrainians in the Czechoslovak Republic was different. The Czechoslovak Republic came to exist in October 1918 and united within its borders territories of the contemporary Czech Republic, Slovakia, and also lands with a Ukrainian and Hungarian population – Sub-Carpathian Ruthenia. The foreign policy of the Czechoslovak Republic changed according to circumstances and was largely conditioned by the attitude of the Czechoslovak leaders and political figures towards the Ukrainian question, the potential for Ukrainian state-building, and Ukrainians in general. There were two main attitudes towards the Ukrainian question in Czechoslovakia: a pro-Russian stance (such as that supported by Karel Kramář)[45] and one which encouraged the idea of Ukrainian statehood, albeit in its particular form (advocated by Tomáš Masaryk).[46] After Sudetenland was given up by the Czechoslovak government to Germany, according to the Munich Agreement of 1938,[47] Slovak and Ukrainian demands for independence increased. Following the Slovak proclamation of independence on 14 March 1939, on 15 March Carpatho-Ukraine also declared its independence with Augustyn Voloshyn as its president. On the same day, the Hungarian Army invaded Carpatho-Ukraine. The

44 See Yekelchyk, *Ukraine*, pp. 128–9.

45 Karel Kramář was a Czech politician and liberal nationalist who favoured close ties between the Czechs and the Russian Empire.

46 Tomáš Masaryk was the first president of Czechoslovakia. Masaryk viewed the Ukrainian question in a pan-Slavic context. See Ievhen Topinka, *Tomáš Masaryk a Ukrajinci. Archiválie* (L'viv: Tsentr Ievropy, 2010).

47 The agreement allowed German annexation of Czechoslovakia's Sudetenland (areas along the Czech border populated largely by ethnic Germans). This agreement was negotiated without the participation of Czechoslovakia.

proclamation of independence in March 1939, although a spontaneous and hasty event, had an impact not only on the Ukrainians of Transcarpathia, but also on the Ukrainian people as a whole. Following the Act of Union of the Ukrainian People's Republic and the Western Ukrainian People's Republic (*Zakhidnoukraïns'ka Narodna Respublika*, ZUNR) on 21 January 1919, the proclamation of independence of Carpatho-Ukraine was the second attempt to declare the self-sufficiency and capacity for state-building by Ukrainians. And although the real act of proclamation of independence, ratified on 15 March 1939 by the Sejm of Carpatho-Ukraine, was more symbolic than factual, it played its part in the creation of the state-building narrative of the Ukrainian nation.

The main Ukrainian military formation in Czechoslovakia was the Carpathian Sich (*Karpats'ka Sich*), a paramilitary organization acting in Carpatho-Ukraine in 1938–9. The Sich was formed in November 1938 from the units of the Ukrainian National Defence (*Ukraïns'ka natsional'na oborona*), and was led by Dmytro Klempush, who started forming the first units of the Sich in the early 1930s. This formation adopted its own uniform and ranks similar to those that existed in the Ukrainian military units of the Austro-Hungarian Army. The Carpathian Sich included a number of women who formed the female unit of the Sich, known as Women's Sich (*Zhinocha Sich*).[48] The Sich benefited from an influx of Galician Ukrainians who had fled Poland and who were keen to support Ukrainian ambitions for statehood. The maintenance and development of the Carpathian Sich was expensive. Augustyn Voloshyn, the president of Carpatho-Ukraine, sought financial support mainly from Ukrainians in the diaspora. By January 1939, there was a budget of 34,688 Czech crowns for the development of the Carpathian Sich.[49]

The Carpathian Sich was viewed as the national army of Carpatho-Ukraine. With 2,000 men in its ranks, it mounted armed resistance to the

48 See Oleksandr Pahiria, 'Zhinocha Sich', *Ukraïna Moloda* 047 (13 March 2010) <htp://www.umoloda.kiev.ua/number/1614/196/56827/> accessed 6 December 2012.

49 Mykola Vehesh, 'Velych i trahediia Karpats'koï Ukraïny', *Dzerkalo Tyzhnia*, Kyiv 10 (485) (13–19 March (2004) <http://www.dt.ua/3000/3150/45817> accessed 9 February 2010.

Hungarian invasion in March 1939. The Sich lost several hundred soldiers in battles with the Hungarians. A number of soldiers fled to Romania, where they were turned over to the Hungarian authorities, and those soldiers who were of Galician origin were in turn surrendered to the Polish authorities. Although unsuccessful, the struggle of the Carpathian Sich for the independence of the Carpatho-Ukraine became the first organized armed resistance in central Europe in the lead up to the Second World War.[50] On 18 March 1939, the Carpathian Sich discontinued its resistance, although some Sich units carried on fighting as partisan elements. The Subcarpathian autonomous region (and afterwards the independent Carpatho-Ukraine) existed for an extraordinarily short period of time: October 1938 until March 1939. Nevertheless, it caused significant political shifts and attracted the attention of all neighbouring countries, and especially other regions under the rule of bordering states populated by Ukrainians.

Ukrainians in the USSR

During the 1930s, Soviet Ukraine was experiencing the full implementation of Stalin's schemes for the 'revolution from above', the Five Year Plans, industrialization,[51] urbanization, and collectivization. The dominant tragedy of the 1930s in Soviet Ukraine was the *Holodomor*,[52] the

50 See Mykola Vehesh, *Karpats'ka Ukraïna. Dokumenty i fakty* (Uzhhorod: Karpaty, 2004).

51 The first Five Year Plan was adopted by the Communist Party in 1928. During the first Five Year Plan, 400 of the 1,500 new industrial plants in the USSR were built in Ukraine. See Subtelny, *Ukraine: A History*, pp. 405–6.

52 The term *Holodomor* is translated from Ukrainian as 'death by hunger'. The events of 1932–3 in Ukraine are also referred to as *Holod* (famine) and in the English-speaking world as 'Ukrainian Famine of 1932–3'. Estimates of the numbers of victims of the *Holodomor* vary from 2.5 to 7.5 million inhabitants of Ukraine. See Oleh Wolowyna and Natalia Levchuk, *Holodomor Losses in Ukraine within the Context*

famine of 1932–3. The artificial starvation of the population had a serious impact on the attitudes of the population towards the ruling authority, and if the famine did not succeed in weakening the national consciousness of Ukrainians, the Great Terror which followed across the whole of the USSR made sure to obliterate the remaining 'bourgeois nationalism' among the Ukrainian population. The policy of 'Ukrainization'[53] which had been introduced earlier was now turned into a battle against Ukrainian nationalists, and Russification was strongly implemented in Ukraine as it was in other non-Russian regions of the USSR.

Following the *Holodomor* and the Stalinist purges, nationalism did not acquire any organized form in Soviet Ukraine as the population of the region was oppressed by the regime and mostly disunited, especially in the borderlands, where political control was especially vigorous. The only nationalist military group that operated on the border of the Soviet Union was the Polissian Sich (*Polis'ka Sich*), led by Taras Bul'ba-Borovets'.[54] The

---

of the 1932–1933 Famine in the Soviet Union. Paper presented at the Association for the Study of Nationalities, New York, 2011; David R. Marples, *Holodomor: Causes of the Famine of 1932–1933 in Ukraine* (Saskatoon: Heritage Press, 2011); Stanislav Kul'chytskyi, 'Velykyi Holod', *Istoriia v shkolakh Ukraïny*, 3 (2003), 51–2; David R. Marples, *Heroes and Villains. Creating National History in Contemporary Ukraine* (Budapest: Central European University Press, 2007); Raphael Lemkin, *Soviet Genocide in Ukraine* (Kyiv: Maisternia Knyhy, 2009); Robert Conquest, *The Harvest of Sorrow: Soviet Collectivization and the Terror-Famine* (Edmonton: The University of Alberta Press in Association with the Canadian Institute of Ukrainian Studies and London, Century Hutchinson, 1986); James E. Mace, *Communism and the Dilemma of National Liberation: National Communism in Soviet Ukraine, 1918–1933* (Cambridge, MA: Distributed by Harvard University Press, 1983).

53 'Ukrainization' is a term used with reference to the Soviet indigenization policy of the 1920s – *korenizatsiia* – 'putting down roots'. This policy encouraged the use of the Ukrainian language and promotion of Ukrainian culture. However, Ukrainization was aimed at strengthening the Soviet power in the Soviet Ukraine. See George O. Liber, *Soviet National Policy, Urban Growth, and Identity Change in the Ukrainian SSR 1923–1934* (Cambridge: Cambridge University Press, 1992) and Mace, *Communism and the Dilemma of National Liberation*.

54 Bul'ba-Borovets' was also known as Taras Bul'ba, after a hero in the novel by Mykola Hohol' (Nikolai Gogol), a romanticized, courageous Cossack who fights against the

Polissian Sich, also known as the Ukrainian Insurgent Army of Bul'ba-Borovets' and later as the Ukrainian People's Revolutionary Army, was an underground military formation founded in Polissia (now northern Ukraine, then under Soviet control). Although the territory where the Polissian Sich was most active was in Soviet Ukraine, its leader Bul'ba-Borovets' was strongly linked to Polish Ukraine. He was born in a village near Równe (Rivne) which was under Polish control until 1939, when it became part of the Ukrainian SSR. Bul'ba-Borovets' was always politically active, but his military activity started in 1932 when he was introduced to the colonel of the former UNR Army, Ivan Lytvynenko, who belonged to the secret service of the former UNR Army in 1926.[55] Lytvynenko was responsible for establishing points of communication in Soviet Ukraine with the aim of uniting all insurgent forces acting on territories populated by Ukrainians. In the case of war with the USSR, Mykola Livyts'kyi, the president of the UNR in exile, stated that nationalist underground groups 'must make sure that, before the foreign troops reach Ukraine, Ukrainian military units are formed locally, and can take control under the slogan of the restoration of the UNR'.[56] Borovets' took an active part in arranging such groups. He crossed the border into Soviet Ukraine, where he had the opportunity to witness the *Holodomor*, which he described in his work *L'udoïdy* (*The Cannibals*).[57] In 1932 Bul'ba-Borovets' founded the Ukrainian National Renaissance (*Ukraïns'ke natsional'ne vidrodzhennia*), an underground organization for which he was imprisoned in the Polish Bereza Kartuska prison camp[58] in 1934–5. He also had links with the OUN,[59]

Poles to protect his motherland. The Ukrainian Insurgent Army of the OUN also penetrated Soviet Ukraine in 1943. It mainly conducted raids, and its activity was limited and not always popular among the local population.

55 See Mykola Livyts'kyi, *DTs UNR v ekzyli mizh 1920–1940* (Munich: Ukraïns'ke informatsiine biuro, 1984), p. 23.

56 *Ibid.*, p. 27.

57 He published this work under a pseudonym Rystrychenko. Cited in Kul'chyts'kyi, *Orhanizatsiia ukraïns'kykh natsionalistiv*, p. 115.

58 *Miejsce Odosobnienia w Berezie Kartuskiej*, translated from Polish as a 'place of isolation at Bereza Kartuska'.

59 Kul'chyts'kyi, *Orhanizatsiia ukraïns'kykh natsionalistiv*, p. 115.

and was believed to have been involved in the *Abwehr*, but denied such involvement in his book *Armiia bez derzhavy*, written in 1952.[60]

Soon after the Soviet annexation of part of eastern Poland to the Ukrainian SSR, Bul'ba-Borovets' established the Polissian Sich with German permission.[61] According to Karel Berkhoff, the Polissian Sich 'had legal status as a police force'.[62] Berhkhoff states that it 'roamed the forests and Pripet marshes from a base in Olevks, apprehended partisans and Jewish civilians, and if it did not kill them at least handed them over to the German authorities.'[63] The Polissian Sich, or the UPA of Bul'ba Borovets, set out to fight against the Soviets first but later, it also engaged in combat against the Germans.[64] When fighting one group, the Polissian Sich would co-operate with the other when it was convenient, in spite of announcing during the early stages of the German occupation that Ukraine should have the same negative attitude to the new 'liberator' as it had to the previous one.[65] From 1943 the Polissian Sich became known as the Ukrainian National Revolutionary Army, and another UPA had started to function at the time in eastern Poland.

Ukrainians in Poland

In the years preceding the Second World War, the situation in eastern Poland was very different from that in the Soviet territories. As a result of the collapse of the Hapsburg Empire, the regions of western Volhynia

60 See Taras Bul'ba-Borovets', *Armiia bez derzhavy* (L'viv, 1993 edn), p. 44.
61 See Lower, *Nazi Empire-Building*, p. 53.
62 Karel C. Berkhoff, *Harvest of Despair: Life and Death in Ukraine under Nazi Rule* (Cambridge, MA: The Belknap Press of Harvard University Press, 2004), p. 64.
63 *Ibid.*
64 Subtelny, *Ukraine: A History*, pp. 473–4.
65 Bul'ba-Borovets', *Armiia bez derzhavy*, p. 63.

(Wołyń, Volyn') and eastern Galicia (Galicja, Halychyna),[66] where Ukrainians constituted a majority, found themselves under Polish rule. Following the 1918–19 Ukrainian–Polish War,[67] in order to avoid further political conflicts on these lands, on 26 September 1922 the Polish Sejm allowed the autonomy of the three administrative regions of eastern Galicia. Ukrainians refused to recognize the Polish state, but on 14 March 1923 the Council of Ambassadors in Versailles reached its decision to consider the Galicia region part of Poland.[68] After this, the Ukrainian relationship with their Polish rulers was even more tense. Subtelny describes the early years of Polish rule in western Ukraine as 'mutual negation',[69] which then grew into an open conflict between the Polish authorities and Ukrainian nationalists.

The seemingly flourishing Ukrainization in Soviet Ukraine inspired some Ukrainian nationalists in western Ukraine to support the ideas that were arising across the border. Thus, the head of the Ukrainian National-Democratic Alliance Dmytro Levyts'kyi wrote in *Dilo* that 'in Soviet Ukraine, the Ukrainian idea is growing, getting stronger and developing.'[70] However, such romantic illusions of the Soviet policy of Ukrainization as an example for the rest of the Ukrainian nationalist movement were short-lived. The early 1930s saw the purging of most of those political figures who had moved to Soviet Ukraine in the 1920s.

Towards the end of the 1920s and throughout the 1930s, the Polish government practised forceful measures against the Ukrainian minority living in eastern Polish lands. Golczewski states that 'drawing all the wrong lessons of its past, the Polish state launched a policy of colonizing its newly acquired lands. Despite its treaty obligations to the western powers, Poland began to

66 As there are accepted anglicized spellings for Galicia and Volhynia, I shall refer to these regions using these spellings.

67 The Ukrainian–Polish War was a conflict in 1918–19 between the Second Polish Republic and the Western Ukrainian People's Republic over eastern Galicia, following the collapse of the Austro-Hungarian Empire.

68 Taras Hunczak, *Ukraïna. Persha polovyna XX stolittia* (Kyiv: Lybid', 1993), p. 204.

69 Subtelny, *Ukraine: A History*, p. 427.

70 *Dilo*, 21 February 1925, cited in Hunczak, *Ukraïna*, p. 204.

pursue polonization.'[71] Ukrainian-language schools were transformed into bilingual institutions in which Polish was the main language; Polish citizens of Ukrainian ethnicity were not allowed to enter L'viv (Lwów) University and there were no alternative Ukrainian universities.[72] Apart from the Polonization of education, eastern Galicia and Volhynia were being forcibly populated by Polish settlers. Subtelny estimates that by 1938, 200,000 Poles were settled in the villages of eastern Galicia and about 100,000 had also moved into Galician towns.[73] The policy of 'pacification',[74] which came as a result of a series of attacks carried out by Ukrainian nationalists against the Polish population in Galicia, was intensive and brutal. Ukrainian community centres and libraries in villages were destroyed by Polish armed units. Ukrainian men were arrested *en masse*; women who were suspected in nationalist activity were also imprisoned. It became obligatory to vote for candidates of Polish ethnicity.[75] Resistance towards the Polish authorities manifested itself in many spheres of Ukrainian society: peasants were badly affected by the economic crisis; relationships between Ukrainian youth and the Polish authorities deteriorated because of 'pacification' and the block on their access to higher education and dissatisfaction with the Polish government among Ukrainian intelligentsia also grew.[76]

The growing aggravation of the Ukrainian population and the increasing control of the Polish authorities produced very fertile ground for Ukrainian radical nationalism in the 1930s. The OUN, now more popular

71 Golczewski, 'Shades of Grey', p. 121.

72 Ryszard Torzecki, *Polacy i Ukraińcy. Sprawa ukraińska w czasie II wojny światowej na terenie II Rzeczypospolitej* (Warszawa: Wydawnictwo Naukowe PWN, 1993), p. 12; also Yekelchyk, *Ukraine*, pp. 121–5.

73 Subtelny, *Ukraine: A History*, p. 429.

74 The pacification of Ukrainians (referred to in Polish as *Pacyfikacja Małopolski Wschodniej*) was a campaign of punitive actions by Polish police against the Ukrainian minority in eastern Galicia. The punishment of thousands of peasants resulted in an increase in animosity between the Polish authorities and the Ukrainian population. See Subtelny, *Ukraine: A History*, pp. 430–1.

75 Subtelny, *Ukraine: A History*, p. 430.

76 For a discussion of the interwar Polish–Ukrainian relations, see Torzecki, *Polacy i Ukraińcy*, pp. 11–13.

than ever, focused on the political assassinations of Polish officials such as Tadeusz Hołówko (in 1931) and Bronisław Pieracki (in 1934).[77] This resulted in mass arrests of Ukrainian nationalists by the Polish authorities. There were attempts at a so-called 'normalization' in 1935–7, when Polish authorities and some parts of the Ukrainian community tried to agree on reducing violence and coming to a compromise. Such attempts were, however, unsuccessful and largely rejected by Ukrainian nationalists. Moreover, at this time, the nationalist movement was being consolidated among the Ukrainian community in Poland, mainly by the OUN.[78]

In 1939, as Germany invaded Poland, the USSR occupied the western lands of Ukraine up to the Curzon line, justifying their actions by the need to protect Poland's Ukrainian minority.[79] A large part of the territory west of the Curzon line found itself under German occupation. Subsequently, Ukrainian nationalist political leaders continued their communication with German political and military circles. Iaroslav Hrytsak suggests that one of the reasons why Ukrainians sought support from the Germans is that 'when an extreme situation arises, our consciousness relies not on new solutions, but on familiar schemes.'[80] Hrytsak states that those who created Ukrainian formations with German help during the Second World War, including the 'Galicia' Division, were former residents of the Austro-Hungarian Empire and thus followed their familiar routes to seek support.[81] Similarly to Hrytsak, Frank Golczewski states that 'Ukrainian nationalist circles, particularly in Galicia, became convinced that Ukrainians and Germans were natural allies against Poland, the Entente, and the Versailles Treaty.'[82]

77 *Ibid.*, p. 13. The OUN also targeted Ukrainians who opposed them. Thus in 1934 they assassinated Ivan Babii, a Ukrainian high-school principal who opposed his students' membership of the OUN. See Yekelchyk, *Ukraine*, p. 128.

78 Torzecki, *Polacy i Ukraińcy*, p. 14.

79 The same applied to Belarusians who found themselves under Soviet rule in 1939. See Yekelchyk, *Ukraine*, p. 132.

80 Iaroslav Hrytsak, 'Svoiu doliu dyviziinyky ne vybyraly…', *Visti Kombatanta* 3 (Toronto and New York, 2007), 63–5 (p. 64).

81 *Ibid.*

82 Golczewski, 'Shades of Grey', p. 121.

Dieter Pohl points out that Germans who entered the western Ukrainian towns had little knowledge of the inhabitants, the topography; they did not speak the local language and thus had to rely on the local interpreters and administrators.[83]

Many active members of the OUN were eager to assist the Germans in the creation of Ukrainian military units within the German Armed Forces in the early stages of the Second World War, explaining their collaboration by the desire to restore Ukraine's independence with German help. In his *Roads to Extinction*, Philip Friedman says that '[a]fter the outbreak of World War II, the Germans constantly favoured the OUN at the expense of more moderate Ukrainian groups'.[84] Indeed, leaders of the German Supreme Command of the Armed Forces (*Oberkommando der Wehrmacht*, OKW) were generally prepared to use anti-Communist East European forces in the context of the war campaign against the USSR.[85] With these aims in mind – an independent Ukrainian state for the leaders of the OUN and the use in combat of eager Ukrainians for the OKW – Ukrainian units started to be formed within the Wehrmacht. Bolianovs'kyi states that '[t]he head of the Abwehr, Admiral Wilhelm Canaris, who, according to his close colleague Karl Heinz Abshagen, "personally knew and valued" Konovalets', took on the establishment of communication with the leadership of the OUN'.[86] Thus, a strengthening of co-operation between Ukrainian nationalist leaders and German officials, especially the *Abwehr*, can be explained by a combination of factors: the frustration of the Ukrainian population with the discriminatory treatment they received

83 Dieter Pohl, 'Anti-Jewish Pogroms in Western Ukraine – A Research Agenda', in Eleazar Barkan, Elizabeth A. Cole and Kai Struve, eds, *Shared History – Divided Memory: Jews and Others in Soviet-Occupied Poland, 1939–1941* (Leipzig: Leipziger Universitätsverlag, 2007) pp. 305–13 (p. 308).

84 Philip Friedman, *Roads to Extinction* (New York: Jewish Publication Society of America, 1980), p. 179.

85 Andrii Bolianovs'kyi, *Ukraïns'ki viis'kovi formuvannia v zbroinykh sylakh Nimechchyny (1939–1945)* (L'viv: L'vivs'kyi natsional'nyi universytet im. Ivana Franka, 2003), p. 570.

86 K.-H. Abshagen, *Canaris: Patriot und Weltbürger* (Stuttgart: Union Deutsche Verlaganstalt, 1954), p. 214, cited in Bolianovs'kyi, *Ukraïns'ki viis'kovi formuvannia*, p. 23.

from the Polish authorities, and later the fear of a potential Soviet invasion, the subsequent growing support for radical nationalism in the region, and the perceived potential for the formation of an independent military force.

As the influence and popularity of the OUN was increasing, towards the end of the 1930s the organization was suffering internal conflicts. On 10 February 1940, Bandera was nominated the chief of the new 'revolutionary' *Provid*.[87] Thus, there were now two leaders of the most popular nationalist organization: Mel'nyk, who was winning support among the older generation, and Bandera, who was radicalizing his branch of the organization. Leaders of various groups, the clergy and other nationalist institutions were divided in their support for either Bandera or Mel'nyk. One of the supporters of the 'conservative' branch of the OUN was Bishop Ivan Buchko, who was a close associate of Sheptyts'kyi.[88] Richard Iarii, however, had used the opportunity of the split within the OUN to move away from the old *Provid*, with whom he was already in conflict, and join the Bandera leadership, bringing his valuable connections with the German intelligence with him. This rupture in the largest and the most influential nationalist organization had significant consequences with regards to the strategic development of Ukrainian nationalism. The OUN-M (Mel'nyk's branch) and the OUN-B (Bandera's branch) were often more preoccupied with internal power struggles than with the common struggle for Ukraine's independence.

In 1939 the *Abwehr* formed the so-called Ukrainian Legion which consisted of OUN members, most of whom were students in Austria and Germany; some were also former soldiers of the Carpathian Sich and Ukrainian deserters from the Polish Army. The two battalions that comprised the Legion were officially known as 'Mountain-Peasant's Help' (*Bergbauernhilfe*). Ukrainians referred to them as 'Military Units of Nationalists' (*Viis'kovi viddily natsionalistiv*). The Legion was commanded by Major Hans Dehmel and Colonel Roman Sushko. It took part in the Polish campaign as part of the 14 Army Group South. Their duties

87 Armstrong, *Ukrainian Nationalism*, p. 58.

88 Buchko later played an important role in helping the ex-soldiers of the 'Galicia' avoid repatriation.

consisted mainly of helping with the organization of local administration, informing the Ukrainian civilian population of the existence of the Ukrainian Legion and recruitment of new soldiers. After the end of the German–Polish war, the Legion was disbanded and its soldiers joined other formations such as the *Werkschutz* (factory guard), the *Bahnschutz* (railway guard), and the *Hilfspolizei* (auxiliary police). The *Werkschutz* was formed by the Wehrmacht in the *Generalgouvernement* in October 1939. It consisted of mostly former residents of Carpathian Ukraine, Galicia and Volhynia. They were later joined by the OUN members, former legionaries. In spring 1940 the unit had almost 1,000 members, half of whom were OUN members.[89] In 1941, the racial policy of the Nazis prevented them from recruiting Ukrainian men as soldiers of the Waffen SS.[90] As the Wehrmacht was less preoccupied with the racial policy, on 25 February 1941, Canaris, the head of the *Abwehr*, issued an order to form a new Ukrainian legion. The OUN-B was seen to be the most active of the Ukrainian nationalist organizations, and so the German military authority decided to form a legion based on the members of the OUN-B, in a similar scenario to that of the formation of the *Bergbauernhilfe*.[91] *Werkschutz*, therefore, served as a transition stage between the *Bergbauernhilfe* and the new Ukrainian legion.

In April–June 1941 two Ukrainian battalions were organized by the *Abwehr*: Special group (*Sondergruppe*) *Nachtigall* and *Organization Roland*, referred to by Ukrainians as the Legion of Ukrainian Nationalists (*Druzhyny Ukraïns'kykh Natsionalistiv*, DUN). Both units consisted of OUN members (especially those of the Bandera branch).[92] The *Nachtigall* battalion was officially known to Ukrainians as the Ievhen Konovalets' Legion. Its 330 soldiers were commanded by Lieutenant Hans Albrecht Herzner and Captain Roman Shukhevych, who had as his adviser the German *Oberleutnant* Theodor Oberländer.[93] *Nachtigall* officer, Myroslav

89 Mykola Klymyshyn, *U pokhodi do voli. Spomyny* (Detroit: Ukraïns'ka knyharnia, 1984), in Bolianovs'kyi, *Ukraïns'ki viis'kovi formuvannia*, p. 40.

90 Stein, *The Waffen SS*, pp. 185–6.

91 Bolianovs'kyi, *Ukraïns'ki viis'kovi formuvannia*, p. 51.

92 *Ibid.*, p. 571.

93 Bihl, 'Ukrainians in the Armed Forces', p. 140.

Kal'ba (whose brother Bohdan was an officer of the 'Galicia' Division) gives his opinion on being in *Nachtigall*:

> We did not volunteer to join *Nachtigall*, we were appointed by the Organization [OUN] to join *Nachtigall* as people who swore loyalty to Ukraine and the Organization and as those who, according to the first point of the Decalogue, promised to '[a]chieve the Ukrainian State or die fighting for it'. We were happy and proud to be the first ones to take up arms in the battle for an Independent Ukraine.[94]

When Germany invaded the USSR, *Nachtigall* was attached to the 1st Battalion of the Regiment *Brandenburg-800* and became part of the 1st Mountain Infantry Division whose orders were to march on L'viv. *Nachtigall* reached L'viv on 30 June 1941 and occupied the city's strategic positions (industrial warehouses, prisons and a radio station).[95] On the same day, the restoration of an independent Ukrainian state and establishment of a Ukrainian government was declared by Stepan Bandera and Iaroslav Stets'ko, the deputy leader of the OUN. This proclamation was condemned by the Nazi officials and resulted in the arrest of the Stets'ko government. During the time of the L'viv pogrom, which started the day after the German Army entered the city, the *Nachtigall* battalion was present in the city, but was on a week-long leave from duty. While most scholars agree that the battalion as a whole did not partake in the atrocities in L'viv, it is likely that some individual members of the battalion might have participated in the pogrom.[96] After the proclamation of independence, both

94 Myroslav Kal'ba, *Nakhtigal' v zapytanniakh i vidpovidiakh* (L'viv: Halyts'ka vydavnycha spilka, 2008), p. 19.

95 Bolianovs'kyi, *Ukraïns'ki viis'kovi formuvannia*, pp. 66–9.

96 For the OUN's involvement in the L'viv pogrom, see John-Paul Himka, *Ukrainians, Jews and the Holocaust: Divergent Memories* (Saskatoon: Heritage Press, 2009); John-Paul Himka, True and False Lessons from the Nachtigall Episode, BRAMA, 19 March 2008 <http://www.brama.com/news/press/2008/03/080319himka_nachtigall.html> accessed 6 May 2011; Ivan Patryliak, *Viis'kova diial'nist OUN (B) u 1940–1942 rokakh* (Kyiv: Kyïvs'kyi natsional'nyi universytet imeni Tarasa Shevchenka Instytut istoriï Ukraïny NAN Ukraïny, 2004), pp. 321–68. See also extracts from 'Materialy Haluzevoho derzhavnoho arkhivu SB Ukraïny', SBU Archives, Kyiv, Ukraine. Among those who question *Nachtigall's* innocence with regard to the pogrom is Sol Littman. He poses the question: '[f]or what purpose was *Nachtigall* – a highly trained Special

Nachtigall and *Roland* were disbanded.[97] Despite their failure to form a nucleus of a Ukrainian army, all but fourteen of the members of the two battalions signed up with the Wehrmacht for one more year and continued to receive military training. Yet at the end of their service, they refused to sign up for further service and most of the men joined the UPA.[98]

The Ukrainian Insurgent Army, formed by the OUN-B, was one of the largest and best-known military structures that fought for Ukraine's independence in the twentieth century. A large portion of the men who formed Bandera's UPA had served in the Ukrainian police under German occupation and in 1943 deserted it to join the UPA.[99] The formation of the UPA was not a trouble-free process. By the time the OUN was ready to expand its military influence to the north-western regions of Ukraine, an organization fighting for the same goal already existed there: the UPA of Bul'ba-Borovets', described above. In 1942 when the OUN-B established its UPA units in Volhynia, it decided to form a larger military force, once again aspiring to see it grow into the nucleus for a Ukrainian army, which the OUN believed would be required for when the Second World War came to an end and the 'third world war' started.[100] Bandera and Bul'ba-

---

Operations regiment specializing in sabotage and subversion – rushed to the city on advance of the regular army units? Surely not to serve as honour guards at funerals or to remain confined to barracks performing housekeeping duties' (Littman, *Pure Soldiers*, p. 30).

97 Bolianovs'kyi, *Ukraïns'ki viis'kovi formuvannia*, pp. 41–74. The *Roland* battalion has enjoyed less scholarly attention than *Nachtigall*. It was led by Ievhen Pobihushchyi, who later joined the 'Galicia' Division. During its training, which was conducted in total secrecy, the *Roland* unit was under Iarii's command. It followed German and Romanian Armies into southern Ukraine.

98 Bihl, 'Ukrainians in the Armed Forces', p. 140.

99 John-Paul Himka, 'Christianity and Radical Nationalism', p. 96.

100 The 'third world war' is frequently mentioned in the memoir literature, and, when interviewed, the former 'Galicians' often refer to it as one of the major factors that led them to believe in the long-term need for the 'Galicia' Division. Although this notion might seem somewhat unrealistic, upon examination of the so-called 'Operation Unthinkable' documentation (see (NA) CAB 120/691, 'Russia. Threat to Western Civilisation. Operation "Unthinkable"', 22 May 1945), produced by the Churchill government, it becomes clear that the plans for the 'third world war' existed not just in the imagination of Ukrainian nationalists; they had the potential of becoming

Borovets' tried to come to an agreement which would clarify power divisions, but the peaceful negotiations were short-lived and they soon grew into open hostility and a power struggle. Bandera's propaganda declared that the OUN-B 'is not some underground activity of hundreds or even thousands of people, it is a national liberation revolution of millions of the Ukrainian masses'.[101] Bandera's OUN issued flyers ordering all nationalists to obey the command of the OUN-B and its main UPA staff.[102]

Having failed to unite the UPA of Bul'ba-Borovets' with the one controlled by the Organization of Ukrainian Nationalists by peaceful means, the OUN-B forcibly assimilated the already existing formation of Bul'ba-Borovets'. Roman Shukhevych, the commander of the disbanded *Nachtigall* battalion, went on to head the UPA. The UPA's weapons were mostly guns and ammunition captured from the Nazis or Soviets. Their uniforms were a mixture of everything from confiscated enemy uniforms (without the insignia) to a variety of civilian clothes adapted for the purposes of guerrilla fighting. The UPA did have some training schools and after 1943 officers often gained their training in the ranks of the 'Galicia' Division, but most schooling came from action. Much of the local Ukrainian population supported the UPA: some out of genuine belief that Bandera's tactics were necessary in the struggle for independence, and others because they had no choice but to support the nationalists. Those Ukrainians who were reluctant to join the nationalist resistance found themselves dealing with serious dilemmas: they feared refusing to co-operate with the UPA (often it would be made up of their relatives or neighbours) as the UPA was known to have employed force when they were denied assistance.[103] On the other hand, if discovered by the Soviets, Ukrainians who supported the UPA

---

reality. For more discussion of 'Operation Unthinkable', see Roger Bruns, *Almost History: Close Calls, Plan B's, and Twists of Fate in America's Past* (New York: Barnes & Noble, 2007).

101 Bandera, cited in Kul'chyts'kyi, *Orhanizatsiia ukraïns'kykh natsionalistiv*, p. 149.

102 Kul'chyts'kyi, *Orhanizatsiia ukraïns'kykh natsionalistiv*, p. 149.

103 One of the most contested pages of the history of UPA is the Volhynia massacre, a cleansing operation carried out by the UPA against the Polish population of the region in 1943–4. See Grzegorz Motyka, *Od rzezi wołyńskiej do akcji 'Wisła'. Konflikt polsko-ukraiński 1943–1947* (Kraków: Wydawnictwo Literackie, 2011).

risked being exiled to Siberia, and if discovered by the Nazis, summarily executed. The UPA succeeded in achieving a monopoly on the nationalist militarized movement in the region until 1943, when the Waffen SS 'Galicia' was formed.

Why a Ukrainian Waffen SS?

By 1941, the generally disunited nationalist groups were in agreement over one idea: the necessity of a Ukrainian military formation. They hoped that despite the clear direction of German policy against the recruitment of East Europeans, sooner or later the Wehrmacht would form a Ukrainian unit. These expectations were rooted in the events which led to the growing Red partisan threat and the German reaction to this, which manifested itself in the formation of the so-called voluntary assistant units (*Hilfswillige* or *Hiwi*) and Eastern Legions (*Ostlegionen*) in 1941–2. These groups recruited prisoners of war and former soldiers of the Russian Liberation Army (*Russkaia osvoboditel'naia armiia*, ROA), the Ukrainian Liberation Army (*Ukraïns'ke vyzvol'ne viisko*, UVV or *Die Ukrainische Befreiungsarmee*),[104] as well as Cossacks of the Don and the Kuban' to fight in the Wehrmacht.[105]

104 The UVV acted as a symbolic body consisting of units that were scattered throughout the German Armed Forces. This 'army' had no political influence and the German officials made it clear to the Ukrainian leadership of the UVV that there would be no tolerance of any attempts to gain political independence for Ukraine. The UVV units consisted of volunteers, the majority of whom were Ukrainians who had fought in the Red Army and had chosen to join the German Army when captured as an alternative to being POWs. Others volunteered in order to fight against the USSR. Another group which joined the UVV units were colonels, majors and lieutenants of the former UNR Army. Bolianovs'kyi states that '[i]n February, 1943 there were approximately 100,000 Ukrainians in units of the Eastern Troops. The majority of them were organized in the UVV (about 75,000 soldiers)' (Bolianovs'kyi, *Ukraïns'ki viis'kovi formuvannia*, pp. 576–7).

105 Kolisnyk, *Viis'kova Uprava*, p. 13.

Unlike the Wehrmacht, being understaffed, the SS could not mobilize its soldiers, but only recruit volunteers. SS forces accounted for about 10 per cent of the Wehrmacht. The SS units, although formed as elite squadrons and having received the best quality training and modern weapons, were regulated by the Wehrmacht at the frontline and often designated to participate in battles at the epicentre of frontline action, and thus, regularly suffered heavy losses. As early as 1940, Gottlob Berger,[106] the head of recruitment of the Waffen SS, had the idea of creating a multi-national mixed German and European army under German control, but his proposals failed as the racial policy did not permit 'non-Aryan' soldiers to join the SS. When Germany started to suffer severe losses at the Eastern Front, the German youth was less willing to voluntarily join the SS ranks. The persistent pressure of losses persuaded the German command to form units, at first consisting of West Europeans and the *Volksdeutsche*.[107]

Eventually, Otto Wächter, *SS-Gruppenführer* and the governor of the Galicia district, received permission from Heinrich Himmler to form the 'Galicia' Division.[108] Wächter stressed the significance of the USSR being Ukraine's greatest enemy and emphasized the willingness of Ukrainians to fight against the Soviet Union. Thus, on 14 April 1943, the chief of *Ordnungspolizei*[109] Kurt Daluege notified General Otto Winkelmann that Himmler had approved the creation of the 'Galicia' as a frontline division. On 28 April 1943, the formation of the 'Galicia' Division was officially announced throughout the Galicia region. On 4 May 1943, the Division's formation was proclaimed by Volodymyr Kubiiovych, who believed that if the Ukrainian Central Committee did not offer their assistance in the creation of the Ukrainian division within the Waffen SS, the Germans would do it anyway, but without taking into account Ukrainian demands. The UTsK formulated these demands; they included an assurance that the

106 Gottlob Berger (1896–1975) held the rank of *Obergruppenführer* during the Second World War. After the war, he was tried and convicted of war crimes in 1949.

107 Stein states that 'by the end of 1944 more than half the men wearing Waffen SS uniforms were not native Germans.' Stein, *The Waffen SS*, p. xxxi.

108 Kolisnyk, *Viis'kova Uprava*, pp. 14–15.

109 The *Ordnungspolizei* or Orpo was the uniformed regular German police in 1936–45.

Division should have a Ukrainian character represented in its name, badges and rank designations; that the Division should have its own Ukrainian commanders and be treated as a separate entity; that it should be used only on the front against the Red Army; that the soldiers be assured of spiritual care from their own Ukrainian chaplains; finally, that whole cadres of young Ukrainian officers and non-commissioned officers be created through special training programmes. An additional demand was made that a military committee be formed to handle all matters concerning the Division and to maintain close links with the Ukrainian Central Committee.[110]

The German authorities in Berlin only accepted some of these demands. Thus, the commanders of the Division were Germans, who had, of course, a pre-'Galicia' history. The most infamous of them was a devoted National Socialist, Fritz Freitag.[111] Another officer, Franz Magill, who was appointed as chief supply officer to the 'Galicia' Division, had also been involved in many atrocities, including commanding the infamous Dirlewanger Brigade, discussed later in the book.[112] In fact, according to Melnyk

> […] the Division, as was the case with many other European Waffen-SS Divisions, effectively became a dumping ground for a great many second-rate German officers and NCOs. Without consideration of their suitability, German cadre personnel were transferred to it from various *Polizei*, SS and Waffen-SS formations, including the 1st *'Leibstandarte'*, 3rd *'Totenkopf'*, 4th *'Polizei'* and 5th *'Wiking'* divisions. Indeed, the service records of the personnel who served with the division reveal that this extended to former concentration camp personnel such as *SS-Untersturmführer* Herbert Hanel.[113]

110 Heike, *The Ukrainian Division*, pp. 19–24.

111 Fritz Freitag (1894–1945) was the commander of the 'Galicia' Division. His pre-'Galicia' history included serving as an Operations Officer with the 1st SS Motorised SS *Infanterie* Brigade, which operated separately or alongside the *Einsatzgruppen* and participated in anti-Jewish campaigns. The memoirs of the 'Galicians' reveal that he was despised by the Division members for his anti-Ukrainian attitude. Freitag committed suicide in May 1945. For further details see Littman, *Pure Soldiers*, pp. 68–9; Melnyk, *To Battle*, 63–8.

112 For more information on the officer and NCO cadre of the 'Galicia' Division see Melnyk, *To Battle*, pp. 61–8.

113 See Melnyk, *To Battle*, p. 67.

Melnyk states that few of these officers were 'well enough disposed towards the Ukrainians to establish cordial relations with them. Most remained distant and aloof, firmly convinced of their superiority.'[114] This, however, suited Himmler, who refused to recognize the 'Galicia' as a Ukrainian formation. For this reason, a lion, the traditional symbol of Galicia, as opposed to the national Trident, was adopted as the emblem of the Division. The title 'Galicia' was also chosen in order to reduce or limit any Ukrainian nationalist feelings that the recruits might have had. In addition, Himmler stressed that the Division's personnel were to be referred to as Galicians and not Ukrainians. Most importantly, discussions of Ukrainian statehood or efforts to revive the Ukrainian state were forbidden among the Ukrainians-Galicians.

The disregard for most of the Ukrainian demands put forward by the UTsK was the basis of a continuous state of dissatisfaction in the Division for the entire period of its existence. It is clear that the Division as such was predetermined by the German authorities in terms of racial selection, political anti-Soviet views, ethnic background and territorial location. This predetermination affected the narrative of the Division members at a later stage, when they were being held by the British authorities at the surrendered enemy personnel (SEP) camp in Italy. The fact that the Division had made demands, albeit disregarded by the German authorities, allowed its members to see themselves as a homogeneous unit with a clear identity and distinct nationalist agenda rather than a spontaneous and acquiescent expression of support for Nazi ideology. This self-image of the Division as nationalistic, and in many ways at odds with the Germans, eventually helped them in achieving their civilianization, as will be illustrated later.

In order to further the recruitment process of volunteers to the 'Galicia', a Military Board (*Viiskova Uprava*) was established. It was headed by Colonel Alfred Bisanz, a German born in western Ukraine, who had been a Colonel in the UNR Army during the First World War and who was subordinate to Governor Wächter. The task of the Board was to develop and maintain communication between the soldiers of the Division and

114 *Ibid.*

their families and to popularize the Division among the general public. The Board was to ensure that the soldiers did not feel isolated among their foreign surroundings and that forceful recruitment was not being carried out by the Germans, as such instances had occurred in the past. Besides this, the Board also issued other conditions, the most important of which was the release of Ukrainian political prisoners by the German forces, in particular former *Roland* and *Nachtigall* commanders Pobihushchyi and Shukhevych.[115] This enabled the Military Board to grow in the eyes of the general public as a kind of military authority, with a wide-ranging influence in the military and political fields. In reality, the power of the Board was very limited even in those areas in which the German authorities allowed Ukrainians to participate, namely, the organization of the mobilization of volunteers, looking after them during their training, and caring for the Division soldiers' families. There were a number of restrictions imposed by the German government, including strict censorship of the books, journals and newspapers available to the soldiers.

The Division won support among the Galician population, especially among the youth and the former officers of the UNR Army. The latter saw in the creation of such a Division the potential fulfilment of their own unfulfilled dreams: the basis for a future Ukrainian army which, after the war, could play a decisive role in the formation of an independent Ukrainian state. Although, at first, it was planned to recruit only Greek Catholic residents of the Galicia district into the Division,[116] in May 1943, over 80,000 Ukrainians volunteered for service, not only from the territories of Galicia, but from all parts of the *Generalgouvernement*.[117] Out of these, 27,000 were found to be fit for military service, 19,000 were enlisted, and 13,000 actually reported for duty in the Division. The first group of volunteers were sent to training camps on 18 July 1943: 350 to the officers' schools in the Reich, 2,000 for non-commissioned officers' training, and

115 See Protocol of the Military Board meeting on 22 August 1947 in Munich, in Kolisnyk, *Viis'kova Uprava*, p. 257.

116 Bolianovs'kyi, *Dyviziia 'Halychyna'*, pp. 322–4.

117 See Report on Recruitment in Melnyk, *To Battle*, p. 325.

2,000 more to the training camp in Heidelager.[118] Others were sent to various other training centres.[119] In the autumn of 1943, *SS Oberführer* Fritz Freitag was appointed Commanding Officer of the Division (he was later promoted to *Brigade*führer and Major General of the Waffen SS). It was with Freitag's arrival in Heidelager and the appointment of Major Heike as Chief of Staff to the Division that intense training began.[120] In July

118 Heike, *The Ukrainian Division*, p. 153.

119 The question of the 'Galicia's' training causes controversy as the 'Galicians' were bound to have received education on National Socialist ideology and some of their training camps were located in close proximity to concentration camps. This is discussed in a number of studies: Rudling, 'They Defended Ukraine', p. 342; Melnyk, *To Battle*, p. 95, Bolianovs'kyi, *Dyviziia 'Halychyna'*, p. 134.

120 The Division's first order was to form a task force which would be used in action against Polish and Soviet partisans in February 1944. Heike gives a detailed description of this order and the situation in which the Division found itself: 'One night in early February 1944, the Higher SS and Police Leader in Cracow, SS Obergruppenführer Wilhelm Koppe [...] passed on the [...] order [...] to immediately form a task force in order to combat Kovpak's Soviet partisan formations that have penetrated into the territories of the Generalgouvernement' (Heike, *The Ukrainian Division*, p. 20). (Sydir Kovpak was one of the leaders of the communist partisan movement and was active in north-western regions of Ukraine only in 1943. The name 'Kovpak's partisans', however, became the general term to describe Soviet partisan formations.) Heike explains that the Division was not ready to engage in combat and so the order was ignored. When, several days later, the second order was received, this time allegedly from Himmler himself, a battle unit was formed and sent off to the region north-west of L'viv. Heike goes on to say that 'not surprisingly, the aforementioned task force did not perform its duties well', due to their lack of training. Heike also mentions that 'reports of the unseemly behaviour of the unit began to arrive at the Division.' He does not elaborate on what exactly this behaviour entailed, but explains it as something that 'should have been expected because the soldiers had not finished their training, and their officers were young and inexperienced'. He goes on to say that '[o]ne should not forget that the battalion had been sent to an area populated largely by Poles. The age-old antagonism between Poles and Ukrainians inevitably manifested itself.' Heike then says that 'the Division's staff heeded all complaints and, if proof was provided, punished the guilty parties' (Heike, *The Ukrainian Division*, p. 22). This demonstrates two points: first, that the 'Galicians' (albeit members of one task force) did engage in 'unseemly behaviour', i.e. violence against civilians when they found themselves among Poles. Second, this shows that in February 1944, the

1944 the 'Galicia' was sent to participate in the Battle of Brody. This battle destroyed the newly-formed Ukrainian Division almost entirely. Of the approximately 11,000 Galician soldiers who were deployed at Brody, only about 3,000 returned to re-join the Division.[121] This heavy loss initiated a new phase of recruitment.

The Waffen SS 'Galicia' continued to be an alternative to the existing underground movements, in particular the UPA. Indeed, in the context of present-day debates, it is still presented as an alternative solution with regard to the Ukrainian nationalist struggle for independence. Both the UPA and the Waffen SS 'Galicia' appear to have been formed with the same principles and objectives of creating a nucleus military formation for an independent sovereign state and to resist the Soviet regime in its attempts to sovietize the 'reunited' post-1939 Ukraine. The ways of achieving these aims were very different, and there was little prospect of the two groups uniting into one larger military structure. The main dissimilarity between the two was the fact that one of them, the UPA, seemed independent (although its leadership co-operated with the Nazis periodically). The 'Galicia', despite claiming to have the ambition of turning itself into an independent army, was ultimately a division of the infamous Waffen SS. The 'Galicia's' association with the Waffen SS created the opportunity to support this structure for those who wished to see a Ukrainian military formation within a regular army – similar to the earlier Ukrainian units in the Austro-Hungarian Army – but it also caused a great deal of criticism among those who did not support any co-operation with Nazi Germany. As far as any prospect of co-operation between the UPA and the 'Galicia' is concerned, it is important to consider the conditions required for the creation of such coalitions and alliances. Unity would have required time and space for rational decisions to be made, for pragmatic debates to take place. Instead, by 1943, the UPA command, as well as that of the Division, was faced with the chaos of war and the pressure of needing to act without

---

'Galicia' as a Division was not ready to engage in combat. For more details, see Heike, *The Ukrainian Division*, pp. 20–4; Bolianovs'kyi, *Dyviziia 'Halychyna'*, pp. 208–9.

121 Hunczak, *On the Horns of a Dilemma*, p. 95; Melnyk, *To Battle*, pp. 149–94.

delay. The UPA had neither time nor resources to engage in extensive training of its soldiers. It sought immediate action: it attempted assassinations of the key figures such as the Chief of Staff of the Nazi SA, Viktor Lutze (May 1943), as well as the Red Army Marshal Nikolai Vatutin (April 1944).[122] By contrast, the Waffen SS 'Galicia's' soldiers underwent military training better than that received by the average German soldier mobilized into the Wehrmacht in 1943–4.

There were a number of the OUN members who supported the formation of the Division, among them Viktor Kurmanovych, Mykhailo Khronoviat and other OUN-M supporters. Kubiiovych did not consult Bandera personally with regard to the formation of the Ukrainian division within the Waffen SS.[123] The OUN-B proclaimed its disapproval of collaboration with the Germans in this way and denounced other nationalist groups who were in favour of it. Although this was Bandera's official line, in practice nothing was done to prevent the formation of the Division. Shukhevych, the commander of the UPA, viewed the 'Galicia' as a valuable resource for Ukrainian youth as it secured military training.[124] The difference between the 'Galicia' Division and other previously established Ukrainian formations within German forces, such as the *Nachtigall* or *Roland* battalions, was that the former was formed within the Waffen SS and not the Wehrmacht and that it never came under the control of either the OUN-M or the OUN-B.

It might seem surprising that some nationalists supported the formation of the Waffen SS division consisting of Ukrainians, when it was the SS who in the years preceding 1943 had repressed Ukrainian nationalism. Despite the nationalists' distrust of the Nazis, their hatred and fear of advancing Communism was greater, and encouraged them not to obstruct the creation of the new formation, even though it had no national insignia and was part of the German Army; their ultimate hope was that it would

122 Lev Shankovs'kyi, *Ukraïns'ka Armiia v borot'bi za derzhavnist'* (Munich: Dniprova Khvylia, 1958), pp. 289–301.

123 See Protocol of the Military Board meeting on 22 August 1947 in Munich, in Kolisnyk, *Viis'kova Uprava*, p. 276.

124 Armstrong, *Ukrainian Nationalism*, pp. 170–1.

become a training base for Ukrainian youth. One person who did not support the formation of the 'Galicia' Division was Roman Dashkevych, a former officer of the UNR Army. Dashkevych believed that, if after the war was over, Ukrainians offered their services to the British, as some of them had hoped to in the case of Germany's defeat, they would not be viewed favourably by the British due to their service in the German Armed Forces.[125] Yet, those who disapproved of the formation of the Division, like Dashkevych, formed a minority among the Ukrainian nationalist elites.

One important achievement of the Ukrainian leadership of the Division was securing the support of the Greek Catholic and the Autocephalous Orthodox Churches. Metropolitan Sheptyts'kyi, who was strongly opposed to the anti-Semitic outrages carried out by the Nazis and condemned the ethnic violence in which Ukrainian nationalists engaged,[126] nonetheless did not object to the creation of the 'Galicia' Division and appointed Vasyl' Laba as a chief chaplain of the Division.[127] The Archbishop of L'viv, Iosyf Slipyi, conducted the mass at St George's Cathedral, one of the largest Greek Catholic Cathedrals in L'viv when the Division was inaugurated.[128] Rev. Laba read the sermon, directed at the new recruits of the 'Galicia', stressing their role as the rebuilders of the Ukrainian army:

> The German government, with the permission of the Führer of the German people, has granted the Galician Ukrainians permission to set up their own volunteer Division of riflemen. On this day of celebration, the Ukrainian people's army is resurrected.

125 See Protocol of the Military Board meeting on 22 August 1947 in Munich, in Kolisnyk, *Viis'kova Uprava*, p. 256.

126 See Himka, 'Christianity and Radical Nationalism', Golczewski, 'Shades of Grey', p. 146; Shimon Redlich, 'Metropolitan Andrei Sheptyts'kyi, Ukrainians and the Jews during and after the Holocaust', *Holocaust and Genocide Studies*, 5/1 (1990), 39–51; Bohdan Budurowycz, 'Sheptytski and the Ukrainian National Movement after 1914', in Paul Robert Magosci, ed., *Morality and Reality: The Life and Times of Andrei Sheptytsky* (Edmonton: Canadian Institute of Ukrainian Studies, University of Alberta, 1989), pp. 47–74.

127 Armstrong, *Ukrainian Nationalism*, pp. 173–4.

128 *Nastup*, 16 May 1943, p. 2, cited in Armstrong, *Ukrainian Nationalism*, p. 174. See also Protocol of the Military Board meeting on 22 August 1947 in Munich, in Kolisnyk, *Viis'kova Uprava*, p. 256.

> The Sich Riflemen return to join the Ukrainian people's army, to restore the link that was severed twenty years ago. At this decisive time we receive from the German government the weapons that will let us join forces with the renowned German army and its allies, to take part in the battle against Bolshevism.[129]

John Armstrong suggests that the reason the Church in general and Metropolitan Sheptyts'kyi in particular agreed to provide chaplains to the Division and thus support its creation was that he 'felt that German defeat was only a matter of time and that the small military support which the division could provide for the faltering Wehrmacht could not be decisive.'[130] Armstrong goes on to suggest that Sheptyts'kyi 'thought the existence of a nationalist military force of some strength would be invaluable in the chaos which would succeed a German collapse and might even be necessary to preserve the lives of a considerable portion of the Ukrainian population of Galicia.'[131] John-Paul Himka suggests that Sheptyts'kyi decided to support the formation of the Waffen SS 'Galicia' Division because 'he feared what the nationalist youth would do in the period between the German withdrawal and the Soviet reoccupation.'[132] Being opposed to Ukrainian participation in anti-Jewish campaigns as well as to the practices implemented by the OUN-B, Sheptyts'kyi

> [...] preferred that young Ukrainians be in a regular army unit, with discipline and with chaplains that he appointed. He considered this the lesser evil even though by this time, spring 1943, he rejected Nazi Germany entirely. His concern, in part, was to support an alternative to the anarchic violence that he associated with the Banderites, having in mind the bloody events of early July 1941.[133]

Thus, despite being part of the German Army, having to swear an oath of allegiance to Hitler,[134] and receiving little support from the OUN-B, the

129 Rev. Laba's speech, 28 April 1943 in Melnyk, *To Battle*, p. 28.
130 Armstrong, *Ukrainian Nationalism*, p. 174.
131 *Ibid.*
132 Himka, 'Christianity and Radical Nationalism' p. 102.
133 *Ibid.*
134 'Galicia's' oath of allegiance read: 'I swear before God this holy oath, that in the battle against Bolshevism, I will give absolute obedience to the commander in chief

'Galicia' managed to secure the support of the Ukrainian population of the *Generalgouvernement* and the Greek Catholic Church. In some ways, the Division came closest to the original aim that had been pursued by other military and paramilitary units: it was part of a regular army and in March 1945 it became the 1st Ukrainian Division of the Ukrainian National Army. In reality, however, the Waffen SS 'Galicia' had little influence on the course of the development of the Ukrainian state-building project.

---

of the German Armed Forces Adolf Hitler, and as a brave soldier I will always be prepared to lay down my life for this oath' (in Melnyk, *To Battle*, p. 57). This oath was replaced by the new oath to Ukraine written by General Shandruk when the 'Galicia' symbolically became part of the Ukrainian National Army. The new oath read: 'I swear to Almighty God on His Holy Gospel and His Living Cross, sparing neither life nor health, always and everywhere to fight with weapons in my hand under the Ukrainian National Banner for my people and for my homeland, Ukraine. Aware of my great responsibility as a soldier of the Ukrainian National Army, I swear that I will carry out all orders of my superiors obediently and without question, and to keep secret all service orders. So help me God and the Holy Virgin, Amen' (in Melnyk, *To Battle*, p. 268). The ceremony of the proclamation of the new oath on 25 April 1945 was conducted in the presence of a limited number of the 'Galicians' as the majority of them were engaged at the frontline. The proclamation and the name change were purely symbolic as the Division remained under German control and subject to the authority of the *Reichsführer-SS*, thus relying with regard to the supplies and equipment on the Waffen SS until it surrendered to the British and Americans. See Melnyk, *To Battle*, p. 268; Shandruk in Slaboshpyts'kyi and Stetsenko, *Ukraïns'ka dyviziia 'Halychyna'*, p. 72 and Shandruk, *Arms of Valor*, pp. 227–48; and Protocol of the Military Board meeting on 22 August 1947 in Munich, in Kolisnyk, *Viis'kova Uprava*, p. 267.

CHAPTER 2

War Crime Allegations and Investigations

The Waffen SS was known for its participation in war crimes and was subsequently recognized as a criminal organization at the Nuremberg Trials. Thus, the significance of the 'Galicia' Division's association with the Waffen SS cannot be underestimated. This association influenced the narratives which were created about the Division by every party involved in the story of the 'Galicia': the members themselves in fact used it to their advantage in their fight against repatriation, for they ascribed their connection with the Waffen SS to their hatred of the 'Bolsheviks'. The Soviets saw the Division's association with the Waffen SS as a reason for its members to be classified as traitors and thus demanded that they be handed over to the USSR authorities. As far as the British authorities were concerned, the 'Galicia's' involvement with the German Army, combined with the Division's nationalistic character, its open hostility towards the Soviet Union, and the statelessness of its members created a complex situation, the resolution of which required a lot of time and resources, which the British were not prepared to dedicate. This resulted in the decisions taken by the UK authorities with regard to the Division's repatriation, civilianization and further settlement, which are analysed in Chapters 3 and 4.

Allegations of involvement in war crimes have been made against the Division since the end of the Second World War. The most significant investigations which addressed the question of 'Galicia's' potential criminality as a division were conducted by the British screening commission and the Soviet repatriation mission which took place immediately after the war, the Deschênes Commission in the 1980s in Canada, and the investigation of the so-called 'Rimini List' in the early 2000s in the UK. While discussing both the accusations and the conclusions of the respective investigations, this chapter will not attempt to establish whether or not the 'Galicians' were war criminals, but will rather examine how the accusation of participation in war crimes affected the general narrative about the Division as well as the specific narratives regarding their repatriation and settlement.

The SS and the Waffen SS

In order to understand why the 'Galicia' Division could be seen as more controversial than, for instance, the Ukrainian Insurgents Army, which has also been subject to accusations of crimes committed against the civilian population,[1] it is necessary to look at it in the context of the Division's allegiance to the *Schutzstaffel* (SS). The SS was established by Hitler in 1925 as an elite section of the *Sturmabteilung* (SA), which had been formed in 1921. In December 1940, Himmler formed the Waffen SS (Armed SS),[2] which, within six months, grew to over 150,000 men. By the end of the war it consisted of 38 Divisions. Most of those who joined the Waffen SS were volunteers (including Ukrainian men who joined the 'Galicia' Division in 1943) and about a third of the Waffen SS soldiers, who joined the organization at the late stage of the Second World War, were conscripts. There were many units which consisted of East European volunteers. These units were known to have participated in atrocities recognized as war crimes. Although the 'Galicia' Division was created towards the end of the Second World War, and thus did not participate in the most infamous crimes of the Nazis, which had already been committed, it shared the notoriety of the Waffen SS in the post-war period.

The Nuremberg Trials recognized that the Waffen SS 'was in theory and practice as much an integral part of the SS organization as any other

1 See Grzegorz Molyka, *Od rzezi wołyńskiej do akcji 'Wisła'.*

2 The foreign units carried the designation *Freiwilligen* (volunteers), or *Waffen* (armed). See Marc J. Rikmenspoel, *Waffen-SS Encyclopaedia* (Bedford, PA: The Aberjona Press, 2004).

branch of the SS.'[3] It was thus concluded by the International Military Tribunal at Nuremberg that 'units of the Waffen SS were directly involved in the killing of prisoners of war and the atrocities in occupied countries.'[4] This, however, did not mean that the Tribunal was to impose a sentence upon the Waffen SS or to convict any individual because of their membership.[5] A number of members of the Waffen SS were tried before Allied military courts. Several hundred of them were convicted and some were executed for specific criminal acts. All officers were kept in POW camps for up to four years after the war; once released, most of them were found to be free of personal guilt, but having belonged to a criminal organization a number of former Waffen SS members were denied some rights which were afforded to other German combat veterans.[6]

Conscripts who were sworn in after 1943 were exempted from the judgement by the Tribunal on the basis of involuntary servitude.[7] Although the 'Galicia' was established in April 1943, most soldiers recruited then were not conscripts, but volunteers. Those who joined its ranks in 1943 did so possibly without complete realization of the full scope of the crimes perpetrated by the Waffen SS, or without complete support of its ideology,[8] but they enlisted voluntarily and therefore could not be exempted from the judgement by the Tribunal on the basis of involuntary servitude. While the 'Galicians' were in the surrendered enemy personnel camps, they were not registered according to the date of their recruitment. Accurate informa-

3 Summary by deputy chief prosecutor Sir David Maxwell-Fyfe, cited in Stein, *The Waffen SS*, p. 250.

4 Judgement of the International Military Tribunal, cited in *ibid.*, p. 251.

5 NCA, II, 5 f., cited in *ibid.*, p. 251 n. 5.

6 *Ibid.*, pp. 251–2.

7 Those members of the Waffen SS who were repatriated to their home countries were put on trial in the courts of their home countries and were punished much more severely, especially those in the USSR.

8 The claims of the lack of awareness of the atrocities which were perpetrated by the Waffen SS and the absence of support of the Nazi ideology by the 'Galicians' are found in memoirs (discussed in the introduction) as well as interview testimonies (personal interviews: interviewee S., 26 December 2006 (Ternopil'); interviewee B., 27 December 2006 (L'viv); interviewee B., 20 May 2007 (London)).

tion about recruitment date of each 'Galician' might have been difficult to obtain, given the chaos of the circumstances and the complexity of often incomprehensible or non-existent documents.[9] Yet there is no evidence that any attempt was being made to investigate which of the 'Galicians' were volunteers and which joined as conscripts. Had these investigations taken place, those soldiers who joined the Division in April 1943 and stayed in the ranks of the 'Galicia' could have been separated from those who had a pre-Division military history and could have been involved in war crimes prior to their joining the 'Galicia'.

The 'Undetermined'

The confusion as to the date when Ukrainians joined the Waffen SS 'Galicia' was not the only factor that caused the UK authorities difficulties in deciding on the categorization of the Ukrainian men. A memo from the British Zone in Europe, dated 11 March 1947 states the advantages and disadvantages of separating Ukrainians into Soviet and non-Soviet citizens. Among the advantages to determining who exactly was of 'Ukrainian extraction' was the possibility for the British Zone authorities to 'get down to a much more firm picture of the type of person we have amongst the undetermined'.[10] The main disadvantage of this pursuit stated by the secretariat and statistics

9 Most of the Divisional archive was burned by the Military Board members towards the end of the war for fear that the documents might be discovered by the Soviets. See Protocol of the Military Board meeting on 22 August 1947 in Munich, in Kolisnyk, *Viis'kova Uprava*, pp. 272, 276. Tolstoy claims that Colonel R. Campbell-Preston, the commanding officer of the 80th (Scottish Horse) Medium Regt., RA 'persuaded the Ukrainians to destroy all compromising indications of citizenship' after he had learned of the forceful repatriation of the Cossacks. See Tolstoy, *The Victims of Yalta*, pp. 603–4.

10 Secretariat and Statistics memo to SO I Secretariat, Subject: Ukrainians – Recording by Nationality, (NA) LFWP/EAW, 11 March 1947.

department was that they 'would have to disclose to the Soviets the number of Soviet Ukrainians that we hold amongst the undetermined. [...] a great number, possibly 50% of them, are of Ukrainian extraction and have come from the portion of the Soviet Ukrain [sic] which has always been Soviet territory.'[11] Another obstacle to separating Ukrainians into 'Soviet' and 'non-Soviet' was to do with the fact that 'no one at the moment seems to be able to give us an absolute definition of a "Ukrainian" [...]' which could become 'a possible source of argument for our future dealings with the Soviets, an argument of course from their direction, in that certain people should be forced to return to the Soviets, when our interpretation of the ruling would be the opposite.'[12] Indeed, when it came to defining what it meant to be 'Ukrainian', the various offices of the British government found it problematic to agree. The 'PW [Prisoners of War] and DP [Displaced Persons] Technical Instruction' on the subject of the 'Displaced Persons Formerly Living in Ukraine' stated that

> [t]he 'Ukraine' is a term used to describe a geographical area which in 1939 lay mostly in U.S.S.R., and partly in Poland and Czechoslovakia & Roumania. The expression 'Ukrainians' therefore means persons who come or came from this general geographical area. They will be mainly Soviet or Polish citizens, but may also contain Czech and Roumanian citizens.
>
> There is no such thing as a Ukrainian nation, and the word 'Ukrainian' cannot be used to describe the nationality of any person.
>
> [...]
>
> (c) If it is desirable to refer either to former inhabitants of the Ukraine by nationalities, or to nationalities by their geographical relationship, the expression Soviet (Ukrainian), Polish (Ukrainian), Roumanian (Ukrainian) or Czech (Ukrainian), or Stateless (Ukrainian), may be used. For persons formerly living in the Ukraine, but whose nationality has not yet been established, the expression Ukrainian 'Undetermined' may be used until such time as they are classified as being of a definite nationality or as being Stateless.[13]

11 *Ibid.*

12 *Ibid.*

13 PW & DP Technical Instruction, Subject: Displaced Persons Formerly Living in the Ukraine, (NA) PDWP/58378, 15 March 1947.

This instruction was aimed to give guidance to the PW & DP Division,[14] who sent a somewhat uncooperative response, saying that '[i]t looks as if we are being very stupid up here, but at the moment we cannot quite see what the difficulty is your end [...]'. They continued to claim that they have been told that

> [...] we may use the term 'Ukrainian' as much as we like, but it may not be used officially as describing a persons [sic] nationality. [...] as there is no Nation called 'UKRAINIA' [sic] and it is only a term descriptive of an area in Europe, parts of which happen to be owned by determined states. In this we think it bears a close relation to the term 'Jew' which describes the religion of a certain sect of people who live in every country in the world.[15]

The comparison of Ukrainians and Jews could be seen as paradoxical in this context, since the Ukrainians in questions had been collaborating with the Nazis, but it made sense to the PW and DP Division to see Ukrainians as a group of people with a shared identity, but who had no formal nationality or citizenship. The PW and DP Division did not envisage any trouble in naming Ukrainian DPs and POWs 'Ukrainian' as long as it was understood that that was not their actual citizenship, but rather a self-identified ethnicity (although the term 'ethnicity' is not used in these documents). The PW and DP Division also did not see any disadvantage with regard to the Soviet authorities' potential reaction to the number of alleged Soviet citizens in the British Zone in 1947. Lieut. Colonel Vaughan-Hughes suggested that he would not worry very much about 'the effect it would have on the SOVIET Mission, who quite candidly are perfectly aware that we have these SOVIET CITIZENS in the Zone [...] and at any time if they had really challenged us in public we could not have denied that we probably have a lot more but have not yet sorted them out.'[16] Lieut. Colonel Vaughan-Hughes' seeming lack of concern at the potential objections by

14 Full title: P.W. and D.P. Division of C.C.G. (B.E.) – Prisoners of War and Displaced Persons Division of the Control Commission for Germany (British Element).

15 Lieut. Colonel G.B. Vaughan-Hughes to Lt. Colonel F.R.C. Bray, Zonal Executive Offices, (NA) PWDP/59808/23, 18 March 1947, p. 1. Emphasis as in the original.

16 *Ibid.*, p. 2. Here and elsewhere the emphasis in the text is as in the original.

the Soviets to the British authorities holding a large number of Soviet DPs or POWs might be partly explained by the fact that the correspondence in question took place in 1947, i.e., after the forceful repatriation of the Cossacks (which took place in 1945) and at the beginning of the Cold War, when the UK government was already less concerned with pleasing the Soviet authorities.

The dilemma of defining 'undetermined' Ukrainians was partly resolved by the final instruction:

> The unqualified term UKRAINIAN may be used ONLY to describe the following:-
> a) Camps or Assembly Centres containing a mixed population of POLISH (UKRAINIANS), CZECH (UKRAINIANS), etc.
> b) Relief Societies, delegations, etc. having an overall responsibility for, or interest in, POLISH (UKRAINIANS), CZECH (UKRAINIANS) etc. or as a general term used in instructions/
> Instructions, plans and letters when referring to POLISH, RUMANIAN, SOVIET and CZECH (UKRAINIANS) as a whole.[17]

The explanation as to why this differentiation was made did not include potential repatriation of the 'Soviet Ukrainians' to the USSR; instead it mentioned the necessity to '[d]ifferentiate for statistical purpose between POLES originating from within the geographical boundaries of POLAND as they exist today and therefore repatriable, and POLISH (UKRAINIANS) who are not repatriable to POLAND.'[18] Another reason for differentiation was '[t]o reduce the large number of DPs at present shown as UNDETERMINED'.[19] It is thus clear that the issue of the confusing citizenship of the Ukrainian DPs and POWs was problematic for both the UK and the Soviet authorities. However, with time, the British

17 PW & DP Division, Zonal Executive Offices, Subject: Ukrainians – PWDP Technical Instruction, March 1947, (NA) PWDP/58636/G, pp. 2–3. Emphasis as in the original.

18 *Ibid.*

19 *Ibid.*

authorities became less anxious about upsetting the Soviet Repatriation Mission by not giving them accurate numbers of the 'doubtful Soviet citizens' they held in the British Zone. This became even less of an issue when the 'Galicians' were moved to the UK.

Whether 'truly Soviet' or not, the 'Galicians' had been in the ranks of the German Army and as such subject to condemnation. This shaped a crucial part of their narrative of denial and justification. In the post-war years, former Waffen SS soldiers organized the Mutual Support Organization of Former Members of the Waffen SS (*Hilfsorganisation auf Gegenseitigkeit der ehemaligen Angehörigen der Waffen-SS*, HIAG) in Germany and lobbied for their personal, political and financial rehabilitation.[20] Similar efforts were made by the former 'Galicia' members, especially those who settled in Canada. They set up a Brotherhood of Former Soldiers of the 1st Ukrainian Division of the Ukrainian National Army (*Bratstvo kolyshnikh voiakiv Pershoï ukrainskoï dyvizii Ukrainskoï natsionalnoï armii*), the Canadian branch of which became a member of the Ukrainian Canadian Congress, a representative body of the Ukrainian Canadian community before the Government of Canada. The members of this Brotherhood tried to integrate into both Ukrainian diaspora and Canadian communities and live their lives without the stigma associated with former Waffen SS members.[21] They were relatively successful in doing so until the mid-1980s, when a Commission of Inquiry on War Criminals in Canada was established.

The Deschênes Commission

Two crucial documents which cover existing accounts of the allegations of the Division's war crime participation are the official Commission of Inquiry on War Criminals Report, dated December 1986, and an unpublished study,

20 Stein, *The Waffen SS*, p. 252.

21 See Vasyl' Veryha, *Za Ridnyi Krai, za narid svii, abo Khto taki dyviziinyky?* (Kyiv: Vydavnytsvto imeni Oleny Telihy, 2006), pp. 34–9 and 175–213.

'Nazi War Criminals in Canada: The Historical and Policy Setting from the 1940s to the Present', prepared by Alti Rodal, Director of Historical Research, Commission of Inquiry on Nazi War Criminals in Canada (the Deschênes Commission) in 1986.[22] Both works help trace the creation of the 'Galicia' narratives, particularly with regard to their participation in war crimes. The Deschênes Inquiry offers an official conclusion concerning the Division's innocence or guilt in war crimes, while the study by Rodal offers a more exhaustive and critical examination of the 'Galicia' as a whole and their alleged war crime participation in particular.

The Deschênes Commission was set up by the Canadian government in February 1985 to launch an investigation into the possibility of Nazi war criminals being present in Canada. This Commission was headed by Jules Deschênes, a Justice of the Court of Appeal of Quebec. The report prepared by the Commission was delivered in December 1986 in two parts: one public and one confidential; this chapter will refer to the public volume of the report. The Commission listed 774 alleged war criminals in Canada; it concluded that out of that list, 341 of them never resided or arrived in Canada, twenty-one had arrived in Canada but had departed to settle in another country, eighty-six had died in Canada and four were not located. The Commission could not find *prima facie* evidence of war crimes in the files of 154 further suspects. In ninety-seven cases, the Commission also did not find *prima facie* evidence of war crimes but suspected that such evidence could exist in the countries of Eastern Europe. The decision of whether or not to circulate these files abroad was left to the government. Grant Purves, who prepared an updated overview of the Deschênes Commission in 1998, writes that thirty-four cases on the 'master list' of 774 individuals 'were outstanding because answers had not been received from foreign agencies.'[23] Purves' analysis suggests that time constraints had prevented

22 I obtained the unpublished manuscript of the chapter on the 'Galicia' Division by Alti Rodal directly from the author. As I received the chapter in a separate document, the page numbers quoted will only correspond to the copy which I was sent by the author and not to the full unpublished document.

23 Grant Purves, *War Criminals: The Deschênes Commission*, Political and Social Affairs Division, revised 16 October 1998, E. The Report of the Deschênes Commission,

the Commission from investigating in full the thirty-eight cases referred to it after October 1986 as well as a list of German scientists and technicians. Purves continues by saying that the Deschênes Commission stated that it found *prima facie* evidence of war crimes 'in just 20 cases and [...] made detailed recommendations to the government about how to proceed in each case.'[24] The use of the expression 'just 20 cases' is fitting with the general tone used by Purves with regard to the findings of the Commission, when it states that

> [t]he [Deschênes Commission] Report found that public estimates of the number of war criminals allegedly living in Canada had become grossly exaggerated, expanding from a 'handful' or 'several hundred' in the mid-1970s to 'thousands' by the mid-1980s. Some exaggeration may have resulted from the casual lumping together of 'war criminals' and 'war-time collaborators', some from blanket accusations against all members of certain military units such as the 'Galicia' or 'Halychyna' Division (which the Commission formally cleared of collective war crimes), and still more from duplication.[25]

---

1. General. <http://dsp-psd.pwgsc.gc.ca/Collection-R/LoPBdP/CIR/873-e.htm> accessed 24 September 2010. I have decided to use both the work of Grant Purves and the original report of the Deschênes Commission, as the latter gives a more detailed overview of the Inquiry, whereas the work by Purves offers a more up-to-date picture of the Commission and its legacy. There are also annual reports which have been produced by the Crimes Against Humanity and War Crimes Programme in Canada between 1998 and 2011. The Programme partners consist of the Canada Border Services Agency, Citizenship and Immigration Canada, the Department of Justice and the Royal Canadian Mounted Police. The main aim of the Programme is 'to deny safe haven in Canada to war criminals or those suspected of being directly involved or complicit in the commission of war crimes, crimes against humanity or genocide.' These reports include updates on trials of suspected war criminals, including those of Ukrainian origin. For further information see <http://canada.justice.gc.ca/warcrimes-crimesdeguerre/researchreports-rechercherapports-eng.asp> accessed 24 January 2013.

24 Purves, *War Criminals*, 1. General.

25 *Ibid.* The alleged numbers of war criminals living in Canada varied according to those who presented the allegations from a 'handful', as suggested by the Department of Justice in 1982, to 6,000 according to Simon Wiesenthal in 1986, as reported in the *New York Daily News*. Sol Littman suggested that there were 3,000 alleged war criminals in his brief before the Commission. These, however, included 'war criminals

Thus, after two years of court hearings, the Deschênes Commission drew the following conclusions with regard to the 'Galicia' Division:

> 58- Charges of war crimes against members of the Galicia Division have never been substantiated, either in 1950 when they were first preferred, or in 1984 when they were renewed, or before this Commission.
>
> 59- Further, in the absence of evidence of participation in or knowledge of specific war crimes, mere membership in the Galicia Division is insufficient to justify prosecution.[26]

These conclusions were based partly on the assumption that the Division underwent a thorough screening by the UK authorities while in SEP/POW camps in Europe, although that screening, as will be discussed in Chapter 3, was far from thorough. This, however, did not discourage the Deschênes Commission from relying on it, as is evident from the conclusions which cite the screening report of 1947:

> The general impression which we have formed of all the men in the camp is favourable, as they strike us all as being decent, simple sort of people. The national emblem of the Ukraine, in the form of a trident, is freely displayed all over the camp, and the inmates clearly regard themselves as a homogeneous unit, unconnected either with Russia or Poland, and do not seem conscious of having done any wrong.[27]

The confidence of the Deschênes Commission in the British screening report's conclusions seems to imply that the Commission was either ill-informed as to the meticulousness of the screening of the 'Galicia' performed

---

and war-time collaborators'. See Jules Deschênes, 'Commission of Inquiry on War Criminals', *Report, Part 1: Public* (Ottawa: Minister of Supply and Services, 1986), pp. 245–7.

26 Deschênes, 'Commission of Inquiry', p. 261. The original text is in bold.

27 British Screening Report, cited in *ibid.*, p. 253. It is surprising that the Commission is quoting from the book by Gordon Richard Bohdan Panchuk, the director of the Canadian Relief Mission for Ukrainian Refugees, and not directly from the original document (NA) HO/213/1851. See Bohdan Panchuk, *Heroes of their Day: The Reminiscences of Bohdan Panchuk* (Toronto: Multicultural History Society of Ontario, 1983), p. 143, paragraph 6; p. 147, paragraph 11 (C).

by the UK authorities in the aftermath of the Second World War, or that it chose not to subject the report to close scrutiny. According to Rodal, a key explanation for the Deschênes Commission's collective exoneration of the Division is what she refers to as the 'ethnic factor',[28] and 'persistent lobbying efforts and backing from a demographically significant Ukrainian ethnic constituency.'[29]

> The ethnic factor then influenced both the deliberations and some of the recommendations of the Deschênes Commission and, even more so, the government's response to the Commission, primarily as a result of intensive and strident lobbying from Ukrainian and other East European ethnic groups in Canada. This was reflected in the collective exoneration in the Deschênes Commission Report of former members of the Ukrainian Waffen SS Division despite the strong probability of criminality for some of its members, and in the misleading assertion that members of the Division 'were individually screened for security purposes before admission to Canada'.[30]

The conclusions of the Commission also stress that no further evidence has been produced to incriminate the 'Galicia' men either immediately after the war or in the 1980s. Therefore, according to the Commission, membership of the Waffen SS alone does not classify the former 'Galicians' as war criminals. The report also states the following:

> 60- No case can be made against members of the Galicia Division for revocation of citizenship or deportation since the Canadian authorities were fully aware of the relevant facts in 1950 and admission to Canada was not granted them because of any false representation, or fraud, or concealment of material circumstances.[31]

Indeed, as will be discussed in Chapter 4, the Canadians were fully aware of the 'Galicia's' association with the Waffen SS when they allowed the former members of the Division to settle in Canada. Thus, there was no question

28 Alti Rodal, 'How Perpetrators of Genocidal Crimes Evaded Justice: the Canadian Story', in John K. Roth and Elisabeth Maxwell, eds, *Remembering for the Future. The Holocaust in an Age of Genocide*, Vol 1, History (Basingstoke: Palgrave Macmillan, 2001), 702–25 (712).

29 *Ibid.*

30 *Ibid*, p. 713. Here Rodal cites Deschênes 'Commission of Inquiry', pp. 12 and 261.

31 Deschênes, 'Commission of Inquiry', p. 261. The original text is in bold.

that the former 'Galicians' misrepresented their identity on arrival, and therefore there were no grounds to withdraw their Canadian citizenship. The final point which the Deschênes Commission makes with regard to the former 'Galicians' is that 'of the 217 officers of the Galicia Division denounced by Mr Simon Wiesenthal to the Canadian government, 187 (i.e., 86 per cent of the list) never set foot in Canada, 11 have died in Canada, 2 have left for another country, no *prima facie* case has been established against 16 and the last one could not be located.'[32] Despite treating the estimates of the alleged war criminals' presence in Canada as being 'grossly exaggerated', the report did issue recommendations to amend the Criminal Code, Extradition Act and issue amendments to laws and procedures governing denaturalization and deportation in order to bring war criminals to justice. As a result of these changes, Canadian prosecutors pressed charges against four men. One case resulted in acquittal, two were dropped when prosecutors were unable to obtain overseas evidence, and one case was stayed because of the poor health of the defendant.[33]

The Deschênes Commission produced a report of substantial size and detail on all alleged war criminals in Canada and it merits a separate study. The 'Galicia' Division, which constituted only one part of the report, was formally cleared of collective war crimes to the delight of the former 'Galicians' and those organizations which defended their innocence. This conclusion, however, infuriated others, who considered the report superficial and inadequate. These varying reactions contributed to the ongoing

32 *Ibid.* Alti Rodal makes an interesting observation regarding the list in question: 'The RCMP's 1965 study of the records of thirty-one former members of the Division residing in Canada (which were included in Simon Wiesenthal's list of 218 [sic] Ukrainian SS officers who may have emigrated to Canada) shows that at least eight were promoted to the rank of Untersturmfuhrer or 2nd Lieutenant in November 1944, and that two had reached the rank of 1st Lieutenant. This too suggests several years of military experience, likely prior to the establishment of the Division in April 1943, either in the Polish army, or with auxiliary police and militia units in the 1941 to 1943 period'. (Alti Rodal, *Chapter XII – Part 3, The Ukrainian 'Halychyna' (Galician) Waffen-SS Division*, Commission of Inquiry on Nazi War Criminals in Canada (the Deschênes Commission), 1986).

33 Purves, *War Criminals*, 1. General.

polarized controversy of the 'Galician' history, rather than offering any closure to it. While agreeing that at the time of the Deschênes Commission there was no evidence of war crimes committed by the Division as a whole, Rodal stresses that there were allegations against individual members of the Division, namely those who had been members of German police units which had committed crimes prior to the formation of the 'Galicia' Division.[34] In her chapter, Rodal quotes Bohdan Panchuk, who prepared a memorandum on the Division in 1948 which stated that 'Ukrainians who had previously been drafted to other German units were offered the opportunity to "volunteer" for transfer from these German units to the Ukrainian Division'.[35] Rodal suggests that these 'would have included individuals scattered throughout various German units, whatever their tasks, in the 1941 to 1943 period.'[36] She also makes the point that after the Battle of Brody in July 1944 '[t]he reconstitution of the Division [...], which added 12,000 men to the 3,000 remaining from the earlier formation, provided a distinct opportunity for integration into the Division of persons with a war criminal background.'[37] Rodal goes on to say that

> [w]ith the advance of the Allies from the West after D-Day and of Soviet troops from the East (Majdanek death camp was liberated on July 24, 1944), the Germans would have sought to organize and place various displaced or disbanded semi-military police and camp guard units in other military formations. It seems highly plausible that members of such units of Ukrainian origin, valued for the years of experience gained in German service, would have been directed to remaining military formations consisting of Ukrainians, such as the Division, then rebuilding its formations after the disastrous battle of Brody.[38]

Rodal makes another important point regarding the narrative which the 'Galicians' promoted while in the SEP camp, namely that most of them had only been in the Division for several months and therefore were soldiers of

34 Rodal, *Chapter XII – Part 3*, p. 8.
35 PAC, RG76, v. 656, f. B53802, pt. 1, Memorandum re: Ukrainian 'Divizia Halychyna', 31 May 1948, p. 4, in Rodal, *Chapter XII – Part 3*, p. 6.
36 Rodal, *Chapter XII – Part 3*, p. 6.
37 *Ibid.*
38 *Ibid.*

the 1st Ukrainian Division of the Ukrainian National Army rather than the Waffen SS 'Galicia'. Rodal looks at this assertion from a different perspective, suggesting that '[t]he argument that most of the former members of the Division served with the Division for only a short period may therefore not remove but rather strengthen the probability of a war criminal element.'[39] While lacking conclusive documentary evidence, the assumption that those Ukrainians who joined the 'Galicia' Division in its post-Brody recruitment phase might have participated in war crimes in the earlier years of the war is highly credible. In the case of the screening of the Ukrainian officers who entered Canada, Rodal points out that

> [t]he BDC [Berlin Documentation Centre] checks undertaken by the RCMP [Royal Canadian Mounted Police] and the Deschênes Commission were limited to the 218 officers of the Division named by Wiesenthal, and, indeed, association with police and other SS formations in the 1940 to 1943 period has been established for only 12 of these officers.[40]

However, according to Rodal, no checks had been made on the Division members admitted to Canada other than those carried out on these officers. Rodal goes on to suggest that '[e]ven from this limited sample, it is clear that there was continuity between the 1941–3 Ukrainian police/military formations and the Division.'[41] Rodal's arguments are extremely important in establishing a more accurate picture of the 'Galician' men's involvement in war crimes outside the Waffen SS 'Galicia' Division.

The fact that the Deschênes Commission lacked further evidence that could have been found in the USSR or the Soviet Bloc countries can be explained by the intensifying Cold War. On 13 July 1948, the governments of the Commonwealth, including Canada, received a telegram from the British Commonwealth Relations Office which proposed ending Nazi war crimes trials in the British Zone of Germany. It stated that '[p]unishment of war crimes is more a matter of discouraging future generations than of

39 *Ibid.*
40 *Ibid.*, p. 7. The Deschênes Commission cites the number of officers named by Simon Wiesenthal as 217, while Rodal cites it as 218.
41 *Ibid.*

meting out retribution to every guilty individual [...] it is now necessary to dispose of the past as soon as possible.'[42] The Cold War made Western powers more inclined to focus their resources on uncovering suspected Soviet agents and Communists, rather than identifying and punishing war criminals. It followed that Canadian immigration policy, and particularly the restrictions against the entry of former 'enemy aliens', was systematically relaxed.[43]

In the light of the above, one point regarding the Deschênes Commission report remains unanswered, namely, whether the findings of the Inquiry might have been different had the Commission travelled to the Soviet Union and its satellites in eastern Europe in order to collect more evidence. Purves argued that this issue caused controversy in Canada in 1985:

> Baltic and Ukrainian groups were completely opposed [to collecting evidence in the USSR and Eastern Europe] because, they argued, Soviet-supplied evidence could not be trusted and would be used to attack any individual or ethnic group opposed to the Soviet state. Representatives of Jewish groups argued that there was important evidence in the Soviet Union, both eyewitness and documentary, and that there was no known instance in Europe or North America of the Soviets having provided a false document or a witness who committed perjury.[44]

The last argument seems tendentious, since it would have been naive to rely solely on Soviet evidence with regard to groups of people who, as in the case of the Waffen SS 'Galicia' or the Latvian Legion, were seen as

42 Purves, *War Criminals*, Background and Analysis, B. The Onset of the Cold War and the Decision to Halt War Crimes Trials <http://dsp-psd.pwgsc.gc.ca/Collection-R/LoPBdP/CIR/873-e.htm> accessed 24 September 2010.

43 *Ibid.* Alti Rodal points out that '[b]etween 1950 and 1955 [...] restrictions on the admission of former members of all Nazi organisations (including the SS and SD) were lifted piecemeal. At the same time, the screening system was dramatically strengthened, but with a view to keeping out Communists, not people with Nazi background.' See Rodal, 'How Perpetrators of Genocidal Crimes Evaded Justice', p. 707.

44 Purves, *War Criminals*, D. Establishment of the Deschênes Commission <http://dsp-psd.pwgsc.gc.ca/Collection-R/LoPBdP/CIR/873-e.htm> accessed 24 September 2010.

'enemies of the people' in the USSR. Naturally, the Soviet authorities could have selectively produced evidence, since Western experts were not allowed access to the Soviet archives. Another point to consider regarding the decision of the Deschênes Commission not to seek further evidence from the USSR is that the Soviet Repatriation Mission was active in the post-war years and, in relation to the 'Galicia' Division case, had full access to the 'Galicians' while they were in the SEP camps in Europe. The Soviet Repatriation Mission interviewed the Division men and found no evidence which would demonstrate their participation in war crimes.

The dilemma of seeking the Soviet and Eastern Bloc-based evidence was resolved in 1985:

> In a formal written decision of 14 November 1985, Justice Deschênes decided that, while he himself should not take part in the hearing of evidence abroad, there was no reason why evidence should not be sought and heard, even in Eastern Bloc countries. But he set strict conditions that would have to be met by host countries: protection of reputations through confidentiality; independent interpreters; access to original documents; access to witnesses' previous statements; freedom of examination of witnesses in agreement with Canadian rules of evidence; and videotaping of such examinations. However, a satisfactory response was not received from the Soviet Union until June 1986 and Justice Deschênes decided there was insufficient time left for the Commission to travel.[45]

Thus, in spite of the Deschênes Commission's efforts to seek overseas evidence, its plan was never realized, depriving the Commission of the additional material to prove innocence or guilt of alleged war criminals, such as the 'Galicians', and consequently leaving the Deschênes Report open to criticism.

45 *Ibid.*

The Rimini List

The cause for the investigation into the alleged war crimes of the Waffen SS 'Galicia' Division in the UK[46] was the existence of the so-called Rimini List.[47] It consisted of the names of Ukrainians who were kept in Rimini at the British SEP camp after the Second World War, in other words, members of the 'Galicia' Division. This list, which named 7,100 men, made newspaper headlines in 2001 following public outrage caused by the television documentary, *The SS in Britain*,[48] which told the story of the alleged crimes committed by the Waffen SS 'Galicia' soldiers. A Metropolitan Police spokesperson issued a statement with regard to this, confirming the receipt of a number of allegations, passed to the Metropolitan Police by the Home Office, and that the case was forwarded to the anti-terrorist squad of Scotland Yard.[49] Lord Janner of the All-Party Parliamentary War Crimes Group and a former president of the Board of Deputies of British Jews responded to the Metropolitan Police comment saying that '[i]f there is

46 After numerous discussions in the House of Commons and the House of Lords, the War Crimes Act 1991 was enacted in the UK. Anhony Sawoniuk, a former member of the Belarusian Auxiliary Police, is the only person who has been convicted under the Act. For a detailed discussion of the War Crimes Act 1991 see Cesarani, *Justice Delayed*, pp. 190–246.

47 This is a list of the 'Galicians' who were held at the SEP camp in Rimini, Italy. The list is permanently classified and is stored at the National Archives in London.

48 Yorkshire Television documentary, *The SS in Britain*, aired on the History Channel on 24 September 1999 in Canada, and on 7 January 2001 in Britain. The figure of 7,100 persons given on the 'Rimini List' is somewhat curious. This number is inconsistent with what is usually given in the literature and documents as the number of 'Galicians' present in the Rimini POW camp in 1947 and those of them who were moved to the UK in the same year; although it varies in different accounts, it is still presented as being around 8,000. The figure of 7,100 might have appeared due to considerable fluctuations in the number of SEPs as a result of escapes.

49 In Kate Taylor, 'Safe Haven in Britain', *The Searchlight Magazine* (February 2001) <http://www.searchlightmagazine.com/index.php?link=template&story=91> accessed 22 September 2010.

sufficient evidence against individuals, it should be put before a jury so that these men can receive the justice that they denied to their victims'.[50] Janner continued by saying that '[t]hanks to the information in this television programme I have asked the Home Secretary [Jack Straw] to investigate these people', and concluded that '[t]he Government's excuse at the time was that they were just ordinary soldiers. It is now clear they were not. The people from this unit who are in Britain and who were involved in genocidal murders should not sleep comfortably in their beds.'[51] According to newspaper reports, of the 7,100 mentioned, around 1,200 people were to be 'investigated either as possible war criminals or as witnesses to atrocities carried out by their former SS colleagues'.[52] The Rimini List was supposed to be cross-referenced by Scotland Yard against the confidential NHS and social security records, which could potentially have been in breach of article 8 of the Human Rights Act.[53]

What is surprising is that it was the public reaction to a television documentary that made the Metropolitan Police and the All-Party Parliamentary War Crimes Group act with regard to the possibility of having thousands of former 'Galicians', alleged war criminals, residing in the UK. The reasons for not looking into the 'Galicia's' suspected involvement in war crimes before the allegations were made public by the TV documentary might well be those given by the British Screening Commission immediately after the Second World War, discussed in the following chapter. The fresh accusations were not left unanswered by the 'Galicians' themselves. The Brotherhood of Veterans of the 1st Ukrainian Division of the Ukrainian National Army issued its response to the accusations stated in the TV documentary:

50 *Ibid.*

51 *Ibid.*

52 Daniel Foggo, 'Police to use NHS records to find Nazi war criminals', *The Telegraph*, 22 June 2003 <http://www.telegraph.co.uk/news/worldnews/europe/1433729/Police-to-use-NHS-records-to-find-Nazi-war-criminals.html#> accessed 2 October 2012.

53 *Ibid.*

> The commentator Mr Ceaserani [sic][54] left the impression that the division veterans in Britain and Canada were never properly investigated, but the fact is that the division was screened the first time in the POW camp Bellaria in Italy by the British and Soviet commissions in 1945 [and] [l]ater by the 'Commission of Inquiry on War Crimes' headed by honorable Justice Jules Deschênes in Canada, which after thorough investigation lasting several years was not able to establish any basis to the accusations of war crimes.[55]

Naturally, the former 'Galicians' regarded the discussed investigations into their alleged participation in war crimes as sufficient in proving their innocence.

The only case from the Rimini List which acquired a high profile is that of Dr Swiatomyr M. Fostun. He was editor of *Ukrainian Thought* (*Ukraïns'ka Dumka*), a diaspora newspaper, published in London, chairman of the Association of Ukrainian Former Combatants in Great Britain, and a former general secretary of the Association of Ukrainians in Great Britain. The television documentary alleged that Fostun had been a concentration camp guard in the infamous Trawniki camp (near Lublin) prior to his recruitment into the Waffen SS 'Galicia'. Daniel Foggo, in his report for the *Telegraph* in June 2003, stated that 'Dr Fostun admitted to this newspaper that he was a guard at the infamous Trawniki camp "for a short time" and went on to join the 14th SS Division.'[56] The aforementioned Lord Janner is recorded as having asked the UK government 'whether they will institute an immediate investigation into allegations, reported in the Sunday Telegraph of 26 January,[57]

54 David Cesarani, the author of *Justice Delayed*, and a commentator in the TV documentary.

55 Brotherhood of Veterans of the 1st-Division of the Ukrainian National Army, Response to the recent TV documentary 'SS in Britain' <http://www.infoukes.com/galiciadivision/ss_in_britain_response/> accessed 22 September 2010.

56 Daniel Foggo, 'Police to use NHS records to find Nazi war criminals', *Telegraph* (22 June 2003) <http://www.telegraph.co.uk/news/worldnews/europe/1433729/Police-to-use-NHS-records-to-find-Nazi-war-criminals.html> accessed 2 October 2012.

57 This refers to Daniel Foggo, 'London man denies role in SS massacres', *Sunday Telegraph* (26 January 2003) <http://www.telegraph.co.uk/news/uknews/1420071/London-man-denies-role-in-SS-massacres.html> accessed 22 September 2010.

that Dr Swiatomyr M. Fostun was guilty of Nazi war crimes'[58] to which Lord Falconer of Thoroton answered that

> [t]he Government are committed to bringing war criminals to justice. This can only be done on the available evidence and in accordance with the rule of law. The Metropolitan Police are currently investigating the allegations against Dr Swiatomyr Fostun and will submit a report to the Crown Prosecution Service should sufficient evidence come to light.[59]

An investigation into Fostun's war activity prior to his joining the ranks of the Division shed no light on the war crime allegations. On 25 July 2004, the eighty-year-old Fostun, together with two other Ukrainian diaspora activists and former Division members,[60] was killed in a car crash in the Zolochiv region of the L'viv oblast'.[61] All three of them were on their way from the sixtieth-anniversary commemoration of the Battle of Brody. With Fostun's death, the inquiry into the Rimini List in the UK received no further publicity.

58 Written Answers, Parliament.uk (5 February 2003) <http://www.parliament.the-stationery-office.co.uk/pa/ld200203/ldhansrd/vo030205/text/30205w01.htm#column_WA36> accessed 22 September 2010.

59 *Ibid.*

60 Among those who were killed in the car crash together with Fostun were eighty-year-old Volodymyr Pihii, a member of the Ukrainian community in England, and Markiian Sheptyts'kyi, the secretary of the national executive of the Association of Ukrainian Former Combatants in Great Britain, treasurer of the St Sophia Ukrainian Religious Society, chairman of the Ukrainian Social Club affiliate to the London branch of the Association of Ukrainians in Great Britain (AUGB) and AUGB executive committee director.

61 Vasyl Pawlowsky, 'Four Ukrainian activists killed in a car accident in Lviv Oblast', *The Ukrainian Weekly*, 1 August 2004 <http://www.scribd.com/doc/12815589/The-Ukrainian-Weekly-200431> accessed 22 September 2010.

The Warsaw Uprising and the Huta Pieniacka Massacre

Among the allegations of war crimes against the 'Galicia' is the Division's alleged participation in the suppression of the Warsaw Uprising. One controversial author, Edward Prus, opens his chapter *Na Warszawę!* (Onwards to Warsaw!) with the following lines:

> Ukrainian nationalists, although they said 'Moscow', had more often the slogan 'Warsaw' in mind. It was closer after all, as well as being occupied. [...] Now that the Warsaw uprising had broken out and had to be suppressed the hope arose that there would be an opportunity to acclaim on its ruins. The regiments of the *SS-Galizien* which were not sent to Slovakia but stationed in Poland waited eagerly for the order to move towards Warsaw. In the meantime they revelled with the verse of the song 'march on Warsaw!'[62]

While this account is not supported with evidence, it is still capable of forming a strong idea of the role of the Ukrainian nationalists in general and the 'Galicia' Division in particular, in the war crimes perpetrated against the Polish population. Investigations, based on research, by historians like Ryszard Torzecki suggest that the 'Galicia' Division took no part in the Warsaw Uprising. Torzecki states that

> [i]n the uprising in Warsaw there were no complete units from the Division SS 'Galizien'. The fact should be noted however, that soldiers trained as officers near Rawicz came together with the Germans to the capital. It should be emphasised that this was an isolated instance, [and] it is not known how many Ukrainians were there and it is not possible to define with certainty what functions they performed. Some of them were also killed.[63]

The atrocities ascribed to the 'Galicians' might in reality have been committed in Warsaw by other military formations which were composed of citizens of the USSR, and therefore could include Ukrainian/Russian-speaking soldiers, assumed by the Warsaw inhabitants to be Ukrainians from the 'Galicia' Division. Torzecki states that 'Ukrainians from the

62 Prus, *SS-Galizien*, p. 196.
63 Torzecki, *Polacy i Ukraińcy*, p. 253.

Soviet Army may also have been found in the units of the ROA[64] which fought in Warsaw, since we know that the Germans reinforced the Vlasov unit with Ukrainians; however these were not people incorporated to the SS "Galizien" and they were treated as Russians.'[65] Torzecki goes on to allege that '[i]t was mainly people from the brigades of O. Dirlewanger, M. Kaminskii (RONA)[66] and the Vlasovites from ROA who were responsible for the cruelty towards the population.'[67]

It is known, however, that a reinforced company of a so-called Ukrainian Self-defence Legion (*Ukraïns'kyi lehion samooborony*)[68] was deployed against insurgents in Warsaw in September 1944. In March 1945, this unit was incorporated into the Division.[69] This, again, stresses the likelihood that some soldiers with a war crimes background, acquired prior to joining the 'Galicia', found themselves in the Division's ranks at the end of the war.

Another allegation of war crime participation relates to the burning of a Polish village located in Tarnopol voivodeship (*województwo tarnopolskie*) now in Ukraine. On 28 February 1944, most of the villagers of Polish ethnicity were murdered in what became known as the Huta Pieniacka massacre.[70] It has been suggested by scholars such as Grzegorz Motyka[71]

64 The Russian Liberation Army (*Russkaia Osvoboditel'naia Armiia*).

65 Torzecki, *Polacy i Ukraińcy*, p. 253.

66 The Russian Liberation People's Army (*Russkaia Osvoboditel'naia Narodnaia Armiia, RONA*) was led by Bronislav Kaminskii (1899–1944). He was executed after trial by court martial in 1944. Following his death, RONA was placed under the command of Christoph Diehm.

67 Torzecki, *Polacy i Ukraińcy*, p. 254. See also Motyka, *Od rzezi wołyńskiej do akcji 'Wisła'*, p. 266.

68 Also known as the Volhynian Self-defence Legion, this group has also been accused of participating in atrocities in the village of Chlaniov in August 1944.

69 Torzecki, *Polacy i Ukraińcy*, p. 253.

70 Huta Pieniacka was a village located in Tarnopol Voivodship, which was under Polish rule until 1939. The site of the former village is currently located in Ukraine in the Brody region of L'viv oblast.

71 Grzegorz Motyka, *Ukraińska partyzantka* 1942–1960 (Warszawa: Instytut Studiów Politycznych PAN Oficyna Wydawnicza RYTM, 2006). See also Motyka, *Od rzezi wołyńskiej do akcji 'Wisła'*, pp. 260–6.

and Sergei Chuev[72] that the planned action to kill the inhabitants of Huta Pieniacka was performed by the *4 Galizische SS-Freiwillige Regiment*[73] and the UPA unit *Siromantsi*. At the beginning of 1944 there was a significant presence of Soviet partisans headed by Dmitry Medvedev and partisans of the Polish Armia Krajowa in Huta Pieniacka.[74] This information reached the Germans and the UPA who both had an interest in attacking Soviet partisans. Motyka states that a sub-division of the '4th Police SS Unit', by which he presumably means the *4 Galizische SS-Freiwillige Regiment*, arrived to make enquiries as to the presence of Soviet partisans. The Poles assumed the Ukrainians from this regiment to be disguised UPA soldiers and killed two of them.[75] According to Motyka, following the death of two soldiers, the SS arranged an 'action of pacification'.[76] The atrocities involved the murder of 'several hundred civilian inhabitants'[77] of the village, allegedly by the soldiers of the UPA and the *4 Galizische SS-Freiwillige Regiment*.

Michael Melnyk gives a somewhat different account of the events in Huta Pieniacka. He suggests that the first attack on the village took place

72 Sergei Chuev, *Ukrainskii legion* (Moscow: Iauza, 2006), p. 347.

73 The history of this regiment is explained by Heike. The *4 Galizische SS-Freiwillige Regiment* consisted of 1,254 soldiers and was made up of the initial wave of volunteers for the Division. Heike states that 'in early February 1944 the fourth regiment was transferred into action against Soviet partisans in Galicia and took part in engagements with the Red Army in Tarnopil. In France the soldiers finished their training in spring and most of them were sent to rejoin the Division at Neuhammer. During training they were also used against French partisans. [...] some soldiers deserted to the ranks of the French partisans' (Heike, *The Ukrainian Division*, p. 155, n. 13). Heike also states that '[i]n the spring of 1944 police regiments 4 and 5, and later 6, 7, and 8, were incorporated into the Division' (Heike, *The Ukrainian Division*, p. 24). Bolianovs'kyi also gives his view of the Huta Pieniacka events and the *4* and *5 Galizische SS-Freiwillige Regimenter*. See Bolianovs'kyi, *Dyviziia 'Halychyna'*, pp. 216–24.

74 Motyka, *Ukraińska partyzantka*, p. 383.

75 *Ibid.*

76 *Ibid.*

77 Motyka states that the village served as a base for the local self-defence against the UPA, and included a group of Jews who were hiding there. Motyka, *Od rzezi wołyńskiej do akcji 'Wisła'*, p. 261.

on 23 February 1944. He claims that the village was 'openly acknowledged to have become a well fortified outpost for both Polish and Soviet led partisan groups', who, according to Melnyk, were known to have fought against the UPA and 'terrorized the local Ukrainian population by raiding the surrounding villages.'[78] Melnyk states that this attack failed and resulted in deaths of two Ukrainian soldiers whose 'bodies [were] reported to have been found naked and mutilated'.[79] The second assault was made five days later, during which eight to twelve Ukrainians were wounded. The 'pacification action' which followed included the destruction of the entire village. Melnyk then goes on to say that the Military Board member, Mykhailo Khronoviat, witnessed the event and reported that once the 'village had finally fallen, [...] the Ukrainians had moved on, a German (*Schutzpolizei*) unit (unspecified) arrived. They destroyed the village, setting fire to the houses, which began exploding because of the ammunition stored in them, and killed many of its inhabitants.'[80]

In 2003, the Commission for the Prosecution of Crimes against the Polish Nation (*Komisja Ścigania Zbrodni przeciwko Narodowi Polskiemu*), drawing mostly on witness statements, investigated the involvement of the 'Galicia' Division in the Huta Pieniacka massacre and also came to the conclusion that it was the *4 Galizische SS-Freiwillige Regiment* that perpetrated the crime.[81] In June 1944, the regiment was disbanded and

78 Melnyk, *To Battle*, pp. 102–3.

79 *Ibid.*

80 *Ibid.*

81 See 'Investigation into the Crime Committed at the Village of Huta Pieniacka. Commission for the Prosecution of Crimes against the Polish Nation', *Institute of National Remembrance* (18 November 2003). <http://ipn.gov.pl/portal/en/19/188/Investigation_into_the_Crime_committed_at_the_Village_of_Huta_Pieniacka.html> accessed 27 August 2012. See also: 'Dokumenty z akt śledczych Okręgowej Komisji Badania Zbrodni przeciw Narodowi Polskiemu' in Władysław Bąkowski, *Zagłada Huty Pieniackiej* (Kraków: Biblioteka Złoczowska, 2001). The Huta Pieniacka massacre, as well as other atrocities allegedly perpetrated by the members of the 'Galicia' Division in the Palikrowy, Vitsyn', Pawłów and Budki Nieznanowskie, receive detailed attention in Rudling's paper, 'They Defended Ukraine', pp. 346–56. While it is not always clear whether these 'pacification actions' were directed against

incorporated into the Waffen SS 'Galicia' Division. This proves two points: first, the Division as a whole was not involved in the massacre of Huta Pieniacka as it was in training until May 1944; it was a Police unit and the UPA soldiers who attacked the village. Second, some of the surviving soldiers of the *4 Galizische SS-Freiwillige Regiment* who might have participated in the atrocities in Huta Pieniacka joined the Division in June 1944. This, once again, supports the hypothesis of scholars such as Rodal, that there were individual war criminals in the Division, such as the *Galizische SS-Freiwillige Regiment* soldiers; the problem is that they were not identified prior to the civilianization and settlement of the 'Galicia' men.

The 'Galicia' Division in Slovakia

Another unexamined aspect of the 'Galician' war-time history is their time in Slovakia. Due to the lack of documentation, the Division's counter-insurgency actions cannot be fully assessed. Once again, opinions are divided on the degree to which the civilian population might have been targeted by the 'Galicia' soldiers in the suppression of the Slovak National Uprising in August–October 1944. Without offering evidential backup, Littman maintains that in Slovakia 'the Division did prove particularly effective in teasing Jews out of their hiding places and [...] [s]ince the Division members were Slavs who spoke a Slavic language, they were adept at luring partisans out of their hiding places by calling to them in Russian.'[82] Julian Hendy, the producer and director of the 'SS in Britain' television documentary, in his submission to the independent television commission, cites an interview with the director of the Museum of National Uprising Jan Stanislav, who

the partisan groups or the civilian population, it is clear that they should have been taken into consideration during the official inquiries and demand further scholarly examination at present.

82 Sol Littman, *Pure Soldiers*, p. 86.

claims that the 'Galicians' participated in terrorist operations and reprisals against the fighters of the National Uprising. According to Hendy, Stanislav insists that the 'Galicia' Division attacked the civilian population:

> In Smerycany, the Wittenmayer unit from the Division burnt the village down using artillery and mortar fire. The civilian population was driven out of the village and 80% of the 120 houses were burnt down. Four people died. During the raid on Nizna Boca, five people died.[83]

Hendy also refers to witness statements given by residents of the village of Nižná Boca who describe their attackers as 'Germans' or 'SS-men'.[84] Hendy, nevertheless, is adamant that the perpetrators of the attacks were Ukrainian and explains their lack of mention in the testimonies stating that

> [t]he soldiers arrived deep in the night. The villagers were in fear of their lives – drunken soldiers speaking German were arresting and shooting their men for no apparent reason. The soldiers who committed the crime wore German SS uniform. It is not surprising the villagers thought they were Germans.[85]

Taras Hunczak offers a remarkably different account of the 'Galicia's' time in Slovakia to the one suggested by Hendy. While recognizing that the 'Wildner Battalion', 900 men commanded by *Obersturmbannführer* Wildner, engaged in 'search and destroy' operations in Slovakia,[86] Hunczak claims that the 'main responsibility of the Division was to provide protection to the arms industry of the region and its workers [...and] the defense of the railroads and numerous tunnels'.[87] In fact, according to

83 Interview with Dr Jan Stanislav, director of the Museum of the Slovak National Uprising, Banska Bystrica, 4 December 1998, cited in Julian Hendy, '"SS in Britain", submission to the Independent Television Commission. The 14th SS Division Galizien and War Crimes in Nizna Boca, Slovakia. October 1944' (Yorkshire Television, October 2001), p. 4.

84 *Ibid.*, pp. 5–6.

85 *Ibid.*, p. 6.

86 Taras Hunczak, *On the Horns of a Dilemma*, p. 107. See also Melnyk, *To Battle*, pp. 195–214.

87 Hunczak, *On the Horns of a Dilemma*, p. 110.

Hunczak, '[b]eing stationed in Slovakia proved to be a home away from home for the Ukrainian members of the Division',[88] as they understood Slovak which 'facilitated the development of friendly relations and even romantic involvements.'[89] Thus, the knowledge of the Slavic language is interpreted by Hunczak as enabling the 'Galicians' to form positive relationship with the local population and by Littman as functional in 'luring partisans out of their hiding places'.[90]

As with most episodes of the 'Galicia's' history, their time in Slovakia receives polarized representation, depending on the commentator. One other reason that might help explain the negative reputation of the Division soldiers in certain circles with regard to their activity in Slovakia is that the Dirlewanger Brigade (*36 Waffen-Grenadier Division 'Dirlewanger'*), the unit which consisted of criminals and military convicts and was infamous for pillaging and looting,[91] was attached to the 'Galicia' Division during the counter-insurgent operations in Slovakia. Heike insists that it was the Dirlewanger men and not the 'Galicians' who were unruly and undisciplined.[92] While highly plausible, the argument that the Dirlewanger men were responsible for the war crimes committed in Slovakia does not take away the potential involvement in atrocities of the 'Galicia' at the time.

It is known that after the Battle of Brody, groups of Ukrainians were sent to other units of the German Army to receive training and experience in action. Towards the end of the war, some of them were moved back to the 'Galicia' Division. As a result, over 1,000 'Galicians' served with the *Wiking* Division[93] (*5 SS-Panzer Division Wiking*), infamous for its anti-Jewish

88 *Ibid.*
89 *Ibid.* See also Melnyk, *To Battle*, pp. 195–214.
90 Littman, *Pure Soldiers*, p. 86.
91 Rikmenspoel, *Waffen-SS Encyclopaedia*, p. 55.
92 Heike also mentions a so-called East Turkish Battle Group (*Osttürkischer Waffenverband*) as such which committed atrocities against the civilian population and ascribed them to the 'Galicia' Division. For the discussion of the *Division 'Dirlewanger'* and *Osttürkischer Waffenverband*, see Heike, *Ukraïns'ka Dyviziia*, pp. 131–3; Heike, *Sie Wollten Die Freiheit*, pp. 150–1; and Heike, *The Ukrainian Division*, pp. 80–1.
93 Hunczak, *On the Horns of a Dilemma*, pp. 110–12.

campaigns. As with most allegations, it is difficult to estimate how many former *Wiking* men actually participated in atrocities and how many of them ended up in the final setup of the Division, yet the possibility of these men's presence in the 'Galicia' and the 1st UD UNA cannot be ruled out.

There are three main narratives which engage in the discussion of the 'Galicia's' association with the Waffen SS and its subsequent supposed participation in war crimes. Those who argue the Division's complete innocence stress the fact that it was formed in 1943 and therefore could not have committed any crimes, as these had all been committed prior to the formation of the 'Galicia', and insist that there has been no sufficient evidence discovered that would point towards the Division's involvement in war crimes post 1943. Another narrative treats the Division's participation in the alleged war crimes as obvious, and claims that inquests into 'Galicia's' involvement in war crimes have been insufficient and produced inaccurate outcomes. Finally, there is the narrative that recognizes that there is no evidence to date against the Waffen SS 'Galicia' as a division, but also point out that there is a high probability of individual war criminals' presence in the ranks of the 'Galicia' Division, something that neither the British Screening Commission at the end of the Second World War, nor the Deschênes Commission in the 1980s, chose to focus on. While it is difficult to give exact estimates of the potential war criminals in the ranks of the 'Galicia' when it was civilianized, their probable existence should not be disregarded.[94]

94 John-Paul Himka's article on the participation of Ukrainians in war crimes during the Second World War does not discuss the 'Galicia' or the war crimes in which it is implicated. It does, however, explain the way in which war criminality is discussed in the diaspora, which is one of the main factors behind the polarisation of the debate. See John-Paul Himka, 'War Criminality: A Blank Spot in the Collective Memory of the Ukrainian Diaspora', *spacesofidentity* 5.1 (2005) 9–24.

CHAPTER 3

Soviet Repatriation Mission and the UK Screening Commission

One of the least studied questions concerning the Division is their escape from repatriation to the USSR, and the role of the British authorities in this. In order to understand why the forceful repatriation of the 'Galicians' did not take place and why the UK Screening Commission was in favour of moving the Division members to the UK the post-war decisions of the British officials have to be contextualized. At this stage, the changing political situation regarding the Soviet Union and the subsequent dilemmas the UK authorities faced when dealing with the Ukrainian surrendered enemy personnel perhaps played a more significant role than the actual war-time history of the Waffen SS 'Galicia'.

The Yalta Agreements

The Yalta Agreements were crucial in the question of the repatriation of Soviet citizens, including those who came from pre-1939 Soviet Ukraine. These agreements were reached during the Yalta Conference (4–11 February 1945) between three heads of government of the United States, the United Kingdom and the Soviet Union: Franklin D. Roosevelt, Winston Churchill and Joseph Stalin. The purpose of the conference was to discuss the reorganization of post-war Europe, including the division of Germany, German war reparations, the formation of the United Nations, and the controversial question of the reorganization of the territory of Poland. It also addressed the critical 'Agreement relating to Prisoners of War and Civilians Liberated by Forces Operating under Soviet Command and Forces Operating under British Command'.[1] The nine articles of the Yalta Agreements regarding repatriation of Soviet citizens and British subjects were reconsidered by the British in May 1946, because 'the text of the Agreement [relating to prisoners of war and agreed at the Yalta Conference] contains no provision laying down what degree of coercion is to be used to secure the repatriation of Soviet citizens who are reluctant to return to their homes'.[2] The 'Galicia' members were among those who were unwilling to return to their country of origin. This memorandum from the UK Secretary of State for Foreign Affairs states that the majority of the Soviet citizens had been repatriated without disturbance, but it also stresses that there were still 'groups of recalcitrants in various theatres whom it may not be possible to repatriate without resort to coercion'.[3] Such groups included the Waffen SS 'Galicia' men, who were in the Italian SEP camp near Rimini in May 1946 as this memorandum was being written.

On 30 January 1946, in the Overseas Reconstruction Committee, the Chancellor of the Duchy of Lancaster questioned the use of force during repatriations, pointing out that 'the consequences might be unpleasant'.[4] It is not further explained what is meant by 'unpleasant consequences', but it was agreed that 'the British Commanders in all European theatres should suspend the forcible repatriation of Soviet citizens'[5] until the Agreement had been reviewed. Such a review took place in May 1946 and it recommended that

> we should apply the principle of compulsory repatriation only to such Soviet citizens as were captured in German uniforms, or were members of the Soviet Armed Forces on or after the 22nd June, 1941, and were not subsequently discharged therefrom, or could be shown to have rendered aid and comfort to the enemy.[6]

1 Repatriation of Soviet Citizens, (NA) CAB/129/10, 20 May 1946, Annex 3, p. 4.
2 *Ibid.*, p. 1.
3 *Ibid.*
4 *Ibid.*
5 Conclusions of a Meeting of the Cabinet held at 10 Downing Street, SW1, (NA) CAB 128/5, 6 June 1946, p. 114.
6 *Ibid.*

This description would unquestionably include the members of the 'Galicia' Division, but there was one more criterion which had to be satisfied for the forceful repatriation to take place: '[o]nly persons who were both citizens of and actually within the Soviet Union on the 1st September 1939, will be regarded as Soviet citizens for this purpose.'[7] This last statement put those Ukrainians who served in the Waffen SS 'Galicia' in a distinctive position: although, as was explained earlier, not all members of the Division were from the district of Galicia, most of them claimed to have come from the region, which became occupied by the Soviet Army only on 17 September 1939. Thus, with no proof of there being Soviet citizens within the Division, the 'Galicians' did not strictly fulfil the criteria for forceful repatriation. This placed the British authorities in a position where they were unable to send the Division to the USSR by force, but were at the same time facing controversy by allowing over 8,000 men who had surrendered wearing German uniforms into the UK.[8] A number of rounds of negotiations took place between the Soviet Repatriation Mission and the British authorities in Europe before the final decision was made.

In the 'Revision of Geneva Conventions on War Victims', in the section on the 'Repatriation after Termination of Hostilities' where the obligatory repatriation of the prisoners of war is discussed, it is noted that '[t]here have been criticisms of our own performance in this matter, both abroad and at home',[9] and it was suggested that the proposal made by the Red Cross Committee 'to prohibit repatriation of prisoners against their own will'[10] should be given further consideration. Thus it could be argued that the scandal that the British authorities caused with the forced repatriation

7 Repatriation of Soviet Citizens, (NA) CAB/129/10, 20 May 1946, p. 2.

8 The lack of proof of the Soviet citizenship, however, did not stop the British in May 1945 from forcefully repatriating the Cossacks, among whom were white Russian émigrés and Tsarist fugitives who had never lived in the Soviet Union, and who had fled their country in 1919. See Nikolai Tolstoy, *The Minister and the Massacres* (London: Century Hutchinson, 1986), p. XIV.

9 Revision of Geneva Conventions on War Victims, 10 March 1949, (NA) CAB/129/33, p. 7. Although the document is dated 1949, it refers to the ongoing criticisms of obligatory repatriations which started immediately after the end of the war.

10 *Ibid.*

of the Cossacks, served as a lesson in dealing with other divisions which could potentially be forcefully repatriated, the 'Galicia' Division being one such case. Thus the 'Galicians' were fortunate in not being among the first on the list for repatriation.[11] However, this fortune alone would not be enough to protect them from being repatriated in the future, as they were still to be subjected to the screening of the Soviet Repatriation Mission, which, if it found the 'Galicians' to be either Soviet citizens or war criminals, was able to demand their obligatory repatriation.

Fears of Soviet Repatriation

Repatriation to the USSR was feared by most Ukrainian displaced persons; the ones who fought against the Red Army, however, feared it most of all. From interviews[12] with the former 'Galicians', it is clear that the Division members did not have any formal information about the Yalta Agreements on repatriation issues. However, there were rumours, which came from two sources in particular. First, religious visitors from Rome, the most influential of whom was Bishop Ivan Buchko, who ran a Ukrainian Help

11 Littman states that on 21 May 1945 the 5th Corps, in charge of the surrendered enemy personnel, including the 'Galicia' men, received an instruction to not regard the Russian Corps (composed of Russian émigrés) as Soviet nationals, and to treat the 15th Cossack Cavalry Corps as Soviet citizens and thus subject to repatriation. Yet the 'Galicia' Division 'disappeared' from the list of those who could potentially be classified as Soviet nationals who could be forcefully repatriated, and no further instructions were issued with regard to the Division until it was moved to northern Italy. See Littman, *Pure Soldiers*, p. 107. It is, however, not surprising that the 'Galicia' was not included in this instruction as there was no clear decision as to the Division's men's nationality or citizenship. The discussions addressing this issue took place later. See Secretariat and Statistics memo to SO I Secretariat, Subject: Ukrainians – Recording by Nationality, (NA) LFWP/EAW, 11 March 1947.

12 Interviewee B., 27 December 2006 (L'viv); Interviewee B., 20 May 2007, 2 December 2007 (London); Interviewee K., 14 April 2010 (Toronto).

Committee (*Ukraïns'kyi dopomohovyi komitet*) and was responsible for visiting Ukrainian Catholics in Western Europe, are said to have brought updates on the Yalta Agreements to the 'Galicia' men in the camp.[13] Second, some of the Division men had witnessed the forceful repatriation of the Cossacks in the temporary camp in Austria, which made them aware that the same fate may have awaited them.

The total number of DPs listed as ethnic Ukrainians was only 9,190 in December 1945. It had risen dramatically to 106,549 by June 1947.[14] However, Ukrainians were not given the status of a national group, as the classification of DPs and of prisoners of war continued to be made in terms of their citizenship and not their nationality or ethnic origin. In his article on the visit to the Rimini SEP camp, Denis Hills,[15] who was sent by Allied Forces Headquarters (AFHQ) Caserta in July 1945 to report on the '10,000 soldiers of the Ukrainian Galicia Division who were being held there as Surrendered Enemy Personnel after giving themselves up to the British in Carinthia',[16] writes that his immediate task to establish the

13 This was suggested in the interviews with the ex-'Galicians' (Interviewee S., 26 December 2006 (Ternopil'), Interviewee B., 20 May 2007 (London)) and correspondence with Rev. Ivan Muzyczka (Ivan Muzyczka to Olesya Khromeychuk, Rome, 11 September 2009, author's private archive).

14 Mark Wyman, *DPs: Europe's Displaced Persons, 1945–1950* (Ithaca, NY: Cornell University Press, 1998), p. 80.

15 Denis Cecil Hills (1913–2004) was a traveller, writer, linguist, military intelligence officer and teacher. In 1947 he wrote a report which condemned forceful repatriation to Eastern Europe and noted the secretive protection and re-routing of many prisoners of war present in the British Zone. At the time, this document was circulated anonymously, as written by 'Capt A'. He explained his involvement with the POWs in the following way: 'Many of them eluded [the orders] with our collusion […] I doctored the nominal roles as best I could. Some Russians I registered as Poles. Some I encouraged to run away from their camps, which were not at all closely guarded […]' (from his obituary by Richard Greenfield, 'Denis Hills. Post-Yalta whistle-blower later sentenced to death by Idi Amin', *The Independent*, 11 May 2004). The article 'You are the Grey Mass', *The Spectator* 23/30 (December, 1989) by Denis Hills, is very popular among the ex-'Galicians' in the UK.

16 Denis Hills, 'You are the Grey Mass', *The Spectator* 23/30 December (1989), p. 14. Around 1,300 'Galicians' surrendered to the American troops and were held as POWs

identity of these men proved to be difficult: '[w]ere they to be listed as "Polish", "Russian" Ukrainians, Soviet, or even, some of them as true Poles? – though General Anders' Army in Italy would have nothing to do with them.'[17] Thus, because of their unclear citizenship, many Ukrainians were classified as 'undetermined' and, until their status could change, they were not eligible for repatriation.

Not all 'Galicians' objected to going back to their native villages, now in the USSR. The estimates of those who went back voluntarily vary between fifty individuals, as stated in the Screening Commission Report,[18] and over 1,000 individuals.[19] Yet for many Ukrainians, including the Division men, going to the Soviet Union equalled death. Mark Elliott has estimated that, after the end of the Second World War, several thousand Soviet citizens chose to commit suicide rather than return the USSR.[20] For the 'Galicians', the 'repatriation fight' began with proving that they were originally from western Ukraine, the part which was under control of Poland, Romania, Czechoslavakia or Hungary. The screening teams, as illustrated by Hills, were more than puzzled:

> My preliminary findings revealed a cartographer's nightmare. There were certainly some genuine Soviet Russians in the division; but with so little time, and without facilities, proper screening was impossible, and any attempt to winkle out 'war

---

in the American Zone and later released. See Bolianovs'kyi, *Dyviziia 'Halychyna'*, p. 354, and Littman, *Pure Soldiers*, p. 96.

17 *Ibid*. General Anders' Army refers to the Polish Armed Forces in the period 1941–2, which got its name from its commander Władysław Anders.

18 Screening Commission Report, (NA) HO/213/1851, p. 4.

19 Littman, *Pure Soldiers*, p. 110, gives the figure of 350 men, while Muzyczka suggests that 735 individuals decided to go back to the USSR. See Radio Svoboda Interview with Ivan Muzyczka by Natalka Kudryk: 'My naïvno mriialy pro vil'nu Ukraïnu', *Radio Svoboda*, 7 May 2010 <http://www.radiosvoboda.org/content/article/2035588> accessed 13 October 2012. Hunczak, on the other hand, claims that '1052 soldiers volunteered to return home' and '176 men decided to join the 11 Corps', the Polish Corps commanded by General Władysław Anders (Hunczak, *On the Horns of a Dilemma*, p. 161).

20 Mark R. Elliott, 'Pawns of Yalta: Soviet Refugees and America's Role in Their Repatriation', *The Journal of American History* 69/4 (March 1983), 1031–3.

> criminals' would have been a farce. I recommended therefore that the Ukrainian formation should be treated as a cohesive whole; and that all should be given the benefit of the doubt and classified as Polish citizens from Polish Galicia.[21]

Despite treating the 'Galicia' as a division which officially was formed from western Ukrainian Galicians, and thus not Soviet citizens, the British authorities allowed the Division to be screened by the Soviet Repatriation Mission. The task of this Mission was to find evidence that would prove the Division's involvement in war crimes, or that there were Soviet citizens among the members of the 'Galicia'.

The Soviet Repatriation Mission

While in the POW camp near Bellaria, Italy,[22] the Division numbered around 11,000. Later, around 500 of them declared themselves to be of German origin and were moved to the camp with German prisoners of war.[23] Others, reinforcing their Polish origins, declared themselves as having served in the Army of General Anders and requested to be moved to the location where Polish regiments were situated.[24] At the same time, a number

21 Hills, 'You are the Grey Mass', p. 14. Here Hills is referring to 'Galicia' members only.

22 This temporary camp is described by Stetkevych as an open field of wheat. The Division men harvested the wheat on the command of the British officers and assembled the camp on the field. This episode illustrates how unprepared the British officials were at the end of the war to deal with the numerous prisoners of war. This lack of preparation contributed to the general inability to carry out thorough screenings of POWs. See Lev Stetkevych, *Iak z Berezhan do Kadry* (Ternopil': Dzhura, 1998), pp. 137–43.

23 See Bolianovs'kyi, *Dyviziia 'Halychyna'*; Veryha, *Slidamy bat'kiv*; Stetkevych, *Iak z Berezhan*.

24 See Stetkevych, *Iak z Berezhan*, p. 140 and Hunczak, *On the Horns of a Dilemma*, p. 161.

of civilians who were unhappy with their status as *Ostarbeiter*[25] joined the Division in hope of better prospects, as they also were fearful of returning to the USSR. It is during the 'Galicia' Division's stay in Bellaria that they were visited by the Soviet Repatriation Mission. Hills states that 'just before the Soviet repatriation mission arrived I warned the Ukrainian camp leaders and their commandant, Major Jaskewycz, to be absolutely firm with the Moscow officers; they were not to fear them and they would not be under duress. I would be present to see fair play.'[26] It has been stressed by the Division members that the British officials often took the role of observers during the visits of the Soviet Repatriation Mission. They did not, however, intervene in the interaction of the Ukrainian prisoners and the Soviet Mission. Even on occasions when the situation became critical (for example, when the 'Galician' prisoners started throwing stones at the representatives of the Soviet Mission), the British officials did not get too involved and, although the UK military made sure to calm the incident, the prisoners who took part in the violent behaviour were not punished.[27]

The members of the Soviet Repatriation Mission were often from the Ukrainian Galicia region themselves and spoke Ukrainian, as opposed to Russian, which might have been meant to make the Mission look more trustworthy.[28] This is how the appearance of the Soviet Repatriation Mission is described in Hills' account:

> When the Soviet team, under General Vasiliev and Colonel Jakovliev, entered the cage the whole Ukrainian division, paraded for inspection, watched them in silence. Major Fedorov sneered at the flimsy bivouac tents where thousands of thin, suntanned men slept in threadbare uniforms on the ground, and at the British-style cookhouses and rations. General Vasiliev was given a ladle of soup to taste and he

25 Eastern Workers or *Ostarbeiter* is the official term introduced in Nazi Germany to denote people of non-German national origin, who inhabited the Reich Commissariat, and who were brought into the German Reich by the German Armed Forces. Their status was legally defined by the Ministerial Council for Defence of the Reich in June 1942.

26 Hills, 'You are the Grey Mass', p. 14.

27 Interviewee B., 15 November 2009 (London).

28 See Stetkevych, *Iak z Berezhan*, p. 147.

> asked if there were any complaints. There were none. Indeed the uncanny silence of the assembled men struck me as unusual and significant. This was a tussle of wills: the Soviet war-machine facing not merely a few thousand unarmed yet determined men but a test of its reputation.[29]

Evidently, the Soviet officers are portrayed as the villains of the story. Hills is very careful not to reiterate that the Division had fought as part of the Waffen SS, or that the Soviet officers had no reason to see the ex-members of the 'Galicia' as anything but their direct enemy. Instead, he reminds the reader of the fact that now the 'few thousand' (in fact over 8,000) Ukrainians are unarmed and defenceless:

> They had their own language, ranks and uniform, their own religion with its Uniate cross and marvellous chants, their own history. They regarded themselves as part of the Ukrainian Freedom Army, using Germany as an ally in their fight against Bolshevism.[30]

Hills is constructing a certain picture of the Division: when for the Soviet Mission they were traitors who betrayed their motherland and fought against their 'brothers', for Hills the Division members were individuals who were united by their national consciousness and stood strong to defend their beliefs. It is not entirely clear why Hills chose to portray the 'Galicians' in such a positive light. It could have been because of his dissatisfaction with how prisoners of war were treated, or because of his political ideas, combined with personal attachment to the Ukrainian men, with whom he spent a great deal of time. Whatever his motivations were, Hills' depiction of the 'Galicia' members added to their overall positive perception by the British authorities, and eventually increased their chances of being allowed to move to the UK.

On their first encounter with the Division, the Soviet Mission promised 'forgiveness' to the 'Galicia' members and assured them that

29 Hills, 'You are the Grey Mass', p. 14.

30 *Ibid.*

the 'motherland'[31] was exhausted after the war and needed each of her sons and daughters. This approach had largely failed and was followed by the interrogations of the 'Galicians'. They were often pressed to speak about their war activities, their political leaders, connections and relatives both in the USSR and abroad. Hills states that '[t]he Soviet officers spent many days interrogating the Ukrainians. They worked relentlessly, without meal breaks, loosening their collars in a tent pitched inside the cage'.[32] He continues to claim that he 'was present at every interview. The men were grilled individually. Asked why they had taken up arms against the USSR they answered – with vehemence as they gained confidence – that they "hated the Bolsheviks for having persecuted them and their families"'.[33] Here again, Hills, with reference to the soldiers' political conviction, reminds the reader that they were joining a fight to protect their families, and were not simply following an imposed ideology. Hills reinforces that '[e]ach prisoner, standing to attention before the trestle tables where the Soviet officers sat, kept his eyes on me at this critical moment as though my uniform were a lifebelt.'[34] The reference to the British uniform is interesting as it stands in opposition to the Soviet one, worn by the Repatriation team. The fact that until recently the 'Galicians' wore a German uniform is not mentioned; now the battle is between the 'understanding West' and the 'unforgiving Soviet Union'. Hills juxtaposes the British and the Soviets in his account of the events:

31 When discussed in the interviews (Interviewee S., 26 December 2006 (Ternopil'), Interviewee B., 27 December 2006 (L'viv), Interviewee B., 15 November 2009 (London)), the concept of a 'motherland' comes across as very confused. The ex-'Galicians' often say that they could not perceive the USSR as their motherland in spite of the fact that the territory where they were born was now part of the Soviet Union. Similar views were expressed by Polish soldiers, many of whom came from Lwów (L'viv), who had fought with the British. They felt that, although they were fighting for their motherland and won the war, they no longer had a motherland to which they could return.

32 Hills, 'You are the Grey Mass', p. 14.

33 *Ibid.*

34 *Ibid.*

> Soon after the [Soviet] mission had left, Brigadier Block, the Area Commander, took me with him into the cage to address the senior officers. It was a dramatic moment, for the fate of the whole division depended on what he was going to say. The Brigadier spoke briefly and to the point. 'You are safe now', he told them. 'The mission from Moscow will not bother you any more. You must continue to trust us, and we will not let you down.' He complimented the soldiers on their good behaviour and asked them not to relax their discipline. While I was interpreting I looked straight at Jaskewycz. His hard, sergeant-major's face was shining with relief.[35]

Hills' observation of the apparently reassured Ukrainians is interesting, as the interviews as well as memoirs speak of an ongoing fear of the Soviet Mission's return and a continuous distrust of the British authorities:[36]

> The Allies, and especially the English, were not interested in who the Division men were and what we had fought for. They only saw in us soldiers in German uniforms, who were also stateless [...]. There was a wide spread pro-Soviet sentiment among the Western Allies at the time. [...] The military and civil services of the Western victors were rife with communist sympathisers and 'liberals' who were prepared to sell anyone for a good profit.[37]

Whether or not much effort was exerted on behalf of the British into protecting the 'Galicians' from the forceful repatriation to the USSR, the Soviets had to conclude that unless the individuals agreed, they could not remove the Division members forcefully. Essentially, General Vasiliev's repatriation mission failed:

> A colonel freshly arrived from Moscow to ginger things up was permitted to address the prisoners by companies. 'You are the grey mass', he cried to the wooden faces gazing at him. 'You have nothing to offer but your hands. The world doesn't want you. For them, you are rubbish. Be warned. Sooner or later the Soviet Union will have you.'[38]

35 *Ibid.*

36 Interviewee B., 20 May 2007, 9 September 2007 (London). See Mykola Virnyi, *Nasha Dolia* (Kyiv: Iaroslaviv Val, 2007), p. 5; Stetkevych, *Iak z Berezhan*, p. 160.

37 Stetkevych, *Iak z Berezhan*, pp. 148–9.

38 Hills, 'You are the Grey Mass', p. 14.

The fact that the Soviet Repatriation Mission failed to prove that the 'Galicians' were Soviet citizens and did not find any evidence of the Division's involvement in war crimes meant that they had no good ground to enforce the Division's repatriation. Still fearful of the prospect of repatriation, but safe from this particular USSR Repatriation Mission, the 'Galicians' moved to the SEP camp near Rimini, Italy.

Rimini SEP Camp

The Rimini camp was much better equipped to receive over 8,000 Ukrainians than the one in Bellaria. The 'Galicians' were making the best of their life in the camp by establishing a so-called 'university' and writing their own newsletter with any available news and fast-spreading rumours about the situation in Ukraine, now entirely part of the Soviet Union. These activities contributed to the creation of a narrative, used by the 'Galicians' themselves as well as the British Screening Commission, which portrayed the Division members as people who were interested in studying and rebuilding their lives. The image of them as members of the Waffen SS was being replaced by that of peaceful, hard-working men, who have been wronged by the Soviet authorities. Their future was still uncertain, information about their potential release from the Rimini SEP camp was not made available and the 'Galicians' feared the possibility of another visit from the Soviet repatriation team and subsequent obligatory repatriation to the USSR. There was still a great deal of confusion and lack of information as to the exact criteria of those who were to be repatriated by force.

Figure 1 Ukrainian SEP Camp in Rimini (Italy), 29 March 1946.

Figure 2 The blessing of Easter bread in the Ukrainian SEP Camp in Rimini (Italy), 13 April 1947.

According to the 'Galicians' themselves,[39] another factor which helped them avoid repatriation was their regular communication with the Vatican. The 'Galicians' were visited by priests from Rome, and occasionally by

39 Interviewee B., 20 May 2007 (London), and Ivan Muzyczka to Olesya Khromeychuk, Rome, 11 September 2009, author's private archive. Also in Hunczak, *On the Horns of a Dilemma*, pp. 161–2.

Bishop Buchko, Papal representative to Ukrainian Catholics in Western Europe. These visits brought information on the developments in the political situation in the USSR and the decisions which might affect the fate of the Division men; the presence of the bishop also enhanced the soldiers' morale and, allegedly, had a positive influence on the treatment they received from the British military, as the Roman clergy treated the 'Galicia' Division as their protégés.[40] As the International Refugee Organization did not recognize the Division members to be eligible for assistance because they were categorized as surrendered enemy personnel, the Central Ukrainian Relief Bureau (CURB) sought assistance from the Vatican to resettle the Division members.[41] In November 1946 CURB's representatives met with the Apostolic Delegate in London to request that the Pope intervene in the decisions being taken with regard to the Division:

> [...] so that when the Allies do withdraw the members of the division be given an opportunity to immigrate to the various countries rather than be forcibly repatriated [...] it was proposed [...] should an agreement with the Italian government fail, [that] they be made citizens of the Vatican State until such time when they may be able to immigrate.[42]

In December 1946, Panchuk also stated that

> [i]t is very important to note that the Vatican is helping mostly those who are ineligible for help by the International Organization [...] the Vatican IS NOT repeat IS NOT confining its help to Catholics, but they are helping many others regardless of

40 Although this is not evident from the declassified archival materials of the British authorities, such a perception was believed to be held among the 'Galicians' themselves, as well as the clergy who came to visit the camp. (Interviewee B., 20 May 2007; 5 December 2007 (London), and correspondence with Rev. I. Muzyczka, Rome–London 2009. Ivan Muzyczka to Olesya Khromeychuk, Rome, 11 September 2009, author's private archive; see also Stetkevych, *Iak z Berezhan*).

41 AO, Panchuk Collection, Box 27, 7 June 1950, cited in Rodal, *Chapter XII – Part 3*, p. 16.

42 AO, Panchuk Collection, Box 27, re: interview with Apostolic Delegate in London, A.J. Yaremovich's 'Report on Interview with Apostolic Delegate', 14 November 1946, cited in Rodal, *Chapter XII – Part 3*, p. 16.

> their religion. The Vatican is getting a very large quota of visas to South American countries, and we should make every effort to obtain as many of these for our S.E.P. and ineligibles who are in Italy, Austria and Germany.[43]

Ivan Muzyczka, a former Division member and now a Ukrainian Greek-Catholic priest in Rome, stated that as soon as the 'Galicians' heard of the possible repatriation while in the British SEP camp, two soldiers escaped from the camp, which, according to Muzyczka, was not a difficult task, and travelled to Rome to notify Ivan Buchko of the possible repatriation. Muzyczka goes on to say that 'late at night Ivan Buchko paid a visit to Pope Pius XII. [...] It seems that the Pope used the appropriate measures to contact the British headquarters in order not to let this [repatriation] take place.'[44] It is not clear if this active protection of the 'Galicia' by the Greek-Catholic Church under the protectorate of Rome was one of the decisive factors which moved 'Galicia' away from the possibility of a forceful repatriation. However, it is certainly a part of the development of a narrative by and about the 'Galicians' which distanced them from belonging to the German Army and brought them closer to being recognized as part of an essentially Ukrainian group. As such, these factors enabled the construction of a narrative by the UK authorities which portrayed the Division as potentially suitable for transportation to the UK. However, the main factor which enabled the Division's relocation to the UK was the conclusion of the British Screening Commission.

43 AO, Panchuk Collection, Box 22, G.R.B. Panchuk to UCRF/UUARC, 12 December 1946, cited in Rodal, *Chapter XII – Part 3*, p. 16.

44 Ivan Muzyczka to Olesya Khromeychuk, Rome, 11 September 2009, author's private archive.

The Refugee Screening Commission Report

The British delegation aimed to assess, in accordance with the Yalta Agreements, whether the ex-'Galicians', or a proportion of them, were legally obliged to be repatriated to the USSR or whether they could be allowed to go to Britain as prisoners of war. If transported to Britain as POWs, the Division members would act as cheap labour, replacing German POWs, who were due to be repatriated. In order to understand the process of the screening of the Division by the British Commission, it is essential to analyse a document which stands out as one of the most important pieces of evidence used in defence of moving the 'Galicians' to the UK and granting them DP status and subsequent civilianization. It explains the preconditions of the Division's arrival in the UK and gives a flavour of how SEP camp screenings were carried out in the British Zone.

The 'Refugee Screening Commission Report on Ukrainians in SEP Camp No 374 Italy'[45] served as the main official basis in making decisions about the Division. The report claims that those in the SEP Camp No 374 'were either captured in German uniform or were working in Germany as civilians and attached themselves to the 1st Ukrainian division shortly before its surrender'.[46] They are suggested to have formerly belonged to three Infantry Regiments, Artillery, Supply Section, Engineer Battalion, Signals Unit, Recruiting Regiment, Workshop Company, Fusilier Battalion, Sanitary Section, Anti-Tank Section, Divisional Staff and Army Staff. Altogether, the report estimates 8,272 men, though 'the number of inmates varies from time to time due to escapes, transfers to hospitals, etc'.[47] These people had not previously been screened and there was little record on individuals or the group as a whole available to the British officials at the time. Few soldiers possessed documents such as German Army pay books,

45 (NA) HO/213/1851, Screening Commission Report, 21 February 1947.

46 *Ibid.*, p. 1.

47 *Ibid.*

and only 'one or two of them had pre-war Polish civilian identity cards',[48] which made it very difficult to accurately identify the individuals. Thus, the Commission interviewed the Ukrainian SEP camp leader Major Jaskewycz and mainly relied on his account of the history of the Division. It would seem convenient to rely on Jaskewycz's narrative for it created no difficult questions, required no further investigation, and fitted well with the general conclusions of the Report, which suggested that Ukrainians were not 'at heart pro-German'[49] and added to a favourable opinion of the 'Galicians' by the British. Such conclusions were in line with the narrative the 'Galicians' were creating about themselves (i.e., by establishing a 'university', practising Greek-Catholicism, etc).

The Report suggests that the Screening Commission selected a sample of the Division's ex-members for questioning. This amounted to a total of 219 people, approximately 2.5 per cent of the total number present in the camp. The issue of having impartial interpreters was not raised by the Commission: '[e]xcept in the case of Mr Brown, who was able to question the men in Russian, Ukrainian-speaking interpreters, who were actually inmates of the camp, had to be used.'[50] To avoid discrepancies, the information received from the 'Galicians' was cross-checked with the narrative offered by Jaskewycz. It is, however, likely that the rest of the men were aware of what Jaskewycz had told the Commission. Predictably, such cross-checking, according to David Haldane Porter, the official in charge of the Screening Commission,[51] did not produce any major inconsistency; 'nor did any particularly suspicious individuals come to light'.[52] Once again, the lack of 'suspicious individuals' was convenient as it did not require the British Screening Commission to investigate the 'Galicians' in more detail.

48 *Ibid.*

49 *Ibid.*, p. 6.

50 *Ibid.*, p. 2.

51 David Haldane Porter was a member of Brigadier Fitzroy Maclean's Refugee Screening Commission. Fitzroy Maclean was a diplomat and a Member of Parliament. He had a reputation as a Soviet specialist. See Stephen Dorril, *MI6* (London: Fourth Estate, 1998), p. 188. See also Littman, *Pure Soldiers*, p. 117.

52 (NA) HO/213/1851, p. 2.

A further significant problem with the report is that it treated the 1st Ukrainian Division of the Ukrainian National Army and the Waffen SS 'Galicia' as two separate divisions, while, as discussed in Chapter 1, the *14 Freiwilligen-Grenadier Division der SS (Galizische Nr. 1)*, formed in the spring of 1943 became known as the 1st Ukrainian Division of the Ukrainian National Army after 25 April 1945, under General Shandruk's command. Subsequently, the members who found themselves in the SEP Camp in Italy joined essentially the same military formation, formally known as either Waffen SS 'Galicia' or the 1st UD UNA, depending on the time of their enlistment. This implies that either the British Commission seemed unaware that the Waffen SS 'Galicia' and the 1st UD UNA were the same formation, or that they chose to treat it as two separate divisions in order to avoid the difficulty of the Division's involvement in the Waffen SS. The report simplifies the issue of the 'two Divisions' by suggesting that there is 'nothing suspicious in some of the men not knowing exactly what unit they were in, and they probably referred to it as the 1st Galician Division because it was for them the first Division to be formed out of Ukrainians from Galicia.'[53]

Porter's team accepts the words of one of the officers who claimed that the 'SS' had been dropped from the Division's title on the request of the Ukrainians, without enquiring any further as to the veracity of such a claim. Furthermore, Porter maintains that the Division should be treated as 'an ordinary German Army Division',[54] which 'seems, however, to have had some SS training, which would account for some of its officers having stated their rank as "Untersturmführer"',[55] a rank of the SS and not that of the ordinary German Army. These deliberate or accidental assumptions of the British had a significant impact on the way the 'Galicia' was being perceived: the Waffen SS carried connotations of committing war crimes; being 'an ordinary German Army Division' took such connotations away, and made the Division members more likely to be accepted to be moved to the UK.

53 *Ibid.*, p. 2.

54 *Ibid.*

55 *Ibid. Untersturmführer* is a paramilitary rank of the *Schutzstaffel* (SS), created in July 1934. It was senior to *Hauptscharführer* (*Sturmscharführer* in the Waffen SS) and junior to *Obersturmführer*.

The report goes on to describe those who belonged to the Division, but whilst these descriptions may be accurate for those individual cases, it is hard to accept the validity of the general conclusions drawn from them, due to the small number of those questioned. The Report states that

> [t]he men we questioned were nearly all of the simple peasant type, and made a good impression, showing no signs of either prevarication or truculence; a high proportion of them, and, from what we have seen, of the whole camp, are under 30 years of age.[56]

This assumption does not match information on the Division's formation, which suggests that the 'Galicia' Division attracted mainly urban volunteers, students as well as former officers who fought in the First World War, rather than the 'peasant types', referred to in the report. Shandruk refers to the 'Galicians' as 'the blossom of Ukrainian intelligentsia from the western Ukrainian lands'.[57] The Military Board members go as far as to suggest that the UPA failed to achieve the desired support and development because the intelligentsia of the Galicia region supported and joined the Division rather than the UPA.[58] However, the image of the simple hard-working Ukrainian men was more convenient for the purpose of them being moved to the UK. The fact that many of the former 'Galicians' were Ukrainian nationalists who were politically active before and during the war could have potentially created further questions as to their suitability to be moved to Britain and civilianized.

The Report also summarizes the ex-soldiers of the Division as a 'decent, simple sort of people' who 'regard themselves as a homogeneous unit, unconnected either with Russia or Poland', and who 'do not seem conscious of having done any wrong.'[59] It is clear that the 'Galicians' had convinced the British officials of their homogeneity; indeed, they did consider them-

56 (NA) HO/213/1851, p. 2.

57 Protocol of the Military Board meeting on 22 August 1947 in Munich, in Kolisnyk, *Viis'kova Uprava*, p. 253. See also Ihor Arkusha, 'Dyviziia SS "Halychyna". Pravda i vyhadky', *Narodnyi ohliadach* (27 April 2007) <http://sd.org.ua/news.php?id=11849> accessed 12 October 2012.

58 See Protocol of the Military Board meeting on 22 August 1947 in Munich, in Kolisnyk, *Viis'kova Uprava*, p. 266.

59 (NA) HO/213/1851, p. 2.

selves to comprise a distinct ethnic Ukrainian group and most of them held nationalistic views, hoping to see Ukraine independent from both Poland and the USSR. However, it would be inaccurate to claim that none of them had any conscious regrets about fighting in German uniforms. The memoirs unanimously state that the 'Galicians' chose to join the ranks of the German Army not out of their political conviction (they claim to have been against the Nazi ideology), but did so only out of necessity in order to be able to fight the Soviets. Similarly, the interviewees either support the claim of choosing a 'lesser evil' or openly express regret in joining the Waffen SS, even though they state that they did so with the best intentions, and for the good of their country.[60] It is important, however, to note that the memoirs were written in the post-war period and the interviews used for this research were conducted over sixty years after interviewees' involvement in the 'Galicia' Division. Thus, the views expressed by the former 'Galicians' could have been more naive during their screening in SEP camp; and the British authorities might have perceived such naivety as a sign of the 'Galicians' simple-mindedness.

The Screening Commission Report states that the three senior officers who were questioned, Sylenko, Nikitin and Jaskewycz, 'were all born in the 1890's [sic] in Russia, became regular Tsarist army officers and fought in the 1914 war against the Germans. After the revolution of 1917 they fought for the Whites against the Bolsheviks in the Ukrainian Army […] all three settled in Poland as political refugees with Nansen passports.'[61] Lieutenant Colonel Sylenko held a passport issued in 1918 by the Democratic Government of Ukraine and produced it to the Commission 'as if it were a valuable objet d'art'.[62] The other senior officers (two Colonels and one Lieutenant Colonel) 'were not available, but I [David Haldane Porter] feel

60 Interviewee S., 26 December 2006 (Ternopil'); Interviewee B., 27 December 2006 (L'viv); Interviewee B., 20 May 2007, 9 September 2007 (London).

61 (NA) HO/213/1851, pp. 2–3. Nansen passports were the first refugee travel documents, internationally recognized ID cards, first issued by the League of Nations to stateless refugees, designed by Fridtjof Nansen in 1922.

62 (NA) HO/213/1851, p. 3.

sure that their story is similar to the history of the others.'[63] It is surprising that senior officers could be unavailable for questioning by the screening commission in a SEP camp. It is equally surprising that Porter regards his feeling that their story would not differ from the one already collected from the other officers as sufficient to draw conclusions.

The Report claims that there is no evidence of any of the men being Soviet citizens by the British definition: '[m]any of the places which they have given as places of birth and/or habitual residence are small villages and hamlets which are not likely to be marked on any but the largest maps',[64] says Porter, and suggests that it is safe to assume that the majority of the men born after 1919 were born in Poland and 'were resident in Poland on 1st September 1939, and that the great majority of those born before Poland existed were not resident in the Soviet Union on 1st September 1939'.[65] While these assumptions might have reflected the reality, it is unclear what prompted them, for, first, only a very small group of people were questioned, and, second, many of those questioned held no passport to prove their identity, and thus could only be identified by self-definition. But Porter's conclusions 'solve' the problem of the 'Galicians' being potential Soviet citizens and thus there was no urgent necessity to repatriate them to the USSR, consequently avoiding another possible scandal as in the case of the forceful repatriation of the Cossacks. Porter goes on to recognize that 'a fair proportion of them [the 'Galicians'] were really civilians such as Todt workers,[66] who had only attached themselves to the regiment shortly before its surrender, as a means of escaping from the Germans.'[67] Despite acknowledging this fact, the probable presence of civilians, possibly from the pre-1939 Soviet Ukraine, was not investigated further by the Commission.

63 *Ibid.*, p. 2.

64 *Ibid.*, p. 3.

65 *Ibid.*

66 The *Organisation Todt* was a civil and military group in Germany. It was named after its founder, a famous Nazi figure and engineer, Fritz Todt. The organization was responsible for a wide range of projects in Germany and the occupied territories.

67 (NA) HO/213/1851, p. 3.

The Report gives its view on the Soviet screening of the Division members and explains that, having arrived to interview the 'Galicians' on 17 August 1945, Colonel Jakovliev began his campaign for voluntary repatriation and decided that in order to 'break down the general resistance to such repatriation' it was necessary for the '"stubborn Fascist minority" [to be] removed from the camp.'[68] According to the Report, eleven men were in fact isolated from the rest of the camp at the request of the Soviet Mission for some period, but were allowed back in as no evidence of the 'terrorization'[69] claimed by the Soviets was found. The Report argues that if the Soviet Mission had any effect on the Ukrainians, it was to convince them never to return to Ukraine and caused 'a great deal of probably justified anxiety to those who still had relatives there.'[70] The Report suggests that the Soviet Mission left with the conclusion that, according to their definition, the Division ex-members in Rimini were Soviet citizens, and, as they had failed to persuade them to return to the USSR voluntarily, the Soviet government would demand their forcible repatriation as war criminals when the Italian Treaty came into force.[71] Thus, according to the Report, the British Screening Commission understood that rapid progress was required in resolving the 'Galicia' question in order to avoid the possibility of the Division's forceful repatriation.

68 *Ibid.*, p. 4.

69 *Ibid.*

70 *Ibid.*

71 Under the Italian Peace Treaty, Italy promised to apprehend and surrender for trial all persons accused of war crimes. It has been stressed by some authors that Stalin personally demanded repatriation of the Division at the Potsdam Conference. See Littman, *Pure Soldiers*, p. 115; Tolstoy, *Victims of Yalta*, pp. 258–68.

David Haldane Porter's Conclusions

At the end of the Report the Commission offers its proposals as to the future fate of Ukrainian surrendered enemy personnel. Despite the fact that no cross-examination was carried out – the interviews merely involved 'taking down through an interpreter the men's answers to a limited number of set questions', and, as far as the Commission was concerned, '[t]he men may be all or in part lying, and even their names may be false'[72] – Porter nevertheless suggests that '[we] can safely assume that by and large the men are what they say they are and did what they say they did.'[73] The Report does, nevertheless, suggest that it would be useful:

> i) To see if any of the men listed in the nominal rolls figure in U.N.W.C.C.[74] or CROWCASS[75] lists or have been specifically accused by the Russian or other Governments of War Crimes.
> ii) To see if any of the units to which the men belong have particularly bad war records.
> iii) To see if the short history of the various units and of the Division as a whole, as ascertained by interrogation, corresponds to the known facts about them. It might be possible to locate some of the German officers of the Division and have them questioned. None are known to be in this area.[76]

The first point was impossible to accomplish given that the 'Galicians' were mostly self-identified and there was no objective record of their true names or personal details other than that offered by the Division members

72 (NA) HO/213/1851, p. 5.

73 *Ibid.*

74 The United Nations War Crimes Commission (also known as the United Nations Commission for the Investigation of War Crimes).

75 The Central Registry of War Criminals and Security Suspects, which was set up to assist the UNWCC and Allied governments in tracing individuals suspected of committing war crimes during the Second World War.

76 (NA) HO/213/1851, p. 5.

themselves. The second point seems to be also overly ambitious: given that the Screening Commission got confused in differentiating the Waffen SS 'Galicia' and the 1st UD UNA, it is unlikely that they would have succeeded in following through the history of particular units of the Division. But this guidance, as well as that expressed in the third point, was never implemented. This reiterates that, as far as the official decisions taken by the British authorities are concerned, the 'Galician' men benefited from a series of incidental, even accidental, episodes, e.g., not cross-referencing the 'Galician' story of the war-time activities with that of German officers, or not having large enough maps to establish their places of birth. All this, combined with the ignorance of the British as to who these Ukrainians actually were and the officials' unwillingness to cause another repatriation scandal, helped the Division members in receiving permission to move to the UK and avoid repatriation.

At the same time, the British Screening Commission was somewhat concerned that a number of the 'Galicians' were genuine Soviet citizens even by the British definition. The Report states that '[w]e may therefore, if we get them all accepted as D.Ps, render ourselves liable to a valid charge of sheltering Russian traitors.'[77] However, it then goes on to say that

> on the nationality issue these men are really having the best of both worlds. They do not qualify as Soviet citizens because their place of birth and/or habitual domicile on 1.9.1939 was in Poland, and they therefore, by our definition, escape all punishment by the Russians for their having assisted the enemy; and they are not presumably eligible now for punishment by the Polish authorities because that part of the country from which they came is no longer part of Poland.[78]

They did, however, according to the Commission, fall under the definition of a 'traitor',[79] being 'people who gave aid and comfort to the enemy'.[80] Porter

77 *Ibid.* The use of 'Russian' as opposed to 'Soviet' reflects the colonial attitude of the British officials, who perceived the population of the Soviet Union as, essentially, Russian.

78 *Ibid.*, p. 6.

79 This definition is referred to in the report as that of Professor Royes. The report does not explain what the role of Professor Royes is and why it is his definition that they employ.

80 (NA) HO/213/1851, p. 6.

concludes by saying that 'this definition undoubtedly applies to most, if not all, of these Ukrainians.'[81] This, however, did not influence the British official's recommendation not to repatriate the 'Galicians'. Porter also explains the reasons that he believes to be behind the Ukrainian soldiers' choice to join the 'Galicia' Division:

a) The hope of securing a genuinely independent Ukraine.
b) Without knowing exactly what they were doing, e.g. because other Ukrainians whom they knew had already volunteered.
c) As a preferable alternative to forced labour etc, or to living in Soviet controlled territory.
d) To have a smack at the Russians, whom they always refer to as 'Bolsh-eviks'.[82]

Seeing the Division members as not 'at heart pro-German',[83] Porter believes that their support for the German Army was 'incidental and not fundamental.'[84] Their desire for an independent Ukraine is seen by the man in charge of the screening as 'naïve and unreal' but 'none the less genuine'.[85] Interestingly, years after the end of the war, the 'Galicians' also referred to their desire to achieve independence as naive. In an interview for Radio Svoboda, Ivan Muzyczka says that Ukrainian men were hoping to 'come out of the forests' when the Germans lose the war and join the Division in order to fight the Soviet Union together with the West and gain 'true democratic freedom' and an independent Ukraine. Muzyczka qualifies these hopes as 'childish dreams' and a 'fantasy'.[86] Among the reasons for choosing the Division over the Red Army, the UPA or forced labour, former 'Galicians' themselves state the opportunity of professional training, the

81 *Ibid.*
82 *Ibid.*
83 *Ibid.*
84 *Ibid.*
85 *Ibid.*
86 Radio Svoboda Interview with Ivan Muzyczka by Natalka Kudryk: 'My naïvno mriialy pro vil'nu Ukraïnu', *Radio Svoboda*, 7 May 2010 <http://www.radiosvoboda.org/content/article/2035588> accessed 13 October 2012.

possibility of promotion within the regular army, career prospects, ability to get food, clothes and ammunition, desire to protect their families, and the feeling of relative safety. In addition, they often claim to have received advice from their fathers or older brothers, who had been serving in the UPA, to join the 'Galicia' Division, as it seemed to offer better personal and strategic prospects.[87] Evidently, these pragmatic reasons were not emphasized by Porter.

The conclusions of the Report mention the behaviour of the Ukrainian surrendered enemy personnel as being 'exemplary':

> [...] they have not indulged in any subversive activities, nor do I [David Haldane Porter] think they will do so in the future. They seem resigned to the fact that there is now no place in Europe for them and that those of them who have wives and families in Soviet Union will never see them again.[88]

Once again, intentionally or due to his ignorance, Porter avoids the mention of many 'Galicians' being highly political individuals, involved in nationalist movements before and during the war. Instead, the Report emphasizes their personal tragedy and reinforces the image of them as people who will cause no trouble if moved from the SEP camp.

Porter suggests that as long as it is in line with Britain's official relationship with the USSR and Poland, and in agreement with the policy as to the eligibility criteria for the DPs, that

> speaking from humanitarian instincts [...] and taking into account the long time that has elapsed from the end of the war [...] all these Ukrainians should be classified as DPs; and I would add, with all the emphasis I could command, that if this is accepted, immediate action, not high-sounding resolutions, is necessary either to ensure that the I.R.O. [International Refugee Organisation] or the I.G.C.R.

87 See Protocol of the Military Board meeting on 22 August 1947 in Munich, in Kolisnyk, *Viis'kova Uprava*, p. 258. Interviewee S., 26 December 2006 ('Ternopil'); Interviewee B., 27 December 2006 (L'viv); Interviewee B., 20 May 2007, 9 September 2007 (London).

88 (NA) HO/213/1851, p. 7.

> [Intergovernmental Committee on Refugees] can give them effective protection as DPs from being handed over to the Soviet Government by the Italian Government from Italy before the Treaty comes into force.[89]

The Screening Report succeeded in being wholly positive about the 'Galicians', as well as remaining in line with Britain's relationship with the USSR and in accordance with the Yalta Agreements. For these reasons, Porter encountered no obstacles in having his proposal accepted by the British government, which thereby allowed the 'Galicia' Division men to be transported to the UK.

This report continues to receive polarized representation by the commentators of the Division's history. Littman calls it 'a masterpiece of bureaucratic report writing in which he [Porter] confesses all of the report's shortcomings yet manages to provide the government with the conclusion it wants.'[90] Hunczak, on the other hand, uses the Report's findings to emphasize that the 'Galicians' were 'thoroughly screened by the British Commission before bringing them to England [sic]'.[91] Hunczak concludes by saying that

> the assessment of the British Government of the Division's past and subsequent decision of the Canadian Government to deal favourably with the members of the Division is a fitting epitaph for a unit that was attacked from various directions for political reasons rather than for what it actually did during the war.[92]

It is hard not to notice the unintended irony in Hunczak's words: Porter's report, as well as the Deschênes Commission, which partly relied on the Screening Report of 1947, do indeed reveal more about the political dilemmas faced by the British and Canadian governments regarding the 'Galicia' rather than what the Division actually did during its active military service. The Screening Report thus serves as neither an accurate record of the Division's situation while in the SEP camp in Rimini, for it bases its

89 *Ibid.*

90 Littman, *Pure Soldiers*, p. 129.

91 Hunczak, *On the Horns of a Dilemma*, p. 162.

92 *Ibid.*, p. 163.

conclusions on just over 200 men, nor as reliable evidence of the Division's innocence of war crimes and ineligibility to be repatriated to the USSR. What it does, however, contribute to the narrative of the Waffen SS 'Galicia' Division is an insight into the way the British dealt with the 'Galician' question and speaks to wider issues of the pragmatic and sometimes haphazard post-war handling of displaced persons, prisoners of war and surrendered enemy personnel by the Allied powers.

In 1947 Porter's impressions of the Division were shared by other officials and reiterated in Hills' account, where he emphasized the 'confusion as to the exact identity and geographical origins of these East European peasants whose homeland was notorious for its impermanent frontiers and shifting governments.'[93] This geographical dilemma was certainly used in deciding not to classify the 'Galicians' as Soviet. The unwillingness of the British 'to face the scandal of a forcible repatriation operation'[94] also added to the positive decision with regard to the Division. Yet, most importantly, it is the seeming lack of evidence of war crimes against the 'Galicia' that allowed them to avoid repatriation. '[T]he scraps of paper with names written on them which the Soviet mission sometimes handed in to Sub-Area HQ were thrown away',[95] without further investigation. The fact that the Soviets had no direct evidence to prove the 'Galicia's' involvement in war crimes meant that the British authorities did not have to help them with the forceful repatriation of the 8,000 Ukrainians.

Like Porter, Hills recognized that 'the real strength of the Ukrainians lay in their cohesion, their relative literacy and extreme national consciousness.'[96] Although generalized, and in part inaccurate, the importance of the collective qualities of the ex-soldiers of the Division was very influential in creating a positive narrative of the 'Galicians' for the British. Their positive qualities included having their own language, religion and history as well as the fact, stressed again and again by British officials, that

93 Hills, 'You are the Grey Mass', p. 14.

94 *Ibid.*

95 *Ibid.*

96 *Ibid.*

the 'Galicians' 'regarded themselves as part of the Ukrainian Freedom Army, using Germany as an ally in their fight against Bolshevism'.[97] From the available documents, it is evident that the decision to allow Ukrainian 'Galicians' to be moved to the UK was taken on the level of the Foreign, War and Home Offices, with the involvement of the Prime Minister, Clement Attlee, himself. Minutes of a meeting which was held at the Home Office (Aliens Department) on 10 July 1947 'to make a preliminary review of the position and prospects of Ukrainian Surrendered Enemy Personnel and their dependents' state that

> [t]he men had surrendered to the British Forces, had been looked after by them for two years in Italy and had been brought here [to the UK] with the Prime Minister's approval as an alternative to being sent back to such fate as might await them in Russia [sic]. Despite some general accusations of brutality which had from time to time been made against the Ukrainians, individual screening had not brought to light any who might be classed as war criminals.[98]

While there are no available documents which would clearly state that these were the exact reasons that influenced the controversial decision of the British authorities to allow over 8,000 Ukrainian enemy personnel to move to Britain, it is clear that this combination of factors led to the Division's move to the UK, making the 'Galician' case unique when compared with other groups, such as the Cossacks, who also saw themselves in particular national terms and as part of an army.

97 *Ibid.*

98 (NA) LAB 8/98 Foreign Office proposals regarding Ukrainian Prisoners of War in Italy to be brought to the U.K. Ukrainian Surrendered Enemy Personnel and their Dependants. 10 July 1947. Those present at the meeting included Carew-Robinson, Roy, Hayman (Home Office), Blomfield (War Office), Boothby and Wilkinson (Foreign Office), Costley-White (Commonwealth Relations Office), Duncan (Scottish Office), Christie (Ministry of Agriculture), Yates (Ministry of Labour and National Service), Hope-Wallace (Assistance Board) and Hawes (Home Office).

CHAPTER 4

Life in the UK and the Migration to Canada

The 'Galicia's' arrival and stay in the UK caused the creation of a narrative by the press and the opposing organizations that was highly critical of the members of the Division. This prompted former 'Galicians' and those organizations who acted in their defence to promote a counter-narrative, representing themselves rather as ex-soldiers of a so-called 'Ukrainian division'. Such a narrative insisted that the Division's members joined the German Armed Forces (frequently referred to incorrectly as the Wehrmacht), in order to fight the Soviets. This kind of narrative also emphasized that once the 'Galicians' were moved from the SEP camp, they wished for nothing more than a chance to rebuild their lives, work hard and become valuable citizens of the UK or Canada.[1] David Haldane Porter's conclusions of the British screening of the 'Galicia', discussed in Chapter 3, were extremely helpful in maintaining this positive narrative. The general perceptions of the Division members offered by the Screening Report were shared by other individuals who supported the 'Galicia' men.

In his letter to the editor of the *Manchester Guardian* in 1947,[2] Tracy Phillips[3] writes that 'these newly-arrived Ukrainians were [...] for good

1 See Vasyl' Veryha, *Za Ridnyi Krai, za narid svii, abo Khto taki dyviziinyky?* (Kyiv: Vydavnytsvto imeni Oleny Telihy, 2006), pp. 34–9 and 175–213.

2 File B53802, Tracy Phillips to the editor of *Manchester Guardian*, 12 June 1947, Public Archives, Canada, p. 1.

3 Tracy Phillips (1890–1959) served as an advisor to the Foreign Office because of his extensive travels and his knowledge of various languages. In 1940 he came to Canada and served as an advisor on European affairs to the RCMP, the Department of External Affairs and the Department of National War Services <http://www.archives.gov.ua/Eng/ukrainian-collections.php#PHILLIPS> accessed 2 March 2009.

reasons, not classed [...] as prisoners of war, but as Surrendered Enemy Personnel'.[4] The 'good reasons', according to Phillips included the fact that

> these Ukrainians are strongly Western-minded folk, many of whom have relatives and friends in the countries of South America, the United States, and Canada [...] The majority are of Eastern Catholic cult and with no tendency towards dictatorship, whether or [sic] German or Russian brand, since they have experienced three years of each.[5]

This implies that the 'Galicians' were suitable for acceptance to enter the UK because of their 'similarity' to Western Europeans. Phillips argues that 'for two centuries up to 1918 they looked West, to a relatively enlightened liberal Vienna, for their standards of agriculture and education. They also looked West, to Rome, for their religion, Christian ethic, and ideas.'[6] An assumption, stressed by Phillips, that the former 'Galicians' rejected the idea of German or Soviet authoritarian rule does not truly reflect political views of all those who found themselves in the Division. As has already been discussed, many of the Division members supported Ukrainian nationalist groups, some of which offered a highly authoritarian approach to leadership. Nevertheless, the nationalism and patriotism of the 'Galicians' at the stage of their screening was seen in the context of them being against the USSR, and thus assumed to be in support of Western political views. The discussion of their potential radical nationalist inclinations was not convenient and thus avoided by those who wished to present them to the British public in a favourable light.

4 File B53802, Tracy Phillips to the editor of *Manchester Guardian*, 12 June 1947, Public Archives, Canada, p. 1. The status of surrendered enemy personnel implied that the Division men had surrendered voluntarily, while the term 'prisoner of war' would imply that they had been captured.

5 *Ibid.*

6 *Ibid.*

Figure 3 On a ship from Italy to the UK, 9 May 1947.

At the POW Camps in Britain

The soldiers of the Division were moved to the UK in May–June 1947. According to Bolianovs'kyi, of the 9,000 Ukrainians who were in Rimini, Italy, on 17 December 1946, by 3 March 1948, 8,361 had been moved to Britain.[7] At first they arrived in Sheffield and then were relocated to POW camps in the suburbs of Glasgow, the Haddington camp near Edinburgh as well as Sheffield, Norwich, Cambridge, Lincoln and Willesden. One hundred and twenty-seven officers were located in Allington in the Midlands, and the largest number of men were held in Hampton Green Camp in Norfolk (1,593 men) and Camp Victoria at Bury St Edmunds (1,196 men).[8] The highest authority to which the camps' administration reported was the

7 Bolianovs'kyi, *Dyviziia 'Halychyna'*, p. 378.
8 (NA) WO/321/13190, Association of Ukrainians in Great Britain to War Office, 19 July 1948.

War Office. The main camps' administration was conducted by the British militia. There was minimal security in place, and the actual administration of each camp, catering and technical personnel as well as the guards, was arranged by the 'Galicians' themselves. The priests who stayed with the Division members in Rimini were also present in the British POW camps; they represented both the Ukrainian Greek-Catholic and the Ukrainian Autocephalous Orthodox Churches. Additionally, every Sunday, the 'Galicians' had an organized attendance of mass at local churches. Overall, the life of the 'Galicians' in the POW camps in the UK was of a better standard than what they had experienced in Rimini.[9]

'The move of the Division members to Great Britain and their allocation to the POW camps became [...] the second stage of their military life', remembers a former 'Galicia' soldier, Fostun.[10] Once moved to Britain, the 'Galicians' underwent a change in their status from 'surrendered enemy personnel' to 'prisoners of war', which they did not receive with delight. Fostun argues that the fact that the 'Galicians' were referred to as SEPs showed that they had chosen to surrender, whereas the new POW status labelled them as 'prisoners'.[11] The Division men had no right of free movement, thus their only contact with the outside world was through postal correspondence and the press.

As the 'Galicians' were recognized as prisoners of war, officially their political activity was limited. This, however, did not stop the active members of the Organization of Ukrainian Nationalists from monopolizing the support of the Division members and having internal political power struggles. According to Fostun, the majority of the 'Galicians' supported the political movement of the OUN, led by Bandera, while some backed Mel'nyk's branch of the OUN. The third informal political group supported the idea of the Ukrainian National Republic; they were people of

9 Swiatomyr Fostun, 'Voïny 1 UD UNA v taborakh viis'kopolonenykh u Velykobrytaniï', in *Persha ukraïns'ka Dyviziia ukraïns'koï natsional'noï armiï: istoriia stvorennia ta natsional'no-politychne znachennia. Materialy Naukovo-praktychnoï konferentsiï. Dopovidi ta povidomlennia* (L'viv: Novyi chas, 2002), pp. 123–5.

10 *Ibid.*, p. 123.

11 *Ibid.*

an older generation who, once they got their civilian status, officially organized themselves to support the Ukrainian National Council (*Ukraïns'ka Natsional'na Rada*). The fourth group were the supporters of the political movement formed by Ivan Bahrianyi, which later became the Ukrainian Revolutionary-Democratic Party (*Ukraïns'ka Revol'utsiino-Democratychna Partiia*) and found its followers among many Ukrainians at the DP camps in Germany and Austria. The fifth group were Ukrainian monarchists, but their influence was limited.[12]

While in the camps, the active social life of the Division members, which included learning and sports, helped in reinforcing a positive image of the Ukrainian POWs as obedient, respectful and respectable people. These qualities were stressed by those who lobbied the governments of the UK and Canada for the Division's civilianization. In the minutes of a meeting held on 11 July 1947 in the Directorate of Prisoners of War, it was stated that the 'development of education especially training of students was looked upon very favourably by the Government', the choirs and orchestras which were organized were allowed 'to tour other camps [...] when work was not so pressing.'[13] The Division members carried on publishing their newspaper, they reorganized their choirs and dance ensembles. Sport activities organized by Ukrainian men found special support among the British. There were twenty-four football teams in seventeen POW camps. The 'Galicians' worked mainly in agriculture, receiving one shilling per working day. All financial questions were administered by the War Office; the employers paid the regional departments and then the money was transferred to the ministry. The camp administration deducted the expenses for clothes, food and shelter, etc., and the rest was given to the POWs as their salary.[14] Shortly before the 'Galicia's' arrival in the UK, in 1946, a congress of Ukrainians took place in Edinburgh, where the later

12 *Ibid.*, pp. 123–5.

13 File B53802, Admission of 'Surrendered Enemy Personnel', Government of Canada Files, Ukrainian Prisoners of War. Minutes of a meeting held on 11 July 1947 in the Directorate of Prisoners of War. Present: DPW, DDPW, Maj Harding PW1, G.R.B. Panchuk (Director of Central Ukrainian Relief Bureau Canadian Relief Mission to Ukrainian Victims of War), pp. 2–3.

14 Fostun, 'Voïny i UD UNA', pp. 125–6.

influential diaspora organization, the Association of Ukrainians in Great Britain (AUGB), was formed. This association lobbied for the release of the 'Galicians' from the camps after the war. It continues to be active in many towns in the UK, with its head office in London. The AUGB became one of the main sources of the creation and shaping of the narratives that were and are still being created about the Ukrainian British diaspora in general, and the Waffen SS 'Galicia' in particular.

Ukrainians in Post-war Britain

Apart from the Division, there were other groups of Ukrainians who found themselves in the UK after the Second World War. One of the groups was made up of officers of Ukrainian origin who had served in Polish military formations. But the largest group consisted of around 21,000–25,000 women and men of Ukrainian origin who arrived in Britain in 1947–8 mainly from Austria and Germany, where they had stayed in the Displaced Persons camps.[15] Many of them were *Ostarbeiter*. In Britain they were given the status of European Voluntary Workers (EVW) and were obliged to work at the government-allocated posts and locations for a period of three years. In spite of the Division forming quite a decided minority of Ukrainians in the UK as result of the war, the move of Ukrainian ex-enemy personnel came to dominate the image of Ukrainians in Britain. The British authorities received much criticism from the British press, politicians and the public for their decision to first allow the 'Galicians' into the UK and later to civilianize them. The importance of both the criticism itself and the official reaction to it lies in the effect it had on the 'Galicia' men's civilianization process.

15 Natalia Sydorenko, *Taborovi budni viis'kovopolonenykh na brytans'kykh ostrovakh (1947–1950)*, in *Persha ukraïns'ka Dyviziia ukraïns'koï natsional'noï armiï: istoriia stvorennia ta natsional'no-politychne znachennya. Materialy Naukovo-praktychnoï konferentsiï. Dopovidi ta povidomlennia* (L'viv: Novyi chas, 2002), pp. 127–46 (127).

As is evident from the press of the immediate post-war period, the media portrayed the members of the 'Galicia' as former concentration camp guards and murderers, and this had a defining influence on public opinion. A typical headline from the time appears in *The People*, which sums up the 'Galicia's' case without much explanation: 'Fought For Nazis – Coming Here'.[16] Another piece presents more details, but these are extremely confused and misleading: 'While I was in various camps in Germany, including one death-camp in Westphalia, Sonderlager 326, I was guarded by Ukrainian volunteers who wore German uniforms'[17] – writes a reader of the *Evening News* from Surrey in response to the 'Galicia's' arrival in the UK. The author then suggests that '[t]hey were, in majority, the members of the Army of the Russian renegade Vlassow [sic]',[18] thus not from the 'Galicia' Division. The author of the article goes on to say that they were

> all brutal, uncouth, and bloodthirsty, using the butt-ends of their rifles, or their bayonets, on helpless POWs at the slightest pretext; and if any of my fellow-readers were sent to the punishment camps around Rawa-Ruska or Lemberg,[19] they will remember the awful atrocities committed by Ukrainian guards upon the Jewish internees who came there from all over Europe.[20]

This article offers a flavour of the consternation that the 'Galicia' men's arrival caused among the British public. There is no documentary evidence of the 'Galicia' as a division being stationed at the death camps; however, as has been pointed out throughout the book, individual members of the Waffen SS 'Galicia' might have been serving at concentration or death camps prior to their joining the Division. The author of the article cited above does not seem to distinguish the 'Galicians' from the Vlasovites, and treats all Ukrainians as the same. The Vlasovites could not have found

16 'Fought For Nazis – Coming Here', *The People*, 25 May 1947 in (NA) HO/213/1851.

17 'Shelter for Brutes', written by Ex-Nr 3,399 (Addington, Surrey), *Evening News*, 4 June 1947 in (NA) HO/213/1851.

18 *Ibid.*

19 The version of L'viv, the city in western Ukraine, used under German occupation. The Polish spelling of the city is Lwów.

20 (NA) HO/213/1851.

themselves in Great Britain after the war in such a large group as the 'Galicia', as the majority of them had been repatriated to the USSR. Still, the author goes on to say: '[y]et I read in my Evening News that the Ukrainians are to be given shelter in Great Britain after having "drifted" from the Russian territories. Who in the name of heaven is responsible for this?'[21] Evidently, most of the general public had no understanding of who was being moved to Britain and what crimes they had or had not committed. Nor was there public awareness of how many soldiers had been repatriated by the British and American authorities to the USSR and that such repatriations were mostly forceful and led to fatal consequences, including suicides, execution or internment in labour camps for those whom the authorities repatriated.

The *Manchester Guardian* also ran a piece on the 'Galicia', offering slightly more accurate, yet still misleading information on the situation:

> About 8,000 men, formerly members of the Ukrainian Division of the German Army, are being brought from Rimini camp, Northern Italy, to Britain for agricultural and other work. The men, who were recruited into the German Army by various methods, came from what was the Polish Ukraine and are regarded by Britain as Stateless persons. On arrival they will be examined again to ascertain whether any of them are Soviet citizens.[22]

Despite being less emotive and trying to explain who the 'Galicians' are, this quotation is inaccurate on many accounts: it says that the Ukrainian Division was of the German Army, but does not specify that it was a part of the Waffen SS. It states that the men were being regarded as 'stateless persons', yet, while it might have been the case *de facto*, the Division men were treated as 'prisoners of war' during their stay in the UK. The article also says that the 'Galicians' will be examined again to ensure they are not Soviet citizens. The screening that this sentence refers to had already taken place while the Division was in Rimini, and no further screening was carried out on the Division in the UK.[23]

21 *Ibid.*

22 '8,000 Ukrainians to work in Britain', *Manchester Guardian*, 26 May 1947 in (NA) HO/213/1851.

23 Michael J. Melnyk believes that some 'Galicians' were screened in the UK and that this screening is likely to have been connected to the attempts of the British Secret

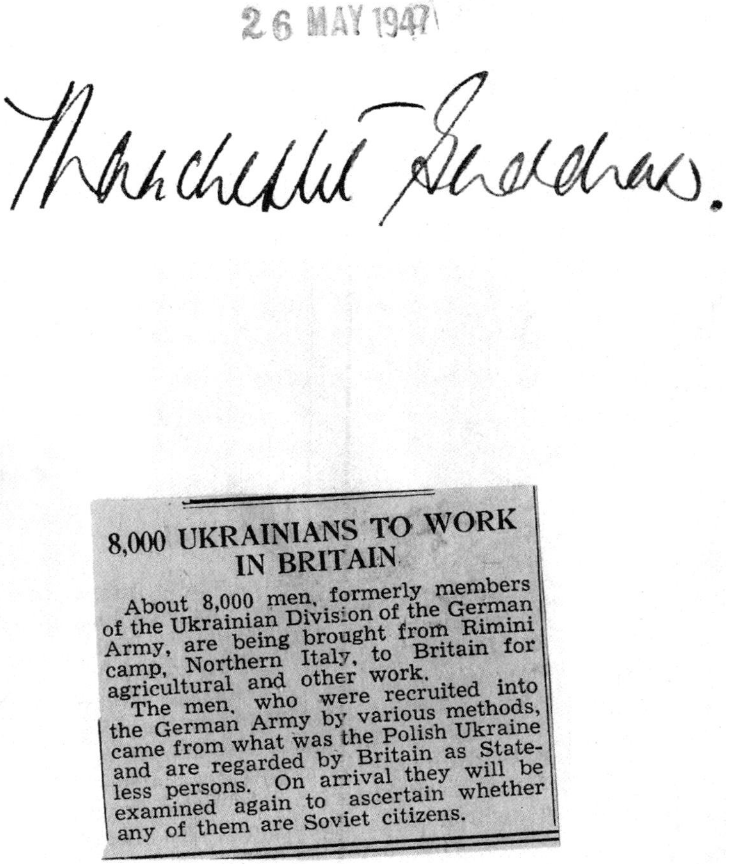
26 MAY 1947

Manchester Guardian.

8,000 UKRAINIANS TO WORK IN BRITAIN

About 8,000 men, formerly members of the Ukrainian Division of the German Army, are being brought from Rimini camp, Northern Italy, to Britain for agricultural and other work.

The men, who were recruited into the German Army by various methods, came from what was the Polish Ukraine and are regarded by Britain as Stateless persons. On arrival they will be examined again to ascertain whether any of them are Soviet citizens.

Figure 4 *Manchester Guardian*, 26 May 1947.

Service to recruit Ukrainians for clandestine operations (from private correspondence with M.J. Melnyk, 3 December 2012). For more details on the Secret Service recruitment operations, see Stephen Dorril, *MI6* (London: Fourth Estate, 1998).

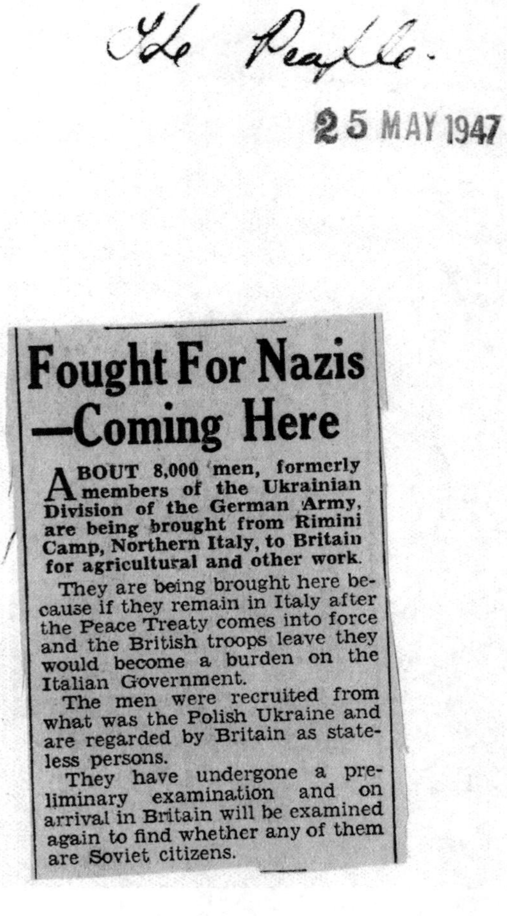
The People.

25 MAY 1947

Fought For Nazis —Coming Here

ABOUT 8,000 men, formerly members of the Ukrainian Division of the German Army, are being brought from Rimini Camp, Northern Italy, to Britain for agricultural and other work.

They are being brought here because if they remain in Italy after the Peace Treaty comes into force and the British troops leave they would become a burden on the Italian Government.

The men were recruited from what was the Polish Ukraine and are regarded by Britain as stateless persons.

They have undergone a preliminary examination and on arrival in Britain will be examined again to find whether any of them are Soviet citizens.

Figure 5 *The People*, 25 May 1947.

The negative reaction of the press to the arrival of over 8,000 Ukrainian ex-soldiers to the UK was bound to have an effect on political decisions. Despite this being the beginning of the Cold War, the UK government was careful in its relations with the Soviet Union. A member of the Foreign Press Association, Felix Wirth, addressed a letter to Tom Driberg, a Labour Party Member of Parliament, in which he asked whether a careful investigation would not reveal that many members of the Division were to be classified as war criminals:

> [w]hatever our quarrel with the Russians, surely the conscience of civilization could not permit to classify these people as innocent political refugees unless we establish that they are definitely not guilty of crimes which cry to heaven unretributed.[24]

Unlike the newspaper articles, Wirth's letter illustrates a level of awareness of the fact that the 'Galicians' were anti-Soviet, but still argues that this alone does not make them 'innocent political refugees'.

Bohdan Panchuk, the director of the Canadian Relief Mission for Ukrainian Refugees, who was lobbying both the Canadian and the UK governments for the 'Galician' men's settlement, writes in his letter to the Office of the High Commission for Canada in London that 'the bulk of the men in question have a total "service career" of only a few weeks to a few months'.[25] He then goes on to explain that '[s]ome have NEVER served in uniform or otherwise but were stragglers who joined the unit during its "migration" from Austria to Italy [...] in the hope that their opportunities for onward immigration would be better from Italy.'[26] Not only does this narrative differ from the one presented to the British Screening Commission, in which the simple 'peasant-types' were thought to have joined the Division 'to have a smack at the Russians'[27] and fight for their nation's independence; it also misses a crucial point about the specificity of the 'Galicia's' recruitment. It seems that Panchuk does not realize that reiterating the fact that a number of 'Galicians' were active members of the Division only for a few months could be inconvenient for the Division men, as that implies that, prior to their joining the 'Galicia', they had been engaged in some other activity potentially involving the war crimes. As has been demonstrated throughout this study, the same argument had been used to condemn the Division and to justify its members, depending on the agenda being followed.

24 (NA) FO 371/66712, Felix Wirth to Tom Driberg, 7 June 1947.

25 File B53802, Admission of 'Surrendered Enemy Personnel', Government of Canada Files. Gordon R. Bohdan Panchuk, M.B.E. to the Office of the High Commission for Canada, London, 7 August 1947, p. 1.

26 *Ibid.*, p. 1.

27 (NA) HO/213/1851, p. 6.

After the Division's move to the United Kingdom, the 'Galicians' were increasingly referred to as the '1st Ukrainian Division of the Wehrmacht' by those who campaigned for their settlement.[28] Panchuk continued to depict the 'Galicians' as totally innocent, and as having found themselves in the Division by accident:

> The largest number however are practically youngsters, who were drawn into the second re-organised division, mostly from youth seized in Western Ukraine when the Germans were retreating before the Red Army, and also from the Labour Camps in Germany.[29]

The problem with this statement is that, although a forceful mobilization did take place when the Germans were retreating, the pre-Brody recruits of the 'Galicia' had not been forcefully mobilized. Yet Panchuk stresses that 'the bulk of these men had little or no choice or alternative insofar as their present position, and were all in one form or another conscripted or forced to join'.[30] Just a quick glance at the memoirs will be enough to see that there was a great desire among the western Ukrainian youth in 1943 to form the Division. It is likely that Panchuk would have been aware of this, and his omission of this aspect of the creation of the Division is very telling of the selectivity with which the narratives about the 'Galicia' have been constructed.

In his letter, Panchuk refers to the 'second re-organized division', presumably meaning the same Waffen SS 'Galicia' that was reorganized after the Battle of Brody in 1944. This, however, is misleading, as there was in fact a 2nd Division of the Ukrainian National Army, the aforementioned anti-tank brigade 'Free Ukraine' (*Vil'na Ukraïna*), which was formed in March 1945, and members of which were mostly taken prisoner by the

28 File B53802, Admission of 'Surrendered Enemy Personnel', Government of Canada Files. Appendix C, British House of Commons. Oral Answers to Questions. Wednesday, 18 June 1947.

29 File B53802, Admission of 'Surrendered Enemy Personnel', Government of Canada Files. G.R.B. Panchuk, M.B.E. to the Office of the High Commission for Canada, London, 7 August 1947, p. 1.

30 *Ibid.*

Soviets (with only approximately a quarter of the 2nd Division managing to surrender to the US Army).[31] Panchuk's often inaccurate or semi-accurate account of the 'Galicia's' story seems to merge different formations, and generally reverts to a strategy of ambiguity. This deliberate blurring of history portrays the Division members as innocent, displaced political refugees from the lands which were annexed by the USSR, and minimizes reference to their association with the Waffen SS, which could decrease their chances of civilianization.

Writing to the Office of the High Commission for Canada, Panchuk carefully draws a comparison between the Division members and the Canadian Armed Forces servicemen. He asks the reader to contemplate the idea of the 'strange "fortunes of war"':

> [...] there are thousands of very loyal and we hope good Canadian citizens, who served in the Canadian Armed Forces, or who are outstanding Canadian citizens, whose fate might have been so very much like the fate of these unfortunate victims of war, and who might have themselves now been in their position, if our fathers had not immigrated to Canada when they did.[32]

Here the 'Galicians' are being portrayed as 'victims of war', countering the accusation of the press which portrayed them as perpetrators. Using the predominant rhetoric of the beginning of the Cold War to the Division's advantage, Panchuk also stresses that 'they are now and have always been FANATICALLY ALMOST, ANTI-COMMUNIST, and would now and always be just as prepared and willing to fight Communism, as they were in 1944–45.'[33] This narrative of the 'victims' who were highly anti-Communist and had joined the Division for 'patriotic and religious reasons'[34] was repeated in every piece of the official correspondence by those who lobbied for the 'Galicia's' settlement.

31 See Burtyk, *Ternystyi shliakh Druhoï Dyvizii UNA*.

32 File B53802, Admission of 'Surrendered Enemy Personnel', Government of Canada Files. G.R.B. Panchuk, M.B.E. to the Office of the High Commission for Canada, London, 7 August 1947, p. 2.

33 *Ibid.* The words are capitalized and underlined in the original.

34 File B53802, Admission of 'Surrendered Enemy Personnel', Government of Canada Files. J. Rudachek to R.N. Munroe, District Superintendent, Immigration Branch,

Publicly, the Ukrainian Relief Bureau presented Ukrainian DPs who had no desire to return to the USSR as suitable for resettlement in the West. Off record, however, Panchuk held a different opinion about some Ukrainian DPs. In his letter to John Karasevich, Panchuk states that '[t]he camps are full of "politicians" who are forever playing politics and games of God knows what instead of getting down to earth and realizing their true position, that they are displaced persons and not wanted by any country except the USSR.'[35] He then goes on to criticize Ukrainian DPs by saying that '[i]nstead of rolling up their sleeves and getting down to work, and learning something and making something of themselves, they find politics [...] more "entertaining".'[36] Being extremely unhappy with the Ukrainians' behaviour in camps, Panchuk's aim of re-settling the Ukrainian DPs is more important than his perception of these people, and he therefore insists on maintaining their image of unfortunate victims:

> This should never be spoken of or quoted publicly. We must defend the principle of the refugees and DPs [...] and victims of war, but, in actual fact, God forbid and protect us if some of these parasitic bandits ever get into Canada.[37]

It is important to stress that Panchuk does not specify which group of displaced Ukrainians he means, and refers to them as DPs or refugees. It is, nevertheless, possible to assume that the group in question is that of the politically active members of the OUN who could be found in most DP and POW camps, including that of the 'Galicia' Division. Panchuk's letter vividly illustrates how a positive narrative was created and for what purpose. In fact, it points to the formation of a double narrative: private and public. The public story of the Division as well as other Ukrainian DPs was presented by Panchuk in the most sympathetic terms in order to

---

Department of Mines & Resources, Winnipeg, Man, Canada, 13 August 1947, p. 1.

35 G.R.B. Panchuk to John Karasevich, 21 December 1946 (GRBPC), quoted in Lubomyr Y. Luciuk, 'Unintended Consequences in Refugee Resettlement: Post-War Ukrainian Refugee Immigration to Canada', *International Migration Review* 20/2, Special Issue: *Refugees: Issues and Directions* (Summer, 1986), p. 474.

36 G.R.B. Panchuk, in Luciuk, 'Unintended Consequences', p. 474.

37 *Ibid.*

juxtapose it with that presented in the British media. The private narrative was used only confidentially, as part of the intelligence gathered by those who visited the camps – intelligence which could have potentially ruined the chances of Ukrainian DPs' settlement, as well as 'Galicia's' civilianization, had it become public.

It is difficult to speculate about the exact reasons behind Panchuk's decision not to make his private opinions about some Ukrainian DPs known to the public and the authorities. It is possible that the motivation behind keeping this information private was that it related only to a minority of Ukrainian DPs, and, if such information were to become public, it would affect the migration and settlement prospects of the majority of Ukrainians who were genuine war refugees. Giving a negative portrayal of his countrymen might have seemed to Panchuk as something which could potentially put the Ukrainian Canadian community in a position of having to alienate themselves from the new wave of Ukrainian refugees in order to preserve their good image as lawful Canadian citizens. Ukrainian Canadians could also decide to defend the post-war Ukrainian migrants in order to protect the positive image of Ukrainian Canadians, which was established by the earlier migrants. Panchuk chose the latter.

In spite of the efforts of Panchuk and others to present the Division members in the most positive light, the perceived political danger of the presence of the 'Galicians' in the UK was high. This is made clear in a letter addressed to the Member of Parliament Richard Crossman by H.L. Hyams, a resident of Coventry:

> While denying asylum to thousands of displaced persons and having no compassion on these poor, homeless, starving creatures, the British government brought into the country 8,000 bloodthirsty cut-throats, part of a German force which was guilty of the most brutal atrocities against defenceless people during the war. One can't help feeling there is something wrong with the mentality of a government. Especially a Socialist government, which on the one hand refuses to give succour to so many helpless creatures whose only 'crime' was they were either Jews or defied the Nazi hordes, and on the other hand opens the doors of this country to scoundrels whose entry is an insult to every decent British subject.[38]

38 (NA) FO 371/66712, a letter by M.L. Hyams to R.H.S. Crossman, June 1947.

Such accusations were made on various levels. The government was under a lot of pressure to resolve the 'Galicia' question and to appease opponents of the Division's civilianization and settlement in the UK. Other similar letters followed, and British government reached the consensus to keep the 'Galicians' temporarily in the UK and to find a new settlement for them once their services were no longer needed.

The Move to Canada

Analysis of correspondence between the Home Office and the government of Canada, and of letters from the voluntary organizations in Canada and the United Kingdom that were lobbying for the 'Galicia's' civilianization, explains the nature of the negotiations that led to the ex-enemy personnel being given the status of civilians and allowed to live and work in the West. The 'Galicia' men were being cast by the Central Co-ordinating Committee of Ukrainian Organizations simply as soldiers who 'fought against Soviet Russia on the German Eastern Front';[39] and the narrative featuring the 'Galicia' as a Wehrmacht Division was being used by officials both in Canada and the UK. The Canadian Deputy Minister refers to them in the following way:

> According to information obtained from the British Authorities these Ukrainians were members of the First Ukrainian Division of the Wehrmacht, which appears to have been formed in 1944 from remnants of what is believed to have been Waffen S.S. Division.[40]

39 File B53802, Admission of 'Surrendered Enemy Personnel', Government of Canada Files. Letter from Theodore Danyliw, Secretary General to Hon. L.B. Pearson, Secretary of State for External Affairs, Ottawa, Canada, 23 March 1950.

40 File B53802, Admission of 'Surrendered Enemy Personnel', Government of Canada Files. Deputy Minister L. Fortier to the Minister of Citizenship and Immigration Walter Harris in Ottawa, Canada on 23 March 1950.

In this version of events, even the date of the Division's formation has been altered, and it seems to have come into existence only after the Battle of Brody. Again, the author of this statement sees no irony in emphasizing the year 1944 as the time when the Division was supposedly formed, even though this strongly indicated that most of the men would have had a pre-Division history of involvement in military activity that would require scrutiny.

The need to resolve the 'Galician' question was becoming more and more pressing. According to the Directive No. 18 of the Allied Control Council, the repatriation of former members of the Wehrmacht was taking place in the UK in 1948.[41] The 'Galician's' could not fall under this order, as prisoners of war were not to be repatriated to 'countries where they might be subjected to racial, religious or political persecution'.[42] The situation required further decision making in order to 'have a clearer idea as to what is likely to be the fate of the Ukrainians.'[43] Meanwhile, the demand for agricultural workers in the UK at a time when there were few prisoners of war left to labour at a very low cost was growing. It was thus convenient to employ those Division members who were fit to work in rural areas of Britain in place of the former German POWs. However, legal employment of the Division members required their civilianization. As the 'Galicians' had been formerly classified as 'surrendered enemy personnel' and 'prisoners of war', the difficulty of their civilianization was more than apparent. Here is what the Under-Secretary of State for Foreign Affairs had to say on the issue:

> Opinion is divided as to their political virtue between those who herald them as the first gallant participators in the struggle against communism and those who regard them as ex-enemy troops whose service in the Wehrmacht, albeit mainly against the Russians [sic], was definitely harmful to the western Allies in that it released German troops to fight on the Western Front.[44]

41 (NA) HO/213/1518, A.A. Stark of the Foreign Office to Mrs Hughes of the Aliens Department at the Home Office, London, 14 June 1948, p. 1.

42 *Ibid.*, p. 2.

43 *Ibid.*

44 (NA) HO/213/1518. Minute sheet by the Under-Secretary of State for Foreign Affairs on 10 June 1948.

The British Under-Secretary of State then goes on to state that: '[t]he division was an SS division and technically all its officers and senior N.C. O's [sic] are liable for trial as war criminals.'[45] The Under-Secretary then explains that 'there is controversy as to whether these Ukrainians were volunteers or conscripts into the SS division.'[46] He then concludes that '[p]robably the fairest interpretation of their conduct is to regard them as Ukrainian separatists, whose age old hatred of the Russians led them to offer their services to the Germans in the hope that in return they would be granted an independent Ukraine.'[47] The repetition by the Under-Secretary of State for Foreign Affairs of the standard narrative promoted by the Galicians themselves is significant, and would have important consequences for their subsequent civilianization. The Under-Secretary reveals that the Foreign Office 'decided to permit those Ukrainian P.O.W's who are suitable for agricultural employment to remain in this country on roughly the same terms as E.V.W's'.[48] The Under-Secretary also recognizes that '[t]here has never been more than a very cursory inspection of these men, which took place before they left Italy and was a sample check only.'[49] However, no order to secure further screening was issued. Instead, the Under-Secretary stresses that '[r]eports have been received that the habits of many of these men border on the primitive and that they are unlikely to be desirable long term residents for that reason.'[50] Thus, no plans for the permanent settlement of the Division men in the UK were made. As an alternative, it was suggested that they be re-settled elsewhere. First, though, the 'Galicia' men had to be civilianized in the UK.

In his letter to the Minister of Justice and Attorney General of Canada, Panchuk writes that

45 *Ibid.*
46 *Ibid.*
47 *Ibid.*
48 European Voluntary Workers. (NA) HO/213/1518. Minute sheet by the Under-Secretary of State for Foreign Affairs on 10 June 1948.
49 *Ibid.*
50 *Ibid.*

> H.M. Government is treating them [the 'Galicians'] in exactly the same way as all other refugees and Displaced Persons. No security objections exist and insofar as emigration is concerned, the Home Office issues them with travel documents and all other facilities in order to assist in the emigration of those persons who have a place to go to and for whom all other arrangements are made.[51]

According to Panchuk's letter 'a certain number have already immigrated to Argentine, France and to other countries, in order to join their immediate and close relatives.'[52] He says that the Government of the United States is also 'prepared to accept applications in the case of those men who have and wish to join close relatives in the U.S.A.'.[53] Despite these changes in the Division members' immigration status, the Canadian government was unwilling to follow the example of Argentina or the USA and allow former SEPs into the country. Yet the positive narrative portraying the former 'Galicians' as an anti-Soviet Wehrmacht unit was successful in at least securing negotiations with the Canadian government about the potential settlement of the Division members in Canada. This was the case only, however, until the Canadian authority representatives started to pay closer attention to the group in question, and realized that the Division had had no connection to the Wehrmacht, but was, in fact, part of the Waffen SS. Canadian immigration law of the time did not permit accepting former combatants who had served in the German Armed Forces voluntarily. The Memorandum for the Cabinet Committee on Immigration Policy stated that '[u]nder existing procedure aliens of Allied or Neutral nationality who served with the Enemy Forces during the war are not admitted to Canada unless they can establish that such service was compulsory. The group of Ukrainians served voluntarily.'[54] This decision was based on the following policy:

51 File B53802, Admission of 'Surrendered Enemy Personnel', Government of Canada Files. G.R.B. Panchuk to the Minister of Justice and Attorney General of Canada, Ottawa, Ontario, 23 November 1948, p. 1.

52 *Ibid.*

53 *Ibid.*

54 File B53802, Admission of 'Surrendered Enemy Personnel', Government of Canada Files. Memorandum for the Cabinet Committee on Immigration Policy. Admission of

> Immigrants who are citizens of Finland, Hungary, Italy and Roumania, who served in the Armed Forces of their own country during the war are not to be refused admission to Canada on account of such service unless recorded on the official list of war criminals.
>
> Immigrants of neutral or allied nationality who have served in the Armed Forces of His Majesty's enemies are to be refused admission unless they can establish that such service was rendered under physical compulsion.[55]

The policy thus stated clearly that Ukrainian men who served in the 'Galicia' were not to be permitted to enter Canada.

As well as the Canadian officials, there were Canadian Ukrainian organizations that strongly opposed the arrival of the Division men in Canada. The Association of United Ukrainians (AUU) expressed its dismay at Panchuk's efforts in petitioning the Canadian Immigration Authorities to admit 'the S.S. Division "Galicia"'[56] to Canada. The AUU stated that '[i]t is clear that Mr Panchuk and his Association either forgets the facts, that no Canadian could forget or feels that Canadians have already forgotten their sons who have fallen on the battlefields of Europe.'[57] The statement continues by saying that

> Ukrainian Division Halychyna (Galicia) was part and parcel of the Hitler army. It was against them that our Canadian boys fought on the battlefields of Italy. Many a Canadian son remained over there, shot by the VERY ONES that Mr Panchuk would wish your Department to bring to Canada.[58]

Here, just as in Panchuk's address to the Government of Canada, a reference to the Canadian soldiers is being employed, but with the opposite intention: to vilify the 'Galicians'. Just as Panchuk referred to the 'Galicia'

Ukrainians (Surrendered Enemy Personnel) from the United Kingdom. 28 October 1948. Emphasis in the last line of the quote as in the original.

55 File B53802, Admission of 'Surrendered Enemy Personnel', Government of Canada Files. Letter to the Associate Commissioner in Ottawa, 19 November 1948, pp. 1–2.

56 File B53802, Admission of 'Surrendered Enemy Personnel', Government of Canada Files. William M. Toresio, President of the Association of United Ukrainian Canadians, Toronto, Ontario, 1 March 1949, p. 1.

57 *Ibid.*

58 *Ibid.*

as a Wehrmacht unit, the Association of United Ukrainians calls it an SS Division rather than Waffen SS. Both expressions are inaccurate and both were used in order to emphasize either the 'innocence' or the 'guilt' of the 'Galician' men.

Despite the vigorous criticism from different organizations of the possibility of allowing the 'Galicians' to enter Canada, and the refusals of the Canadian government to allow the Division men to migrate to Canada, the lobbying efforts continued on both official and personal levels. The Canadian government was 'under considerable pressure to admit a number of these aliens from the United Kingdom'.[59] The High Commissioner for Canada in the UK wrote to the Secretary of State for External Affairs in August 1950, quoting a letter from the Foreign Office which was written in defence of the 'Galicia' men. This letter repeats the rhetoric of the Division being well-behaved and suitable for integration into the Western society:

> While in Italy these men were screened by Soviet and British missions and neither then nor subsequently has any evidence been brought to light which would suggest that any of them fought against the Western Allies or engaged in crimes against humanity. Their behaviour since they came to this country has been good and they have never indicated in any way that they are infected with any trace of Nazi ideology.[60]

The High Commissioner also quotes the Foreign Office's reference to the 'Galicia' as the '1st Ukrainian Division of the Wehrmacht, which was formed about September, 1944 and which was only in action once (against the Red Army in Austria during April 1945)',[61] thus again separating the pre-Brody and the reorganized Waffen SS 'Galicia'. The letter then goes on to mention the '14th Galician Grenadier Division' and states that 'this

59 File B53802, Admission of 'Surrendered Enemy Personnel', Government of Canada Files. M.L. Keenleyside, Deputy Minister to M.H. Werahef, Esq. of the Office of the High Commissioner for Canada, London, UK, 1 February 1949.

60 File B53802, Admission of 'Surrendered Enemy Personnel', Government of Canada Files. L.D. Wilgress, High Commissioner for Canada in the UK to the Secretary of State for External Affairs, Canada, 5 September 1950, p. 1. From the Foreign Office letter dated 4 September 1950.

61 *Ibid.*, p. 1.

was also a Wehrmacht unit, an attempt made by the Germans to make it into an S.S. Division having apparently been resisted by the Ukrainians themselves.'[62] Thus, even in 1950 and even at the level of the Foreign Office and the High Commissioner, there was misinformation produced and reproduced as to the nature of the Waffen SS 'Galicia'. This misleading information was used to pressurize the Canadian government into allowing the 'Galicia' men into Canada. The letter quoted by the High Commissioner concluded that

> [f]rom the reports of the special mission set up by the War Office to screen these men, it seems clear that they volunteered to fight against the Red Army from nationalistic motives [...]. Although Communist propaganda has constantly attempted to depict these, like many other refugees, as 'quislings' amd [sic] 'war criminals' it is interesting to note that no specific charges of war crimes have been made by the Soviet or any other Government against any member of this group.[63]

This last statement reflects the nature of politics in 1950, when the Cold War had already started and criticism of the Soviet Union was accepted and even welcomed by the governments of the UK and Canada. This had not been the case immediately after the Second World War, when the British officials were more cautious when dealing with the Soviets.

A change in Canadian Immigration Law allowed a fresh discussion about the possibility of admitting the 'Galicians' to Canada. A number of individuals were being permitted to come to Canada as part of the government's plan

> [...] to foster the growth of the population of Canada by insuring the careful selection of as large a number of immigrants as can advantageously be absorbed in the national economy, without making a fundamental alteration in the character of the population.[64]

62 *Ibid.*

63 *Ibid.*

64 Administration of Order in Council P.C. 2856. Document No. 174 50, 23 June 1950. Signed by W.E. Harris <http://www.international.gc.ca/department/history-histoire/dcer/details-fr.asp?intRefid=7987> accessed 19 August 2010.

These immigrants potentially included the Division members and the criticisms to the government of the possible admittance of the 'Galicians' continued. The Executive Committee of the Canadian Jewish Congress (CJC) was very critical of a speech given by Walter Harris, the Minister of Citizenship and Immigration on the question of the 'Galicia' men. In his letter to Harris, Samuel Bronfman, the national president of the CJC, stated that he was 'dismayed at the intention [...] of permitting the entry to Canada of the Halychyna division of Ukrainians who fought against the Allies during the course of World War Two.'[65] He continued with the following statement:

> [...] information in our files discloses that this group enlisted as volunteers in the German SS as an infantry Division[.] We believe that the Nuremberg Military tribunal in declaring the SS a criminal organisation encompassed all voluntary groups such as the Halychyna Division.[66]

Harris issued an immediate reply to the accusation made by Bronfman, and explained that his 'remarks in the House may have been misunderstood'.[67] He continued his clarification:

> I meant to convey the idea that we had not investigated any particular individual, but had that to do yet, before granting admission. It seems that someone has taken the opposite meaning: that we had given approval to the whole group. This is not the fact.[68]

65 File B53802, Admission of 'Surrendered Enemy Personnel', Government of Canada Files. Samuel Bronfman, National President of the Canadian Jewish Congress to Hon. Walter Harris, the Minister of Citizenship and Immigration, Ottawa, Ontario, 4 July 1950.

66 *Ibid.*

67 File B53802, Admission of 'Surrendered Enemy Personnel', Government of Canada Files. Walter Harris, the Minister of Citizenship and Immigration, Ottawa, Ontario to Samuel Bronfman, National President of the Canadian Jewish Congress, Montreal, 5 July 1950.

68 *Ibid.*

This, however, became a fact in September 1950 when the efforts of the pro-Division lobbying came to a successful conclusion. Combined with the new piece of immigration law, the government of Canada took the decision to allow the former 'Galicia' men to settle in Canada stating that

> Ukrainians (surrendered enemy personnel) presently residing in the United Kingdom may be admitted to Canada not-withstanding their services in the German Army provided they are admissible according to the provisions of Order-in-Council P.C. 2856,[69] are in good health, and are in possession of a travel document or affidavit establishing the identity of the holder which may be accepted in lieu of a passport.[70]

An additional factor that facilitated the admission of the 'Galicia' members to Canada was the Canadian government's decision, taken in March 1950, to allow the *Volksdeutsche* Waffen SS members to come to Canada. Rodal states that

> [t]he decision to admit Volksdeutsche Waffen-SS members set a precedent that helped break the government's resistance to persistent lobbying from the Ukrainian community for the group admission of some 2000 former members of the Ukrainian Halychina [sic] Waffen-SS Division.[71]

69 Administration of Order in Council P.C. 2856: '1. By the enactment of Order in Council P.C. 2856, dated 9th June, 1950, approval was given to certain proposals designed to give effect to the expressed policy of the Government to foster the growth of the population of Canada by insuring the careful selection of as large a number of immigrants as can advantageously be absorbed in the national economy, without making a fundamental alteration in the character of the population. [...] 6. immigrants, [...], must satisfy the Minister of Citizenship and Immigration, whose decision shall be final, that: (a) they are suitable immigrants having regard to the climatic, social, educational, industrial, labour or other conditions or requirements of Canada; and (b) they are not undesirable owing to their peculiar customs, habits, mode of life, methods of holding property, or because of their probable inability to become readily adapted or integrated into the life of the Canadian community and to assume the duties of Canadian citizenship within a reasonable time after their entry' <http://www.international.gc.ca/department/history-histoire/dcer/details-fr.asp?intRefid=7987> accessed 19 August 2010.

70 File B53802, Admission of 'Surrendered Enemy Personnel', Government of Canada Files. Directive No. 26. H.Q. Files: 500–1 B-53802. Ukrainians (Surrendered Enemy Personnel) in the United Kingdom, 25 September 1950.

71 Rodal, 'How Perpetrators of Genocidal Crimes Evaded Justice', p. 706.

Thus, Panchuk's efforts to secure the settlement of the 'Galicians' as civilians were successful. The 'Galician' men managed to avoid repatriation and to become civilianized and relatively settled in the West. As no trials or full screening of individuals had been carried out by the British or Canadian authorities, and the Division was only cleared of collective war crime allegations, if there were war criminals among the Waffen SS 'Galicia' men, they remained unpunished, while those ex-members who had committed no crime continued to live with the brand of war criminal. Thus, the complex process of the 'Galicia's' progression from a failed military formation to the status of SEPs, POWs and, finally, civilians, remains in some ways incomplete even now. The civilianization and settlement of the Division did not stop the polarization of the narratives that surround it, which continues unabated to the present day.

CHAPTER 5

Contemporary Perceptions of Second World War Collaboration in Ukraine[1]

The late twentieth century has seen a turn toward the study of memory, particularly in relation to the Second World War. Eyewitnesses' and survivors' testimonies began to play an important role in the writing of history of the period, especially with regard to the Holocaust. The distinction between memory and history, however, became somewhat blurred. In his work on the 'memory of sovereignty and sovereignty over memory', Timothy Snyder explains that memory and history cannot be studied separately 'and yet without separate conception the study of neither can proceed.'[2] This is true about the study of the memory of the Waffen SS 'Galicia' Division, when in contemporary debates 'memory' and 'history' are often used interchangeably, especially by politically motivated groups or individuals. Snyder goes on to suggest that '[m]emory cannot be studied as memory, at all. Our recollections are always recollections of something, and unless we have an independent source of knowledge about this something, we can learn nothing about how memory works.'[3] This independent source of knowledge is seldom available when it comes to memory of traumatic and controversial events such as those in which the 'Galicia' was involved. The

1 My paper 'The Shaping of "Historical Truth": Construction and Reconstruction of the Memory and Narrative of the Waffen SS "Galicia" Division', *Canadian Slavonic Papers/ Revue canadienne des slavistes* LIV/3–4 (September–December 2012), 443–69, is based on this chapter.

2 Timothy Snyder, 'Memory of sovereignty and sovereignty over memory: Poland, Lithuania and Ukraine, 1939–1999', in Jan Werner Muller, ed., *Memory and Power in Post-War Europe. Studies in the Presence of the Past* (Cambridge: Cambridge University Press, 2002), pp. 39–59 (p. 39).

3 *Ibid.*, p. 40.

individual accounts of events like the Huta Pieniacka massacre, the Battle of Brody, the surrender of the Division, its relocation to the UK can, of course, be cross-referenced with the available documentary evidence; yet the popular knowledge of these events is often based on memory or even post-memory of those directly or indirectly involved in the very event.[4] In fact, an event does not even need to take place to be meaningful and thus 'memorable' to people. Events acquire their meaning through the importance attributed to them by those who remember them.[5] It is also essential to take into account the fact that the original meaning of an event is easily lost or altered during the process of its recounting and recollection, as, in order to construct a testimony of an experience, one has to go through the process of memory retrieval.

Truth and Memory

One of the opening sentences of a former Division member's memoir is '[t]ime flies, and with it flies our life, and so 54 years later we look at things differently'.[6] The meaning applied to the association with the Waffen SS in 1943 might have gone through several stages of alteration for the 'Galicians' before they came to write their memoirs. In the introduction to his novel about the Second World War, a former 'Galician', Swiatomyr Fostun, lists the Ukrainian men who fought in the Soviet Army, the German Army, the 'Galician' Division, the Ukrainian Liberation Army, the General Anders' Corps as well as the UPA as having all marched an equally 'thorny road of

4 For post-memory, see Marianne Hirsch, *Family Frames: Photography, Narrative, and Postmemory* (Cambridge, MA: Harvard University Press, 1997).

5 See Giovanni Levi, 'Historians, Psychoanalysis and Truth', in Anna-Marija Castrén, Markku Lonkila and Matti Peltonen, eds, *Between Sociology and History. Essays on Microhistory, Collective Action, and Nation-Building* (Helsinki: Finnish Literature Society, 2004), 71–87 (p. 80).

6 Stetkevych, *Iak z Berezhan*, p. 6.

a soldier'.[7] Here these Ukrainian men are not separated into traitors and freedom fighters. Over thirty years after the war, Fostun unites all of them under one description of the 'active participants of the gigantic military struggle'.[8] In other words, the years that have passed since the war have brought new experiences and, subsequently, new understandings of the war-time events. This, in turn, created new memories of the past events.

In his work on the 'retranscription' of memories, Sigmund Freud uses the term *Nachträglichkeit*, explained as *effets d'après-coup* or 'afterwardsness'.[9] Freud describes this as the process of 'the material present in the form of memory traces being subjected from time to time to a *rearrangement* in accordance with fresh circumstances'.[10] This idea suggests that memory is dynamic: operating in the present, memory traces must include the awareness of that which was not known when the remembered event took place, and they thus influence the meaning of that event. While Freud looks at individuals' traumatic experiences and their recollections, the methods used by psychoanalysis can be equally useful when analysing traumatic experiences and memories of groups. With regard to the 'Galicians', the idea of *Nachträglichkeit* is very applicable, as by the time they came to write their memoirs or give interviews, they were already aware of what they might not have known during the war, perhaps most significantly, the full scale and consequences of the Holocaust, and so for some of them their (re)constructed memory of the events they had experienced acquired more of a traumatic significance. In this sense, not only their present recording of the past events changes, the past itself changes also 'as the new meanings

7 Swiatomyr Fostun, *Shliakhamy smerty. Povist' z chasiv II svitovoï viiny* (Buenos Aires: Iulian Serediak, 1979), p. 7.

8 *Ibid.*

9 See Guiseppe Civitarese, *The Intimate Room. Theory and Technique of the Analytic Field* (London: Routledge, 2010) pp. 96–112; Jacques Lacan, Ècrits (New York: Norton, 2005); Jean Laplanche, *Problématiques VI: L'après-coup – La Nachträglichkeit dans l'après-coup (1990–1991)* (Paris: PUF, 2006); Lis Moller, *The Freudian Reading: Analytical and Fictional Constructions* (Philadelphia, PA: University of Pennsylvania Press, 1991).

10 Sigmund Freud in a letter to Fliess, 6 December 1896, in Civitarese, *The Intimate Room*, p. 96. Emphasis as in the original.

come to be assigned to it'.[11] This, of course, reveals the problematic nature of the assumption that memory offers a direct access to the original meaning of past events. Thus, 'versions of the past or present that are to a greater or lesser extent *true* do not exist, but only ones that are to a greater or lesser extent *viable*, or capable of being experienced.'[12] In this sense, the 'Galicians'' memories of the war-time events are not necessarily more or less 'true' depending on when they were recorded or recollected; the very remembering of these events is part of the process of recategorization and recontextualization of traumatic experiences. That is not to say, of course, that these memories cannot be manipulated or used for particular purposes.

Jeffrey Olick and Joyce Robbins explain the importance of control over a group's memory. They state that '[t]he dominance of national memory over other memories [...] not only excludes other contestants for control over the national identity but maintains the primacy of national over other kinds of identity for primary allegiance.'[13] In the contemporary Ukrainian portrayal of the Second World War, politically framed national identity plays a vital role in the battle of memories and narratives. The memory and perception of those who received the 'Galicians' in the UK was affected by the constructed national identity of 'Britishness' (or 'Englishness') and the popular idea of heroic victory in the Second World War. Being seen as 'the other', the enemy, the Division received a negative reaction, which had an effect not only on the 'Galicians' themselves, but also on the second and even third generation of Ukrainians in the diaspora. The shared memories and, to an extent, the shared identities of the contemporary generations in Ukraine and the diaspora continues to form the narrative of the 'Galicia' Division's history in the present-day debate.

11 Civitarese, *The Intimate Room*, p. 104.

12 *Ibid.*, p. 106. Emphasis as in the original.

13 Jeffrey K. Olick and Joyce Robbins, 'Social Memory Studies: From "Collective Memory" to the Historical Sociology of Mnemonic Practices', *Annual Review of Sociology* 24 (1998), 105–40 (p. 127).

Memorialization of the War in Ukraine

One way of understanding how the 'Galicia' members are remembered is through the question of their recognition as veterans. In Ukraine, those who fought for the UPA or the 'Galicia' Division, as well as members of smaller nationalist military groups, are not officially recognized as veterans of the Second World War.[14] A plan, initiated by Ukraine's former President Viktor Yushchenko, to reconcile the Red Army veterans and those who fought for the independence of Ukraine in other military and paramilitary formations, and to recognize them officially as veterans of the Second World War, did not bring any results.[15] It produced a number of public debates which only proved that there was no agreement between the east and south of Ukraine, which predominantly see the 'Galicians' and the UPA soldiers as Nazi collaborators, and the western Ukrainian population, which generally regard them as heroes and freedom fighters.[16] This thus-far irresolvable debate continues to this day with groups such as

14 While the UPA members have no official status as war veterans, some local authorities, especially those in western regions of Ukraine (e.g., Ivano-Frankivs'k and L'viv *oblasts*), where, at the time of writing, the Svoboda party has a majority, took a decision to pay an additional 50–200 hryvnias to former UPA members. See 'Upivtsiam dodaly 100 hryven' do pensiї', *Hazeta po-ukraïns'ky*, No 1047 (23 June 2010) <http://gazeta.ua/post/344378/comm> accessed 24 August 2012.

15 For more details, see 'Yushchenko calls for reconciliation between veterans', *Kyiv Post* (11 May 2005) <http://www.kyivpost.com/content/ukraine/yushchenko-calls-for-reconciliation-between-vetera.html?flavour=mobile> accessed 23 August 2012.

16 Some scholars suggested an alternative to the reconciliation of all veterans, namely, a 'pact of forgetting' (based on the Spanish *Pacto de Olvido*), as a way of dealing with the past by 'forgetting' it, and instead focusing on the necessary reforms. For more details on the reconciliation debate and why the Spanish scenario is not likely to work in the Ukrainian case, see Oxana Shevel, 'The Politics of Memory in a Divided Society: a Comparison of Post-Franco Spain and post-Soviet Ukraine', *Slavic Review* 70/1 (Spring 2011), 137–64.

the nationalist Svoboda party[17] considering it their duty to memorialize nationalist figures, and their opponents, such as the Communist Party of Ukraine preventing these attempts from succeeding.[18]

Official commemoration of the Division is problematic, and generally not highly visible. There is one small museum dedicated solely to the history of the 1st Ukrainian Division of the Ukrainian National Army. The museum is located in L'viv Secondary School No. 34, and has no regular opening hours. Its creator is Ihor Fedyk, a history teacher who writes a blog

17 *Vseukraïns'ke ob'iednannia 'Svoboda'* (the All-Ukrainian Union 'Svoboda'), a far-right political party led by Oleh Tiahnybok. Until 2004, the party was called the Social-National Party of Ukraine. It defends the idea of *natiocratia*: the right of indigenous people to have control over their territory. The term was coined in 1935 by Mykola Stsibors'kyi, a member of the OUN leadership and theoretician. See Oleksandr Sych, 'Natsiokratiia – politychnyi ideal natsionalizmu', *VO Svoboda. Ofitsiina storinka* (17 March 2009) <http://www.svoboda.org.ua/dopysy/dopysy/010221/> accessed 23 August 2012. The influence of the Svoboda party in Ukraine has grown over the past few years. The party made significant gains during the 2009 and 2010 local elections in the west of the country, and managed to secure representation in the national parliament in the parliamentary elections in 2012.

18 The following incident illustrates the ongoing 'war for heroes' between the far left and the far right political groups in Ukraine. The L'viv regional council, run by the Svoboda, issued a decree on 16 March 2012 to introduce a regional Hero of Ukraine Stepan Bandera Award of 20,000 hryvnias (under 2,000 euros) to be awarded to individuals for significant contributions to the national state-building process (*L'vivs'ka oblasna rada XV sesiia VI sklykannia. Rishennia No 423 vid 16 bereznia 2012 roku* (author's private archive). This decree was immediately disputed by the Anti-Fascist Committee of Ukraine. See Complaint to O.A. Vasylenko, L'viv regional attorney, from 1st Secretary of the L'viv Regional Committee of the Communist party of Ukraine and deputy head of the Anti-Fascist Committee of Ukraine, Oleksandr Kalyniuk. *Skarha v poriadku st. 12 Zakonu Ukraïny 'Pro prokuraturu' 2012* (author's private archive). For the list of the first winners of the award, see 'Oholosheno peremozhtsiv oblasnoï premiï imeni Heroia Ukraïny Stepana Bandery', *L'vivs'ka Hazeta* (26 June 2012) <http://www.gazeta.lviv.ua/news/2012/06/26/3506> accessed 22 August 2012. The ceremony to present the award for the first time was symbolically scheduled for 30 June 2012, the seventy-first anniversary of the proclamation of Ukraine's independence by Iaroslav Stets'ko of the OUN-B (also known as the Act of the Ukrainian State).

on Ukrainian history, including questions of Ukrainian nationalism.[19] The fact that this museum is difficult to access, almost hidden, even in a city like L'viv where nationalist memories dominate, speaks to the highly sensitive nature of the memory of the 'Galicia' Division. In general, museums tend to either avoid the mention of the Division and focus on the Sich Riflemen or the OUN and UPA, or mention it as the 1st UD UNA in the larger context of the 'liberation struggle', avoiding the issue of collaboration.

A similarly ambiguous monument is the one that commemorates a 'Galician' soldier in L'viv's Lychakiv cemetery. The monument bears the inscription: 'here rests an unknown warrior of the "Galicia" Division, who gave up his life in the Battle of Brody in July 1944 for the freedom of the Ukrainian people.' The monument fails to mention the 'Galicia's' involvement in the Waffen SS, thereby contributing to the narrative of the Division as having fought solely for Ukraine's independence, and obscuring the connection with the German Army.

Apart from the official commemorative practices the 'Galicia' Division is remembered in other ways. In April 2012 in L'viv, an organization of young nationalists, 'Autonomous Resistance', together with representatives of the Svoboda party, organized the third annual march in honour of the 'Galicia'.[20] Around 1,500 people marched the streets of L'viv carrying banners which depicted the 'Galicians' as heroes of Ukraine and stressed that the association of the Division with what was referred to as the 'Wehrmacht' (the Waffen SS was not mentioned) was merely a strategic move for the otherwise nationalistic formation. Another unusual enterprise which references the 'Galicia' Division is a L'viv taxi company.[21] Unlike the nationalist youth, the taxi company emphasizes the Division's association with the German Armed Forces by decorating its cars with a sign reading 'SS Halychyna'. The owner of the company insists that his project is not

19 See Ihor Fedyk, 'Heroï nashoï istoriï', *Vholos* (27 February 2012) <http://vgolos.com.ua/blog.431.html?page=1> accessed 22 August 2012.

20 'U L'vovi provely marsh vyshyvanok na chest' dyvizii "Halychyna"', *Vholos* (28 April 2012) <http://vgolos.com.ua/politic/news/46260.html> accessed 3 December 2012.

21 'U L'vovi z'iavylos' taksi SS "Halychyna"', *Ukraïns'ka Pravda* (12 October 2012) <http://life.pravda.com.ua/society/2011/10/12/87447/> accessed 3 December 2012.

purely business oriented, but that it also has patriotic motivations.[22] Indeed, the drivers of the taxis in question give a short history of the Division to their customers, thus 'educating' their clients and spreading the memory of the 'Galicia'. What unites these two unofficial ways of commemorating the 'Galicia' is that neither of them offer a picture of the Division based on factual information. They present a particular idea of the Division shedding no light on the historical reality: the demonstration celebrates a 'Wehrmacht' formation, while, judging by media reports, the information provided by the taxi drivers is sketchy at best.

Institutionalized Memory

'Through its cultural heritage a society becomes visible to itself and to others. Which past becomes evident in that heritage and which values emerge in its identificatory appropriation tells us much about the constitution and tendencies of a society',[23] suggest Jan Assmann and John Czaplicka. The way an event is represented in texts or in oral tradition forms a perception of not only that event, but also the group in question. With regard to Ukraine, Andrii Portnov suggests that the lack of consistent state policy of memory in post-Soviet Ukraine in a way supports the relative stability of the society's development, because having several regional centres that propagate their own version of history means that none of the individual narratives is able to become the state narrative.[24] While agreeing that a variety of interpretations of historical events is present in contemporary Ukraine, it is difficult to deny the influence of the state and state-funded institutions on the presentation of history, especially through secondary and higher education.

22 *Ibid.*

23 Jan Assmann and John Czaplicka, 'Collective Memory and Cultural Identity', *New German Critique*, 65 (1995), 125–33 (p. 133).

24 See Andrii V. Portnov, 'Memory Wars in Post-Soviet Ukraine (1991–2010)', in Uilleam Blacker, Alexander Etkind, Julie Fedor, eds, *Memory and Theory in Eastern Europe* (Palgrave Macmillan, forthcoming).

Adopted in 2001 by the Ministry of Education, Science, Youth and Sport of Ukraine, the programme of teaching the history of Ukraine in high schools allowed for nine lessons on the history of the Second World War. These included a number of issues such as the partisan movement, the activity of the OUN and UPA and even their relationship with Armia Krajowa.[25] The programme emphasized the contribution of the Ukrainian intelligentsia to the victory over Nazi Germany.[26] In the 2012 version of the programme, there are seven teaching hours (out of the total of fifty-two hours of Ukrainian history in grade 11)[27] which are dedicated to the history of the Second World War. The learning objectives of the programme include the assessment of the different points of view on the activities of the OUN and UPA as well as a comparison of different attitudes of the population and political forces towards the war. The subject of collaboration is also included in the programme. This, theoretically speaking, should signal a move towards the depoliticization of taught history and the inclusion of various points of view. Yet when one continues to read the programme, one also notices other learning objectives, such as the description of the 'heroic events of the Great Patriotic War'. In fact, the term 'the Great Patriotic War (1941–5)' appears each time the term 'World War Two (1939–45)' is mentioned.[28] Thus the new school programme in history does not aim to offer an objective portrayal of the history of the Second World War, but,

25 The Home Army (*Armia Krajowa*, AK,) formed the resistance movement in Nazi-occupied Poland. For details on AK's relationship with UPA, see Grzegorz Motyka and Rafał Wnuk, *Pany i rezuny. Współpraca AK-WiN i UPA w latach 1945–1947* (Warszawa: Oficyna Wydawnicza Volumen, 1997).

26 For more details see Fedir H. Turchenko, Petro P. Panchenko and S.M. Tymchenko, eds, *Novitnia Istoriia Ukraïny. Chastyna druha 1939–2001. 11 klas* (Kyiv: Heneza, 2001).

27 Grade 11 is the final year of secondary education in Ukraine. The pupils are 16–17 years old.

28 *Prohrama dlia zahal'noosvitnikh navchal'nykh zakladiv. Istoria Ukraïny 10–11 klasy. Riven' standartu* <http://osvita.ua/school/materials/program/30993/> accessed 14 November 2012. See also Andrii Portnov, '"Nestacha porozhniaka", abo novyi pidruchnyk z istorii vid Tabachnyka', *Zakhid.net* <http://zaxid.net/home/showSingleNews.do?nestacha_porozhnyaka_abo_noviy_pidruchnik_z_istoriyi_vid_tabachnika&objectId=1236705> accessed 7 February 2013.

once again, reflects the political position of the current Ministry, which, under Dmytro Tabachnyk, has turned towards a Russian-style glorification of the Soviet victory.[29] Just as in 2001, in 2012 there is no provision for the study of the 'Galicia' Division's history. It is up to the teacher whether she or he will take the liberty to dedicate any part of the lesson time to a discussion of Ukrainian participation in the Waffen SS.[30]

Developing Halbwachs' idea that the past is stored and interpreted by social institutions, Daniel Levy and Julian Dierkes state that 'collective memories inform institutional arrangements [...] and these institutional arrangements structure the subsequent understanding of collective memories.'[31] Levy and Dierkes go on to explain that politicians, legislators and administrators are not the only factors which determine 'the shape of national memories', but they suggest that 'state actors are a dominant force that supplies categories to articulate and legitimize nationhood.'[32] Ukraine suffers from a fundamental political division, and the political factions often base their arguments on opposing interpretations of national history. The already dichotomous memory of the Waffen SS 'Galicia' is a key part of these political and institutional discourses. The 'Galicians' are

29 An alternative history textbook has been written by Andrii Zakaliuk, a history teacher in a L'viv school. His book is an introduction to Ukrainian history and has been used by some schools in L'viv as supplementary material for the study of Ukrainian history. See 'U L'vovi prezentuvaly posibnyk z istorii Ukraïny dlia 5 klasiv', *20 khvylyn* (8 August 2012) <http://20minut.ua/Новини-Львова/news/У-Львові-презентували-посібник-з-історії-України-для-5-класів-10239321.html> accessed 15 November 2012. Alternative textbooks, like the one by Zakaliuk, are now banned by the Minister of Education, Tabachnyk. See 'Tabachnyk vymahaie vid L'vova vidmovytysia vid al'ternatyvnoho pidruchnyka istorii', *Ukranews*, 10 October 2012 <http://ukranews.com/uk/news/ukraine/2012/10/10/80714> accessed 15 November 2012.

30 For interviews with Ukrainian secondary school teachers on the question of the 'Galicia' Division, see Ella Schindler, 'Mynule – sudyty chy vyvchaty?', *Visti Kombatanta* 1 (2007), 34–5.

31 Daniel Levy and Julian Dierkes, 'Institutionalising the Past: Shifting Memories of Nationhood in German Education and Immigration Legislation', in Jan Werner Muller, ed., *Memory and Power in Post-War Europe. Studies in the Presence of the Past* (Cambridge: Cambridge University Press, 2002), pp. 244–64.

32 *Ibid.*

seen as traitors by those who oppose the current nationalist movement. This group often comprises supporters of Communist, socialist and other left-wing parties as well as supporters of President Viktor Yanukovych's ruling Party of Regions. The pro-'Galician' view is strongly backed by the nationalist groups, one of the most prominent examples of which is the already mentioned Svoboda party. There is also a smaller group of politicians who position themselves in the middle and have more flexible interpretations of history, which tend to depend on the political climate, but these politicians are a minority and do little to actively neutralize the polarized historical debates.

The division is especially visible during electoral campaigns. On 14 October, on the religious holiday of *Pokrova*,[33] Ukrainians traditionally celebrate Cossackdom as the protective military force of the Ukrainian state. This day has also been assumed to be the day of the formation of the UPA by Bandera's OUN in 1942, and is thus also celebrated by UPA veterans. In 2012, the *Pokrova* holiday fell two weeks before the parliamentary elections, and thus represented a chance not to be missed by those competing in the elections. The opposing political groups vocally exploited the 'heroes' and 'anti-heroes' of the Second World War, either celebrating or condemning them in order to make a statement about the contemporary political situation. Thus, many cities in Ukraine witnessed a 'Resistance March', celebrating the 70th anniversary of the UPA, mostly under the banners of the Svoboda party, desperate to win enough votes in order to gain representation in the parliament. Meanwhile, on Shevchenko Boulevard in Kyiv, by the monument to Lenin, the Communists staged a mock trial of Roman Shukhevych, the UPA commander and formerly the *Nachtigall* battalion officer, and the OUN leader, Stepan Bandera. Cardboard cutouts of both men bearing the sign of 'fascist collaborator' were 'hanged' by the communists in a symbolic execution.[34] This episode is indicative

33 *Pokrova* (the Intercession of the Theotokos) refers to the holiday of the protection of the faithful through the intercessions of the Holy Virgin Mary.

34 See 'U mistakh Ukraïny proishly zakhody z nahody stvorennia UPA', *BBC Ukraïna*, 14 October 2012 <http://www.bbc.co.uk/ukrainian/politics/2012/10/121014_kyiv_lviv_svoboda_march_ek.shtml> accessed 28 October 2012.

of the general polarization of the use of Second World War history in contemporary Ukraine for political purposes: it is telling that these high-profile public events were initiated and organized by political parties and organizations, and occurred directly before parliamentary elections. It is unlikely that these 'commemorations' would have occurred spontaneously.

Co-operation versus Collaboration

The politicized polarization of debates on the Division was also evident in the interviews collected in May 2009 for this study, and which focus on two interlinked questions. The first of these concerns how the contemporary narratives of the Second World War in general, and the issues of collaboration in particular, are presented to the public, and the second relates to the role of national institutions in creating the official narrative of the 'Galicia'.[35] The subject of Ukrainian collaboration is the one which divides the political interpretations of the Second World War period most

35 The interviews, which I collected in Kyiv and L'viv in May 2009, represent a number of case studies: the Ukrainian National Memory Institute (then supported by Viktor Yushchenko); the Svoboda party (a far-right political party); the L'viv Regional Committee of the Communist Party of Ukraine; and the *Mankurty* blog (run by an ethnic Russian who lives in L'viv). These case studies involve interviewees with strong political standpoints. They reflect, however, a variety of widespread beliefs in the popular discourse in Ukraine with regard to the question of the Second World War and Ukrainian collaboration. Although the official position of the current government of President Yanukovych (which affects the funding and, subsequently, the approach of institutions such as the Ukrainian National Memory Institute) on the question of memory of the Second World War is very different from that of Yushchenko, who was in power when the interviews were carried out, the answers given to me by the interviewees remain relevant, as they represent the contemporary perspective of a variety of people on the role of the institutions and public debates in the creation of a private and public narrative of the Second World War.

drastically. 'The question of collaboration is timely but tricky',[36] suggests Vladyslav Verstiuk, the vice chairman of the Ukrainian National Memory Institute at the time of the interview:[37]

> Collaboration is discussed in relation to the 'Galicia' Division. The majority of Ukrainian academics are almost subconsciously ready to find some reasons *not* to see the Division as collaborators. France had a state and a government, its citizens who fought with the Nazi Germany were collaborators. In Ukraine the situation was different. There was some co-operation, but not the classic form of collaboration.[38]

Vladyslav Verstiuk is not the only one who cites the French example in order to illustrate the specificity of the Ukrainian version of co-operation with the Axis powers. Yurii Mykhal'chyshyn, deputy head of the L'viv branch of the Svoboda party specializing in political education, and from 2012 a Member of the Ukrainian Parliament also believes that the Ukrainian case should be seen as unique:

> We refuse to call it collaboration. Ukrainians took part in World War Two as a separate side. The term 'collaboration' is appropriate for the French example, as they had to invent their resistance movement after the war. Our involvement with the Third Reich we see as a political tactic, not collaboration.[39]

36 Interviewee Vladyslav Verstiuk, 15 May 2009 (Kyiv).

37 Vladyslav Verstiuk was a vice chairman of the Institute under Ihor Yukhnovs'kyi. In 2010 the management of the Institute was replaced in accordance with the preferences of the new government. Thus, the current chairman of the Institute is Valerii Soldatenko, who was a senior member of the Institute of Party History (under the Central Committee of the Communist Party in Ukraine) in 1976–84. His views differ from those of his predecessor and this is reflected in the work of the Institute.

38 Interviewee Vladyslav Verstiuk, 15 May 2009 (Kyiv). Emphasis, as in the original speech.

39 Interviewee Yurii Mykhal'chyshyn, 12 May 2009 (L'viv). Yurii Mykhal'chyshyn holds extreme right views. His position on the 'Galicia' as well as Ukrainian collaboration in general finds support in western regions of Ukraine. In 2010, Mykhal'chyshyn ran an unsuccessful campaign to become the mayor of L'viv, but he was elected a member of L'viv City Council. In 2012 Mykhal'chyshyn was successful in becoming a Member of the Ukrainian Parliament, for the Svoboda party.

The Svoboda party has always been very active in celebrating the 'Galicia' as part of the heritage of the Ukrainian state-building process. In 2004, the Svoboda-run local government of Ternopil' renamed one of the main streets of the city the 'Street of the Warriors of the "Galicia" Division', thereby, according to the party, 'restoring historical justice with regards to the respectful residents of the city'.[40] In April 2009, the party set up twenty advertising boards in L'viv commemorating the 'Galicia' as having 'defended Ukraine' and describing the Division as a 'treasure of the nation'.[41] This caused a wave of negative responses, for example, from the Polish Embassy, the Communist Party and various non-nationalist groups.[42] Mykhal'chyshyn explains that such memorialization activities are supported by the party on a regular basis, and does not see the presentation of the Division as the 'treasure of the nation' as problematic, but rather as part of the 'historical truth'.[43]

Oleksandr Kalyniuk, 1st Secretary of the L'viv Regional Committee of the Communist Party of Ukraine and deputy head of the Anti-Fascist Committee of Ukraine, explains his view on the contemporary treatment of history with regard to the 'Galicia' Division:

> [...] those advertising boards [in L'viv] said that it is a 'treasure of the nation' and that the 'Galicia' was a Ukrainian division which fought for Ukraine in 1943. So I would like to say that the only bit that is true on this advertising board is that they fought in 1943, the rest is a lie and a mythologization. [...] And if someone is telling me that it is a treasure of the nation – I say it is the shame of the nation.[44]

40 Bohdan Chervak, 'Dyviziia "Halychyna": bezporadnist' vlady i "patriotiv"', *VO Svoboda. Ofitsiina storinka*, 23 April 2009 <http://www.svoboda.org.ua/dopysy/dopysy/010361/> accessed 28 October 2012.

41 *Ibid.*

42 See 'Reklamy dywizji SS na ulicach Lwowa', *Gazeta.pl*, 17 April 2009 <http://m.wiadomosci.gazeta.pl/wiadomosci/1,17915,6510598,Reklamy_dywizji_SS_na_ulicach_Lwowa.html> accessed 28 October 2012.

43 Interviewee Yurii Mykhal'chyshyn, 12 May 2009 (L'viv).

44 Interviewee Oleksandr Kalyniuk, 11 May 2009 (L'viv).

The term 'collaboration' itself causes a great deal of disagreement: 'the collaborators are all those who helped the Germans and fought on their side (the German police, SS Galicia, *Nachtigall*, *Roland*, etc.)',[45] argues Kalyniuk:

> I heard the Banderites themselves say that it is called Fascism in Italy, Nazism in Germany, and what we have here is called Ukrainian Nationalism. [...] Someone said that it is easy to fool a small amount of people but it is hard to fool a large group. People will know the truth.[46]

Ironic as it might seem, coming from a member of the Communist Party, the idea of an open discussion on the question of Ukrainian collaboration finds many supporters. Among them is Oleksandr Khokhulin, the creator of the *Mankurty* blog,[47] well known in L'viv as a political and cultural commentator, and a self-identified *moskal'*,[48] who light-heartedly noted: '*moskali* are talking about nothing else but [Ukrainian] collaboration. But "true Galicians" do not talk of collaboration, they commemorate their heroes. There is no healthy discussion of the subject in Ukraine.'[49]

The facilitation of a critical discussion on the collaboration of Ukrainian nationalist organizations and individual Ukrainians with Nazi Germany is difficult in Ukraine. There are some debates and conferences on these issues, but they tend to separate into groups who share the same views and rarely represent a constructive dialogue between opposing parties.[50] There is no doubt that a discussion of questions of collaboration

45 *Ibid.*
46 *Ibid.*
47 The blog discusses the issues of ethnic minorities (the Russian community in particular) in contemporary Ukraine, especially in the city of L'viv, which is often regarded in Ukraine as the epicentre of nationalism.
48 'Moskal'' is a derogatory term for someone from Russia or an ethnic Russian. It was used to refer to the inhabitants of the Grand Duchy of Moscow and later the Russian Empire. In the eighteenth–nineteenth centuries, this term was also used to refer to soldiers of the Russian Imperial army.
49 Interviewee Oleksandr Khokhulin, 11 May 2009 (L'viv).
50 For two different examples of academic conferences, see 'World War Two and the (Re) Creation of Historical Memory in Contemporary Ukraine', 23–26 September 2009 (Kyiv, Ukraine) <http://ww2-historicalmemory.org.ua/conference_e.html> accessed

and nationalism, including the discussion of the existence of the 'Galicia' Division as well as other controversial and insufficiently researched topics, must be developed. There is also a need to foster a debate within civil society in Ukraine which is firmly placed outside the immediate sphere of the political. The importance of this comes from both the failure of previous historiographical accounts to develop narratives that go beyond attempts to justify or condemn the Division and because of the inability of state funded and state controlled institutions to discuss the context and concept of collaboration directly and openly, rather than using it as a political weapon. Of course, the question of collaboration is a political one and always will be; but it has been reduced to an impoverished type of politics, represented by forms of historiography which are only designed to celebrate or condemn, or which subscribe to an overly narrow notion of party politics which serves the interest of those parties themselves and does not contribute to clarification and a genuine attempt to understand the historical framing and legacy of the past. Thus, although the political manipulation of history seems to be inevitable, it is vital for the development of an unconstrained and impartial historiography that scholarly debate is kept clearly outside of political manipulations. This demands the creation of an uncontrolled space for academic debate, which would provide an opportunity for scholars to remain outside any immediate political influence and for non-governmental institutions dealing with the creation of historical research to remain truly non-governmental. But is this achievable in contemporary Ukraine?

'There are two dominant types of historical memory in Ukraine: the national memory and the Soviet memory', states Verstiuk, adding that 'different political forces use history in order to receive certain political dividends'.[51] As for the institutions, Verstiuk believes that

7 December 2012 and 'Collaboration between the Soviet Union and Germany: Causes and Consequences', 5–6 November 2011 (Kyiv, Ukraine) <http://hsozkult.geschichte.hu-berlin.de/termine/id=16932> accessed 7 December 2012.

51 Interviewee Vladyslav Verstiuk, 15 May 2009 (Kyiv).

> [t]he move from the discourse of the Great Patriotic War to the Second World War in Ukraine is still incomplete. Academic discussions have moved towards the idea of World War Two, but public and political circles still talk in terms of the Great Patriotic War.[52]

In 2009, the National Memory Institute produced an analytical report of a national survey on the attitudes of Ukrainians to the Second World War.[53] According to this survey, 57.4 per cent of Ukrainians consider the 'Great Patriotic War' to be the most accurate name for the last world war, while the term 'Second World War' was supported by 32.3 per cent of those surveyed.[54] When asked which factors were the most influential in the respondents' perception of the war as the 'Great Patriotic', 67.2 per cent singled out the Russian media as having most impact on their view of the war, 62.6 per cent referred to the Soviet legacy and 61.5 per cent to the older generation, while 55 per cent thought the programmes of the secondary and higher education to be vital in the formation of their perceptions of the war. Thirty-nine per cent of those who see the war as the Second World War believed that the school and university programme was decisive in forming their opinion of the war.[55]

Oleksandr Khokhulin sees the contemporary portrayal of the Second World War as problematic:

> [...] recently I read a piece about World War Two which said that 'three sides met in a mortal duel'. It made me laugh; there is something wrong with the arithmetic here. There can only be two sides in a duel. Any attempts to add a third [Ukrainian] side are incorrect.[56]

52 *Ibid.* As is evident from the earlier cited Ministerial school programme, the term 'Great Patriotic War' is now back in official use.

53 Analitychnyi zvit za rezul'tatamy sotsiolohichnoho doslidzhennia 'Stavlennia naselennia Ukraïny do problem pov'iazanykh iz II svitovoiu viinoiu', *Vseukraïns'ka sotsiolohichna sluzhba* (Kyiv, 2009).

54 *Ibid.*, p. 5.

55 *Ibid.*, p. 7.

56 Interviewee Oleksandr Khokhulin, 11 May 2009 (L'viv).

Khokhulin believes that 'there are no chances to reconcile the veterans: everything is being done to discourage them from reconciliation.'[57] As far as the National Memory Institute is concerned, he views it as 'a mockery of history, memory and the nation.'[58] Khokhulin is not alone in his criticism of the institutions. Mykhal'chyshyn argues that the regional position of the institutions is incorrect. 'Western Ukraine celebrates the anti-communist movement but it also celebrates 9th May – Victory Day – which is evidence of political schizophrenia', states Mykhal'chyshyn. He goes on to argue that '[t]he position of Ukrainian institutions should be Ukraine-centric.'[59] Such a position does not involve the pursuit of objectivism when it comes to the presentation of history, confesses the Svoboda activist, 'we believe that our form of history is the most adequate for the interests of our electorate and the population of the regions which we consider to form our stronghold.'[60] As for the 'black and white' portrayal of history, Mykhal'chyshyn states with confidence that the Svoboda party has no problem with the idea of a biased interpretation of events, as long as the colours are defined by the party itself.[61]

Just like the nationalist Mykhal'chyshyn, the Communist Kalyniuk thinks that 'institutions have a huge role in forming public opinion about history'.[62] He suggests that the local government 'is supporting the idea of glorification of the collaborators.'[63]

Each interviewee has a very clear opinion of what constitutes the 'truth' and what does not. These strongly expressed opinions, although coming from opposing camps, unite in their view that state-supported institutions are not accomplishing their tasks effectively. So what prevents them from offering an independent, if not objective, representation of the history to the general public?

57 *Ibid.*
58 *Ibid.*
59 Interviewee Yurii Mykhal'chyshyn, 12 May 2009 (L'viv).
60 *Ibid.*
61 *Ibid.*
62 Interviewee Oleksandr Kalyniuk, 11 May 2009 (L'viv).
63 *Ibid.*

The Future of the Past

The question of the Waffen SS 'Galicia', as well as the general discussion on the collaboration of Ukrainians with Nazi Germany in the Second World War, is one that requires a detailed, micro-analytical examination, rather than the biased, broad brushstrokes of politically motivated arguments. The Division's history begs a number of controversial questions, both about their military activity in relation to war crimes as well as their remarkable civilianization and resettlement in the West. The contemporary relevance of the Division's narratives, and their use for political ends, requires an equally scrupulous analysis. The importance of the national institutions in the formation of the narratives of the 'Galicia's' history is undeniable. At present, Ukraine lacks a calm and unrestricted discussion on the role of Ukraine in the Second World War, and especially on the question of collaboration and the phenomenon of the 'Galicia' Division, as well as a way of presenting these problems to the public; this should be the role of public institutions. The failure of institutions to fulfil this role is vital, as the degree of openness, honesty and maturity with which the question of the collaboration and nationalism of the 'Galicia' Division is dealt in Ukraine might be seen as a measure of the development and strength of the nation's political, academic and cultural status.

Discussing the case of Germany, Levy and Dierkes explain that after the Second World War 'the two post-war German states had to reform their history schooling and purge narratives of nationalistic elements.'[64] Such a process never took place in the independent Ukraine, which, of course, faced a very different situation in the early 1990s. Instead of being deconstructed and critically analysed, formerly Soviet as well as nationalistic interpretations of collective memory that suited the government in power continued to influence not only the general idea of national identity, but also textbooks and the education system as a whole. Thus, during the years of Yushchenko's administration, nationalism was presented in positive terms

64 Levy and Dierkes, 'Institutionalising the Past', p. 245.

and manifestations of it were celebrated (e.g., a decree conferring upon Stepan Bandera the status of national hero was passed on 22 January 2010). Now that Viktor Yanukovych's Minister of Education, Dmytro Tabachnyk, himself a historian, is re-interpreting the collective memory of the nation, the rhetoric of nationalistic heroism is replaced by narratives of the heroic struggle in the 'Great Patriotic War' and memorialization of appropriate figures in this context. An example of this is the unveiling of the monument to Stalin in Zaporizhzhia on 5 May 2010, which was subsequently blown up by a group of nationalists on 31 December 2010. The erection of this monument was initiated by the local Communist Party, but the central authorities did not object to it being unveiled. In addition, the police were encouraged by the government to find those who destroyed the monument and arrest them on charges of terrorism.[65] Thus, instead of encouraging an open and critical approach to the collective national memory, successive Ukrainian governments replace one set of interpretations with another, leaving no room for a neutral discussion of Ukraine's controversial historical pages and thereby complicating further the unresolved conflicts with regard to the national past and the Ukrainian identity.

The appointment of the new government in Ukraine in March 2010 brought about changes with regard to the way history is presented by the national institutions. The position of the current government, as represented by figures such as Tabachnyk, is more authoritarian than it was in Yushchenko's time.[66] In spite of these changes, one concern remains the same: the approach which national institutions take towards history under

65 Olesia Oleshko, 'People who don't like Stalin may be going to jail', *Kyiv Post* (14 January 2011) <http://www.kyivpost.com/content/ukraine/people-who-dont-like-stalin-may-be-going-to-jail-94839.html?flavour=mobile> accessed 18 December 2012.

66 In 2010, Ruslan Zabilyi, a Ukrainian historian, was detained by SBU agents who confiscated his research material. This provoked protest in the international academic community with a number of scholars objecting to the Security Service's actions, even though many of them disagreed with Zabilyi's political views and his perception of Ukrainian history. See 'Petition by historians in response to detention of their colleague Ruslan Zabily', *Human Rights in Ukraine* (15 September 2010) <http://khpg.org/en/index.php?id=1284550630> accessed 27 August 2012.

the current government, just as during Yushchenko's time, is politically framed. There is very little prospect of widespread, independent academic discussion.[67] Access to vital archives has been restricted by the state, making the possibility of research into controversial subjects, such as the Second World War, difficult. Ukrainian scholars who deal with the Second World War and the role of Ukraine in it face the dilemma of either going along with the rhetoric approved by the government (in Yuschenko's time it was a nationalistic rhetoric, and under Yanukovych it is counter-nationalistic) or forming 'oppositional' cliques that stand by their traditional (left or right) views of history.

Attempts to politically frame history are inevitable, especially in a country which tends to present its historiography through nationalistic or anti-nationalistic prisms even before politicians get involved. Such framing often employs 'macro-narratives', which are unhelpful in the formation of a productive and nuanced debate. Thus the challenge for Ukrainian historiography is to offer an alternative to such 'macro-narratives' and to minimize the overlap of the political framing within academic debate. This could be achieved through promoting and maintaining state detachment from scholarly debate, and securing genuinely independent funding for impartial, politically unengaged scholarship. Additionally, working in collaboration with other scholars when it comes to controversial and polarized topics, and involving a large variety of multilingual sources for historical research, will assure minimal selectivity in the examination of the complex and controversial pages of Ukrainian history, such as the analysis of the 'Galicia' Division's history and narratives.

67 There are some venues for an open debate in Ukraine, but they usually operate on insufficient funding and reach very limited audiences. For instance, see 'Pam'iat' iak pole zmahan'', *Ukraïna Moderna*, 15/4 (2009) <http://www.uamoderna.com/arkhiv/40-menuprochasopys/archivzhurnalu/15/11-pamiat152009> accessed 29 August 2012. This volume includes a number of articles by leading scholars in the field of memory studies. Among the topics discussed in the volume is the question of the Second World War. The authors include Georges Mink, Andrzej Nowak, Grzegorz Motyka, Myroslav Shkandrij, Omer Bartov and many others.

Conclusions

In the aftermath of the Second World War, there were about 2.3 million Ukrainian Displaced Persons, most of whom were *Ostarbeiter* from pre-1939 Soviet Ukraine.[1] During the repatriation process, a large number of displaced Ukrainians returned to the USSR voluntarily or were repatriated against their will, yet about 200,000 DPs of Ukrainian origin refused to return to the Soviet Union.[2] Many of those who decided to remain in Western Europe or seek routes to migrate to the USA or Canada had reasons not to return to the USSR. These reasons included their or their family members' involvement in nationalist activities or military resistance. Only just over 8,000 of the 200,000 DPs were former members of the Waffen SS 'Galicia' Division. Despite this, however, the Division's collaboration with Nazi Germany became associated with the wider Ukrainian community in the West. As a result of the controversy which surrounded the 'Galicia', the Division's history remained poorly examined: much of what is known about the 'Galicia' comes either from works written by the Division members themselves or those who vigorously criticize them. Both strands produce powerful and still influential narratives, yet very few of them go beyond justification or condemnation of the Division and actually look into the contextual setting which allowed for this formation to exist and for its former members to be allowed to move to the West.

In his *Ordinary Men*,[3] Christopher Browning suggests that it was not only the different strands of anti-Semitism found in Germany after 1933 that

1 Subtelny, *Ukraine: A History*, pp. 554–5. Marta Dyczok gives a similar estimate, suggesting that in May 1945 approximately three million of the displaced people in Europe were Ukrainian. Marta Dyczok, *The Grand Alliance and Ukrainian Refugees* (Oxford: Macmillan Press in association with St Antony's College, 2000), p. 42.

2 Dyczok, *The Grand Alliance*, p. 42. See also Subtelny, *Ukraine: A History*, pp. 554–5.

3 Christopher R. Browning, *Ordinary Men: Reserve Police Battalion 101 and the Final Solution in Poland* (New York: HarperPerennial, 1993). Reserve Police Battalion 101

were supported by 'ordinary Germans', but that a number of other factors played a part in the rise in support for the Nazis.[4] Browning also points out that 'before the Final Solution was implemented [...] the Nazi regime had already found willing executioners for 70,000 to 80,000 mentally and physically handicapped Germans, tens of thousands of the Polish intelligentsia, tens of thousands of non-combatant victims of reprisal shootings, and more than 2 million Russian POWs.'[5] This in no way aims to belittle the scale of the Holocaust and the tragedy of the Jewish population of Europe. Browning tries to explain the realities of the Nazi regime and, in order to do so accurately, he examines all aspects of the regime, rather than focusing on the Holocaust alone. Such a contextual approach can in fact help us to understand the Holocaust itself. In the same way, the question of the existence of the 'Galicia' Division has to be looked at in the larger context of the pre-war and wartime history of Ukraine and the position of Ukrainian nationalist movements in these periods. In this context, the absence of an explanation of the growing popularity of radical nationalism in Ukraine leads to a failure to understand why there were over 80,000 Ukrainian men who were willing to join a Waffen SS division. When the background information of the period is combined with the individual testimonies of the 'Galicians' and the archival material, it becomes apparent that there was no one reason for the existence of the Waffen SS 'Galicia'. This formation was not solely a product of the growing anti-Semitism in western Ukraine, nor of the popularization of Nazi ideology, nor of the desire of the nationalist leaders to form an independent Ukrainian army. The 'Galicia' was formed as a result of a complex combination of factors, rooted in the specificity of Ukrainian nationalism and the changing situation throughout Europe.

With regard to war crimes allegations, part of the complexity of the Division's history lies in the fact that the wartime history of the 'Galicia' as a division and the histories of its members are not entirely the same thing. If treated as a whole, the Division is not held responsible for war

---

was a unit of the *Ordnungspolizei* who played an important role in the implementation of the 'Final Solution'.

4 *Ibid.*, p. 202.

5 *Ibid.*, p. 203.

crimes, yet if individual members' histories were to be traced, it would become apparent that a number of Ukrainians who became members of the Division towards the end of the war had previously been engaged in units that were formally held responsible for committing war crimes. At the same time, the tracing of the individual histories might reveal that many of the 'Galicians' had no part in war crimes in which the Division has been implicated. As for the civilianization process of the 'Galician' men, this part of the Division's history makes the Waffen SS 'Galicia' stand out among other military and paramilitary groups that were fighting on the German side during the war. Like the question of war crime allegations, the fact that the Division was not repatriated to the USSR remains at the centre of the discussion of the 'Galicia's' history. In order to understand how the remarkable decisions of the UK authorities with regard to the Waffen SS 'Galicia' were made, while similar groups such as the Cossacks received the opposite treatment, it is important to contextualize every step of the process of the Division's civilianization.

The kind of contextualization described above is indispensable when examining the conditions in which the 'Galicia' Division was created and existed. Similarly, it is necessary to contextualize the presentation which the Division has received since the end of the war. In other words, in order to understand why the Division has been presented in a particular light by different commentators in the post-war Europe or North America as well as in contemporary Ukraine, the political climate of each of these periods has to be examined. All narratives about the Division came to exist for reasons relevant to the time in which they were produced, starting from the end of the war and until the present day. It is therefore essential to study not only all the narratives about the Division, but also how these narratives came to exist and the influence they subsequently had. It is to this process that this study aims to contribute.

> [...H]istory for historians, as well as in a general sense, is essentially a continuous reinterpretation of something that is already known [...] The basis of the historian's task is not to retrieve something that has been forgotten. The myths [...] matter to the historians merely for the significance they have had in the relationship between men [sic].[6]

6 Levi, 'Historians, Psychoanalysis and Truth', p. 81.

The many myths of the 'Galicia' Division matter precisely because of the significance they carry today. If these myths receive more attention in more open discussion, the groups and individuals who reproduce them will be encouraged to re-evaluate their position. This might make a start in the discussion of other aspects of the Second World War, a period which, in Ukraine in particular, consists of a series of ossified myths that still have the power to determine the relationships between people.

> [...T]he task of the historian is to achieve empathy with the protagonists of the event he or she is writing on; and [...] there are always (at least) two sides. The *Verstehen* [...] can be achieved only by empathy with the other, not through mere pity or shame, guilt or rage, but through learning, study and an effort at understanding.[7]

An attempt to understand the 'other' among both the critics and the defenders of the Division would manifest steps towards changing the current patterns of using history for political ends. Such a move would bring the historiography of the Second World War closer to a balanced and nuanced view on hotly disputed topics, such as that of the Waffen SS 'Galicia' Division, and may even, if political manipulation can be minimized, help to diffuse wider social tensions.

7 Omer Bartov, 'German Soldiers and the Holocaust. Historiography, Research and Implications', in Gulie Ne'eman Arad, ed., *History and Memory. Passing into History: Nazism and the Holocaust beyond Memory* (Tel Aviv: Tel Aviv University, 1997), p. 181.

Bibliography

Agamben, Georgio, *Infancy and History* (London: Verso, 2007).

——, *Remnants of Auschwitz* (New York: Zone Books, 2002).

Analitychnyi zvit za rezul'tatamy sotsiolohichnoho doslidzhennia 'Stavlennia naselennia Ukraïny do problem pov'iazanykh iz II svitovoiu viinoiu' (Kyiv: Vseukraïns'ka sotsiolohichna sluzhba, 2009).

Anderson, Benedict, *Imagined Communities* (London: Verso, 1983).

Andreyev, Catherine, *Vlasov and the Russian Liberation Movement: Soviet Reality and Emigré Theories* (Cambridge: Cambridge University Press, 1987).

Arkusha, Ihor, 'Dyviziia SS "Halychyna". Pravda i vyhadky', *Narodnyi ohliadach* (27 April 2007) <http://sd.org.ua/news.php?id=11849> accessed 12 October 2012.

Armstrong, John Alexander, *Ukrainian Nationalism, 1939–1945*, 2nd rev. edn (New York: Columbia University Press, 1963).

——, 'Collaborationism in World War II: The Integral Nationalist Variant in Eastern Europe', *Journal of Modern History* 40/3 (September 1968), 396–410.

Assmann, Jan, *Religion and Cultural Memory* (Stanford, CA: Stanford University Press, 2006).

——, and John Czaplicka, 'Collective Memory and Cultural Identity', *New German Critique* 65, Cultural History/Cultural Studies (Spring–Summer, 1995), 125–33.

Axis History Factbook <http://www.axishistory.com/index.php?id=1959> accessed 18 February 2011.

Bąkowski, Władysław, *Zagłada Huty Pieniackiej* (Kraków: Biblioteka Złoczowska, 2001).

Bartov, Omer, 'German Soldiers and the Holocaust. Historiography, Research and Implications', in Gulie Ne'eman Arad, ed., *History and Memory. Passing into History: Nazism and the Holocaust beyond Memory* (Tel Aviv: Tel Aviv University, 1997), 162–89.

——, *Mirrors of Destruction. War, Genocide, and Identity* (Oxford: Oxford University Press, 2000).

Berkhoff, Karel C., *Harvest of Despair: Life and Death in Ukraine under Nazi Rule* (Cambridge, MA: The Belknap Press of Harvard University Press, 2004).

——, and Marco Carynnyk, 'The Organization of Ukrainian Nationalists and Its Attitude toward Germans and Jews: Iaroslav Stetsko's 1941 *Zhyttiepys*, *Harvard Ukrainian Studies* 23/3–4 (1999), 149–84.

Bhabha, Homi, *The Location of Culture* (London: Routledge, 1994).
——, ed., *Nation and Narration* (London: Routledge, 1990).
Bihl, Wolfdieter, 'Ukrainians in the Armed Forces of the Reich: the 14th *Waffen* Grenadier Division of the SS', in Hans-Joachim Torke and John-Paul Himka, eds, *German-Ukrainian Relations in Historical Perspective* (Edmonton: Canadian Institute of Ukrainian Studies Press, 1994), 138–62.
Blosfelds, Mintauts, *Stormtrooper on the Eastern Front. Fighting with Hitler's Latvian SS* (Barnsley: Pen & Sword, 2008).
Bociurkiw, Bohdan R., 'Sheptyts'kyi and the Ukrainian Greek Catholic Church under Soviet Occupation, 1939–1941', in Paul Robert Magocsi, ed., *Morality and Reality: The Life and Times of Andrei Sheptyts'kyi* (Edmonton: Canadian Institute of Ukrainian Studies Press, 1990), 101–24.
——, *The Ukrainian Greek Catholic Church and the Soviet State (1939–1950)* (Edmonton: Canadian Institute of Ukrainian Studies Press, 1996).
Bolianovs'kyi, Andrii, *Dyviziia 'Halychyna'. Istoria* (L'viv: IU, 2000).
—— *Ukraïns'ki viis'kovi formuvannia v zbroinykh sylakh Nimechchyny (1939–1945)* (L'viv: LNU im. Ivana Franka, 2003).
Bonnard, Pascal, 'Pam'iat' pro radians'ke mynule ta ievropeis'ki normy vyznannia rozmaïttia kul'tur: superechlyvi modeli etnichnoï klasyfikatsiï u Latviï', *Ukraïna Moderna* 4 (2009), 219–37.
Booth, James, *Communities of Memory* (Ithaca, NY: Cornell University Press, 2006).
Boshyk, Yuri, ed., *Ukraine during World War II: History and Its Aftermath – A Symposium* (Edmonton: Canadian Institute of Ukrainian Studies, University of Alberta, 1986).
Brandon, Ray, and Wendy Lower, *The Shoah in Ukraine. History. Testimony. Memorialisation* (Bloomington, IN: Indiana University Press, 2008).
Brotherhood of Veterans of the 1st-Division of the Ukrainian National Army, 'Response to the recent TV documentary "SS in Britain"' <http://www.infoukes.com/galiciadivision/ss_in_britain_response/> accessed 22 September 2010.
Browning, Christopher, *Ordinary Men: Reserve Police Battalion 101 and the Final Solution in Poland* (New York: HarperPerennial, 1993).
——, *The Origins of the Final Solution: The Evolution of Nazi Jewish Policy, September 1939–March 1942* (Lincoln, NE: University of Nebraska Press, 2004).
Brüggemann, Karsten, and Andres Kasekamp, 'The Politics of History and the "War of Monuments" in Estonia', *Nationalities Papers* 26/3 (2008), 425–48.
Bruns, Roger, *Almost History: Close Calls, Plan B's, and Twists of Fate in America's Past* (New York: Barnes & Noble, 2007).
Budurowycz, Bohdan 'Sheptytski and the Ukrainian National Movement after 1914', in Paul Robert Magosci, ed., *Morality and Reality: The Life and Times of Andrei*

Sheptytsky (Edmonton: Canadian Institute of Ukrainian Studies, University of Alberta, 1989), 47–74.

Bul'ba-Borovets', Taras, *Armiia bez derzhavy* (L'viv: Poklyk sumlinnia, 1993).

Burds, Jeffrey, 'Comments on Timothy Snyder's article "To Resolve the Ukrainian Question Once and for All: The Ethnic Cleansing of Ukrainians in Poland, 1943–1947", *Journal of Cold War Studies*, Vol. 1. No. 2 (Spring 1999)', <www.fas.harvard.edu/~hpcws/comment13.htm> accessed 30 January 2013.

Burke, Peter, 'History as Social Memory', in Thomas Butler, ed., *Memory: History, Culture and the Mind* (Oxford: Blackwell, 1989), 97–113.

——, *New Perspectives on Historical Writing* (University Park, PA: Pennsylvania State University Press, 1991).

Burtyk, Ivan, *Ternystyi shliakh Druhoï Dyvizii UNA: stvorennia UNK i Druhoï Dyvizii UNA* (New York: Ob'iednannia Voiakiv i Pryiateliv Druhoï Dyvizii UNA, 1994).

Caldicott, Eric, and Anne Fuchs, eds, *Cultural Memory* (Oxford: Peter Lang, 2003).

Cesarani, David, *Justice Delayed: How Britain Became a Refuge for Nazi War Criminals* (London: Heinemann, 1992).

——, *Report on the Entry of War Criminals and Collaborators into the UK, 1945–1950* (London: All Parliamentary War Crimes Group, House of Commons, 1988).

Chernov, Viktor, and Andrei Shliakhtunov, *Pribaltiiskie Waffen-SS. Geroi ili palachi* (Moscow: Lin-Inter, 2004).

Chuev, Sergei, *Ukrainskii legion* (Moscow: Iauza, 2006).

Civitarese, Guiseppe, *The Intimate Room. Theory and Technique of the Analytic Field* (London: Routledge, 2010).

Connerton, Paul, *How Societies Remember* (Cambridge: Cambridge University Press, 1989).

Conquest, Robert, *Harvest of Sorrow: Soviet Collectivization and the Terror-Famine* (Oxford: Oxford University Press, 1986).

Dallin, Alexander, *German Rule in Russia, 1941–1945: A Study of Occupation Policies* (London: Macmillan, 1957).

Davies, Norman, *Europe. A History* (Oxford: Oxford University Press, 1996).

——, 'The Misunderstood Victory in Europe', *The New York Review of Books* (25 May 1995), 7–10.

Dean, Martin, *Collaboration during the Holocaust: Crimes of the Local Police in Belorussia and Ukraine, 1941–44*. (New York: St Martin's Press, published in association with the United States Holocaust Memorial Museum, 2000).

Deschênes, Jules, 'Commission of Inquiry on War Criminals', *Report, Part 1: Public* (Ottawa: Minister of Supply and Services, 1986).

Donald, James and Stuart Hall, eds, *Politics and Ideology* (Milton Keynes: Open University Press, 1986).

Dontsov, Dmytro, *Natsionalizm* (London and Toronto: Ukraïns'ka vydavnycha spilka, 1966).

Dorril, Stephen, *MI6* (London: Fourth Estate, 1998).

Dyczok, Marta, *The Grand Alliance and Ukrainian Refugees* (Oxford: Macmillan Press in association with St Antony's College, 2000).

Esbenshade, Richard, 'Remembering to Forget: Memory, History, National Identity in Postwar East-Central Europe', *Representations* 49 (1995), 72–96.

Fedyk, Ihor, 'Heroï nashoï istoriï', *Vholos* (27 February 2012) <http://vgolos.com.ua/blog.431.html?page=1> accessed 22 August 2012.

Ferkuniak, Dmytro, *Uryvky z shchodennyka* (Drohobych: 'Vidrodzhennia', 2003).

Foggo, Daniel, 'London man denies role in SS massacres', *Sunday Telegraph* (26 January 2003) <http://www.telegraph.co.uk/news/uknews/1420071/London-man-denies-role-in-SS-massacres.html> accessed 22 September 2010.

——, 'Police to use NHS records to find Nazi war criminals', *Telegraph* (22 June 2003), <http://www.telegraph.co.uk/news/worldnews/europe/1433729/Police-to-use-NHS-records-to-find-Nazi-war-criminals.html> accessed 2 October 2012.

Fostun, Swiatomyr, *Shliakhamy smerty. Povist' z chasiv II svitovoï viiny* (Buenos Aires: Iulian Serediak, 1979).

——, 'Voïny 1 UD UNA v taborakh viis'kopolonenykh u Velykobrytaniï', in *Persha ukraïns'ka Dyviziia ukraïns'koï natsional'noï armiï: istoriia stvorennia ta natsional'no-politychne znachennya. Materialy Naukovo-praktychnoï konferentsiï. Dopovidi ta povidomlennia* (L'viv: Novyi chas, 2002), 123–6.

Foucault, Michel, *The Archaeology of Knowledge* (London: Routledge, 2008).

——, *Language, Counter-memory, Practice* (Ithaca, NY: Cornell University Press, 1977).

Freud, Sigmund, *Moses and Monotheism* (New York: Vintage Books, 1967).

Friedman, Philip, *Roads to Extinction* (New York: Jewish Publication Society of America, 1980).

Gellner, Ernest, *Nations and Nationalism* (Oxford: Basil Blackwell, 1983).

Ginzburg, Carlo, 'The Philosopher and the Witches: an Experiment in Cultural History', *Acta Ethnographica Academiae Scientarum Hungaricae* 37 (1991–2), 283–92.

——, 'Shared Memories, Private Recollections', in Gulie Ne'eman Arad, ed., *History and Memory. Passing into History: Nazism and the Holocaust beyond Memory* (Tel Aviv: Tel Aviv University, 1997), 353–64.

——, and Carlo Poni, 'The Name and the Game: Unequal Exchange and the Historical Marketplace', in Edward Muir, and Guido Ruggiero, eds, *Microhistory and the Lost People of Europe*, trans. Eren Branch (Baltimore, MD: Johns Hopkins University Press, 1991), 1–10.

Gitelman, Zvi, 'The Decline of the Diaspora Jewish Nation: Boundaries, Content, and Jewish Identity', *Jewish Social Studies* New Series, 4/2 (Winter 1998), 112–32.

Gogun, Alexander, *Mezhdu Gitlerom i Stalinym. Ukrainskie povstantsy* (St Petersburg: Neva, 2004).

Golczewski, Frank, *Deutsche und Ukrainer 1914–1939* (Paderborn: Ferdinand Schöningh Verlag, 2010).

——, 'Shades of Grey: Reflections on Jewish-Ukrainian and German-Ukrainian Relations in Galicia', in Ray Brandon, and Wendy Lower, eds, *The Shoah in Ukraine: History, Testimony, Memorialization* (Bloomington, IN: Indiana University Press, 2008), 114–55.

Greenfield, Richard, 'Denis Hills. Post-Yalta whistle-blower later sentenced to death by Idi Amin', *The Independent* (11 May 2004) <http://www.independent.co.uk/news/obituaries/denis-hills-549904.html> accessed 20 September 2010.

Gross, Jan, *Neighbors: The Destruction of the Jewish Community in Jedwabne, Poland* (Princeton, NJ: Princeton University Press, 2001).

——, *Revolution from Abroad. The Soviet Conquest of Poland's Western Ukraine and Western Belorussia* (Princeton, NJ: Princeton University Press, 1988).

Halbwachs, Maurice, *On Collective Memory*, edited by Lewis A. Coser (Chicago, IL: University of Chicago Press, 1992).

Hall, Stuart, David Held, Don Hubert, and Kenneth Thompson, eds, *Modernity. An Introduction to Modern Societies* (Oxford: Blackwell, 1996).

Hatch, J. Amos and Richard Wisniewski, eds, *Life History and Narrative* (London: Falmer, 1995).

Heike, Wolf-Dietrich, *Sie Wollten Die Freiheit. Die Geschichte der Ukrainischen Division 1943–1945* (Dorheim: Podzun, 1973).

——, *Ukraïns'ka Dyviziia 'Halychyna'. Istoriia formuvannia i boiovykh dii u 1943–45* (Ternopil': Mandrivets', 2012).

——, *The Ukrainian Division 'Galicia', 1943–1945. A Memoir* (Toronto: Shevchenko Scientific Society, 1988).

——, *Ukraïns'ka Dyviziia Halychyna: Istoriia formuvannia i boiovykh dii u 1943–45* (Toronto: Zapysky/Naukove tovarystvo im. Shevchenka, 1970).

Hendy, Julian (producer), *SS in Britain*, Yorkshire TV, Leeds (2000).

——, '"SS in Britain", submission to the Independent Television Commission. The 14th SS Division Galizien and War Crimes in Nizna Boca, Slovakia. October 1944' (Yorkshire Television, October 2001).

Hilberg, Raul, *The Destruction of the European Jews* (Chicago, IL: Quadrangle Books, 1961).

Hills, Denis, 'You are the Grey Mass', *The Spectator* 23/30 (December 1989).

Himka, John-Paul, 'Christianity and Radical Nationalism: Metropolitan Andrei Sheptytsky and the Bandera Movement', in Catherine Wanner, ed, *State Secularism and Lived Religion in Soviet Russia and Ukraine* (New York: Oxford University Press, 2012), 93–116.

——, 'Falsifying World War II history in Ukraine', *Kyiv Post* (8 May 2011).

——, 'The Lviv Pogrom of 1941: The Germans, Ukrainian Nationalists, and the Carnival Crowd', *Canadian Slavonic Papers/Revue canadienne des slavistes* LIII/2–4 (June–September–December 2011), 209–43.

——, 'The Organization of Ukrainian Nationalists and the Ukrainian Insurgent Army: Unwelcome Elements of an Identity Project', *Ab Imperio*, 4 (2010), 83–101 <http://www.academia.edu/499198/The_Organization_of_Ukrainian_Nationalists_and_the_Ukrainian_Insurgent_Army_Unwelcome_Elements_of_an_Identity_Project> accessed 30 January 2013.

——, *Ukrainians, Jews and the Holocaust: Divergent Memories* (Saskatoon: Heritage Press, 2009).

——, 'Be Wary of Faulty Nachtigall Lessons' *Kyiv Post* (27 March 2008) <http://www.kyivpost.com/opinion/oped/28686/> accessed 11 February 2013.

——, 'True and False Lessons from the Nachtigall Episode', *BRAMA* (19 March 2008) <http://www.brama.com/news/press/2008/03/080319himka_nachtigall.html> accessed 6 May 2011.

——, 'Obstacles to the Integration of the Holocaust into Post-Communist East European Historical Narratives', *Canadian Slavonic Papers/Revue canadienne des slavistes* L/3–4 (September–December 2008), 359–72.

——, 'War Criminality: A Blank Spot in the Collective Memory of the Ukrainian Diaspora' *spacesofidentity* 5.1 (2005) 9–24.

Hirsch, Marianne, *Family Frames: Photography, Narrative, and Postmemory* (Cambridge, MA: Harvard University Press, 1997).

Höhne, Heinz, *The Order of the Death's Head: The Story of Hitler's SS* (London: Secker & Warburg, 1969).

Hrycyszyn, Michael, *God Save Me From My Friends. A Ukrainian Memoir* (Cambridge: Pegasus Elliot Mackenzie Publishers, 2006).

Hrytsak, Iaroslav, 'Svoiu doliu dyviziinyky ne vybyraly…', *Visti Kombatanta* 3 (2007), 63–5.

——, 'Ukraïns'ka istoriohrafiia. 1991–2001: Desiatylittia zmin', *Ukraïna Moderna*, 9 (2005) 43–68.

——, *Strasti za natsionalizmom, Istorychni eseï* (Kyiv: Krytyka, 2004).

——, *Mizh dvoma totalitaryzmamy. Ob'iednannia ukraïns'kykh zemel' ta radianizatsiia zakhidnoï Urkaïny 1939–1941* (L'viv: Vesna, 2000).

Hrytsak, Pavlo, *Vezhi i kulemety, spohady z dyvizii i bol'shevyts'koho polonu* (Munich: Vydannia bratstva kol. Voiakiv 1-oï Dyvizii UNA, 1959).

Hunczak, Taras, *U mundyrakh voroha* (Brody: Prosvita, 2005).

——, *On the Horns of a Dilemma* (New York: University Press of America, 2000).

——, *Ukraïna. Persha polovyna XX stolittia* (Kyiv: Lybid', 1993).

'Iak tvorylasia lehenda pro Nachtigall', *Dzerkalo tyzhnia* (16 February 2008), <http://www.ssu.gov.ua/sbu/control/uk/publish/article?art_id=74855&cat_id=74589> accessed 12 August 2012.

Iggers, Georg G., *Historiography in the Twentieth Century: from Scientific Objectivity to the Postmodern Challenge* (Hanover, NH: Wesleyan University Press, 1997).

Joachim, Joesten, 'Hitler's Fiasco in the Ukraine', *Foreign Affairs* 21/2 (January 1943), 331–9.

Judt, Tony, 'The Past Is Another Country: Myth and Memory in Post War Europe', in Jan Werner Muller, ed., *Memory and Power in Post-War Europe. Studies in the Presence of the Past* (Cambridge: Cambridge University Press, 2002), 157–83.

Jurado, Carlos Caballero, *Foreign Volunteers of the Wehrmacht, 1941–45* (London: Osprey, 1983).

Kal'ba, Myroslav, *Nakhtigal' v zapytanniakh i vidpovidiakh* (L'viv: Halyts'ka vydavnycha spilka, 2008).

Kamenetsky, Ihor, *Secret Nazi Plans for Eastern Europe: A Study of Lebensraum Policies* (New York: Bookman Associates, 1961).

Kappeler, Andreas, 'Ukrainian History from a German Perspective', *Slavic Review* 54/3 (1995), 691–701.

Khromeychuk, Olesya, 'The Shaping of "Historical Truth": Construction and Reconstruction of the Memory and Narrative of the Waffen SS "Galicia" Division', *Canadian Slavonic Papers/ Revue canadienne des slavistes* LIV/3–4 (September–December 2012), 61–86.

King, Nicola, *Memory, Narrative, Identity. Remembering the Self* (Edinburgh: Edinburgh University Press, 2000).

Kolisnyk, Roman, *Viis'kova Uprava ta ukraïns'ka Dyviziia Halychyna* (Kyiv: Iaroslaviv Val, 2009).

——, Bohdan Matsiv, and Leonid Mukha, eds, *Dyviziia 'Halychyna' v zapytanniakh i vidpovidiakh veteraniv* (L'viv: Halyts'ka vydavnycha spilka, 2009).

Korduba, Feliks, *Dyvizion tiazhkoï artyleriï pid Brodamy* (Drohobych: 'Vidrodzhennia', 2003).

Kosyk, Volodymyr, ed., *Ukraïna v Druhii Svitovii viini u dokumentakh. Zbirnyk nimets'kykh arkhivnykh materialiv (1944–1945)* (L'viv: L'vivs'kyi natsional'nyi universytet imeni Ivana Franka; NANU, 2000).

Krawchenko, Bohdan, *Social Change and National Consciousness in Twentieth Century Ukraine* (Basingstoke: Macmillan in association with St Antony's College, Oxford, 1985).

Kubiiovych, Volodymyr, *Ukraïntsi v Heneral'nii Hubernii, 1939–1941. Istoriia ukraïns'koho tsentral'noho komitetu* (Chicago, IL: Vydavnytstvo Mykoly Denysiuka, 1975).

——, 'Pochatky Ukraïns'koï Dyvizii "Halychyna"', *Visti Bratstva Kol. Voiakiv 1 UD UNA*, 3–4 (1954). <http://www.google.com/gwt/n?u=http%3A%2F%2Flib.galiciadivision.com%2Farticles%2Fkubijovich.html> accessed 7 February 2013.

Kul'chyts'kyi, Stanislav, *Orhanizatsiia ukraïns'kykh natsionalistiv i Ukraïns'ka povstans'ka armiia* (Kyiv: Naukova Dumka, 2005).

——, 'Velykyi Holod', *Istoriia v shkolakh Ukraïny* 3 (2003), 51–2.

Kuropas, Myron, *The Ukrainian Americans. Roots and Aspirations 1884–1954* (Toronto: University of Toronto, 1991).

Laplanche, Jean, *Problématiques VI: L'après-coup – La Nachträglichkeit dans l'après-coup (1990–1991)* (Paris: PUF, 2006).

Lappin, Eleonore, *The Death Marches of Hungarian Jews Through Austria in the Spring of 1945*, Yad Vashem Articles Archive (19 February 2009) <http://www1.yadvashem.org/yv/en/exhibitions/death_march/articles.asp> accessed 1 October 2012.

Lazurko, Roman, *Na shliakhakh Ievropy* (Chicago: Vydavnytstvo Bratstva kolyshnikh Voiakiv 1 UD UNA, 1971).

Levi, Giovanni, 'Historians, Psychoanalysis and Truth', in Anna-Marija Castrén, Markku Lonkila, and Matti Peltonen, eds, *Between Sociology and History. Essays on Microhistory, Collective Action, and Nation-Building* (Helsinki: Finnish Literature Society, 2004), 71–87.

Levy, Daniel, and Julian Dierkes, 'Institutionalising the Past: Shifting Memories of Nationhood in German Education and Immigration Legislation', in Jan Werner Muller, ed., *Memory and Power in Post-War Europe. Studies in the Presence of the Past* (Cambridge: Cambridge University Press, 2002), 244–64.

Liber, George O., *Soviet National Policy, Urban Growth, and Identity Change in the Ukrainian SSR 1923–1934* (Cambridge: Cambridge University Press, 1992).

Littlejohn, David, *The Patriotic Traitors: A History of Collaboration in German Occupied Europe, 1940–1945* (London: Heinemann, 1972).

Littman, Sol, *Pure Soldiers or Sinister Legion, The Ukrainian 14th Waffen-SS Division* (London: Black Rose Books, 2003).

Livyts'kyi, Mykola, *DTs UNR v ekzyli mizh 1920–1940* (Munich: Ukraïns'ke informatsiine biuro, 1984).

Logusz, Michael O., *Galicia Division: The Waffen-SS 14th Grenadier Division, 1943–1945* (Altglen, PA: Schiffer Military History, 1997).

Lotnik, Waldemar, *Nine Lives: Ethnic Conflict in the Polish-Ukrainian Borderlands* (London: Serif, 1999).

Lower, Wendy, *Nazi Empire-Building and the Holocaust in Ukraine* (Chapel Hill, NC: University of North Carolina Press in association with the United States Holocaust Memorial Museum, 2005).

Luciuk, Lubomyr Y., 'Unintended Consequences in Refugee Resettlement: Post-War Ukrainian Refugee Immigration to Canada', *International Migration Review*, 20/2, Special Issue: *Refugees: Issues and Directions* (Summer 1986), 467–82.

Lysiak, Oleh, *Za strilets'kyi zvychai* (Munich: Vydannia Bratstva kol. Voiakiv 1-oï UD UNA, 1953).

Mace, James E., *Communism and the Dilemma of National Liberation: National Communism in Soviet Ukraine, 1918–1933* (Cambridge, MA: Harvard University Press, 1983).

Mackiewicz, Józef, *Kontra* (London: Kontra, 1993).

Magnusson, Sigurdur Gylfi, 'The Singularization of History: Social History and Microhistory within the Postmodern State of Knowledge', *Journal of Social History* 36 (Spring 2003), 701–35.

Magosci, Paul R., *The Roots of Ukrainian Nationalism: Galicia as Ukraine's Piedmont* (Toronto: University of Toronto Press, 2002).

Malkosh, Volodymyr, *Ukraïns'ka dyviziia 'Halychyna' v svitli 'lehionovoï' polityky XX storichchia* (Ivano-Frankivs'k: Lileia-NV, 2007).

Margolian, Howard, *Unauthorized Entry: The Truth about Nazi War Criminals in Canada, 1946–1956* (Toronto: University of Toronto Press, 2000).

Marples, David R., *Holodomor: Causes of the Famine of 1932–1933 in Ukraine* (Saskatoon: Heritage Press, 2011).

——, 'Beyond the Pale?: Conceptions and Reflections in Contemporary Ukraine about the Division Galizien', *Journal of Ukrainian Studies* 33–4 (2008–9), 337–50.

——, *Heroes and Villains. Creating National History in Contemporary Ukraine* (Budapest: Central European University Press, 2007).

Martynowych, Orest T., 'Sympathy for the Devil: The Attitude of Ukrainian War Veterans in Canada to Nazi Germany and the Jews, 1933–1939', in Rhonda L. Hinther and Jim Mochoruk, eds, *Re-imagining Ukrainian Canadians: History, Politics, and Identity* (Toronto: University of Toronto Press, 2011).

Melnyk, Michael James, *To Battle. The Formation and History of the 14th Galician Waffen-SS Division* (Solihull: Helion & Company, 2002).

Mick, Christoph, 'Incompatible Experiences: Poles, Ukrainians and Jews in Lviv under Soviet and Nazi Occupation, 1939–1944', *Journal of Contemporary History* 46/2 (2011), 336–63.

Midzhak, Oleksa, *Pomsta komunistam. Poryv: Pravda pro Pershu Ukraïns'ku Dyviziyu (UNA) 'Halychyna' (Statti, narysy, spohady)* (L'viv: 'Osnova', 1994).

Mikhnovs'kyi, Mykola, *Samostiina Ukraïna* (London: Nakladom Viddilu Soiuzu Ukraïntsiv u Velykii Brytaniï u Volverhemptoni, 1967).

Mitchell, Ian, *The Cost of a Reputation* (Lagavulin: Topical Books, 1997).

Moller, Lis, *The Freudian Reading: Analytical and Fictional Constructions* (Philadelphia, PA: University of Pennsylvania Press, 1991).

Motyka, Grzegorz, *Od rzezi wołyńskiej do akcji 'Wisła'. Konflikt polsko-ukraiński 1943–1947* (Kraków: Wydawnictwo Literackie, 2011).

——, *Ukraińska partyzantka 1942–1960* (Warszawa: Instytut Studiów Politycznych PAN Oficyna Wydawnicza RYTM, 2006).

——, and Rafał Wnuk, *Pany i rezuny. Współpraca AK-WiN i UPA w latach 1945–1947* (Warszawa: Oficyna Wydawnicza Volumen, 1997).

Motyl, Alexander J. *The Turn to the Right: The Ideological Origins and Development of Ukrainian Nationalism, 1919–1929*. (New York: Boulder, 1980).

Mukha, Leonid, *Z Avstriï na Kolymu* (L'viv: Liha-Pres, 2010).

Nahaievs'kiyi, Ivan, *Spohady pol'ovoho dukhivnyka* (Toronto: Ukraïns'ka Knyzhka, 1955).

Newland, Samuel J., *Cossacks in the German Army 1941–1945* (London: Frank Cass, 1991).

'Oholosheno peremozhtsiv oblasnoï premiï imeni Heroia Ukraïny Stepana Bandery', *L'vivs'ka Hazeta* (26 June 2012) <http://www.gazeta.lviv.ua/news/2012/06/26/3506> accessed 22 August 2012.

Oleshko, Olesia, 'People who don't like Stalin may be going to jail', *Kyiv Post* (14 January 2011) <http://www.kyivpost.com/content/ukraine/people-who-dont-like-stalin-may-be-going-to-jail-94839.html?flavour=mobile> accessed 18 December 2012.

Olick, Jeffrey K., and Joyce Robbins, 'Social Memory Studies: From "Collective Memory" to the Historical Sociology of Mnemonic Practices', *Annual Review of Sociology* 24 (1998), 105–40.

Olszański, Tadeusz Andrzej, 'Konflikt polsko-ukraiński 1943–1947', *Więź* 11–12/397 (1991), 214–33.

Ortyns'kyyi, Liubomyr, *Vylim z Brids'koho kitla/Uryvky z spomyniv* (L'viv: 'Osnova', 1994).

Pahiria, Oleksandr, 'Zhinocha Sich', *Ukraïna Moloda* 047 (13 March 2010) <htp://www.umoloda.kiev.ua/number/1614/196/56827/> accessed 6 December 2012.

'Pam'iat' iak pole zmahan", *Ukraïna Moderna*, 15/4 (2009) <http://www.uamoderna.com/arkhiv/40-menuprochasopys/archivzhurnalu/15/11-pamiat152009> accessed 29 August 2012.

Panchuk, Bohdan, *Heroes of their Day: The Reminiscences of Bohdan Panchuk* (Toronto: Multicultural History Society of Ontario, 1983).

Pan'kivs'kyi, Kost', *Roky nimets'koï okupatsiï 1941–1944* (New York: Newark, 1983).

Patryliak, Ivan, *Viis'kova diial'nist' OUN (B) u 1940–1942 rokakh* (Kyiv: Kyïvs'kyi natsional'nyi universytet imeni Tarasa Shevchenka Instytut istoriï Ukranïy NAN Ukranïy, 2004).

Pawlowsky, Vasyl, 'Four Ukrainian activists killed in a car accident in Lviv Oblast', *Ukrainian Weekly* (1 August 2004) <http://www.scribd.com/doc/12815589/The-Ukrainian-Weekly-200431> accessed 18 November 2012.

'Petition by historians in response to detention of their colleague Ruslan Zabily', *Human Rights in Ukraine* (15 September 2010) <http://khpg.org/en/index.php?id=1284550630> accessed 27 August 2012.

Piotrowski, Tadeusz, *Poland's Holocaust: Ethnic Strife, Collaboration with Occupying Forces and Genocide in the Second Republic, 1918–1947* (London: McFarland, 1998).

Pobihushchyi, Ievhen, *Mozaïka moïkh spomyniv* (Ivano-Frankivs'k: Lileia-NV, 2002).

Pohl, Dieter, 'Anti-Jewish Pogroms in Western Ukraine – A Research Agenda', in Eleazar Barkan, Elizabeth A. Cole, and Kai Struve, *Shared History – Divided Memory: Jews and Others in Soviet-Occupied Poland, 1939–1941* (Leipzig: Leipziger Universitätsverlag, 2007) 305–13.

——, *Nationalsozialistische Judenverfolgung in Ostgalizien 1941–1944: Organisation und Durchführung eines staatlichen Massenverbrechens* (Munich: R. Oldenbourg Verlag, 1997).

Poliuliakh, Ivan, *Nazustrich tankam* (Drohobych: 'Vidrodzhennia', 2003).

Portnov, Andrii V., 'Memory Wars in Post-Soviet Ukraine (1991–2010)', in Uilleam Blacker, Alexander Etkind, Julie Fedor, eds, *Memory and Theory in Eastern Europe* (Palgrave Macmillan, forthcoming).

——, '"Nestacha porozhniaka", abo novyi pidruchnyk z istoriï vid Tabachnyka', *Zakhid.net* <http://zaxid.net/home/showSingleNews.do?nestacha_porozhnyaka_abo_noviy_pidruchnik_z_istoriyi_vid_tabachnika&objectId=1236705> accessed 7 February 2013.

'Prohrama dlia zahal'noosvitnikh navchal'nykh zakladiv. Istoriia Ukraïny 10–11 klasy. Riven' standartu' <http://osvita.ua/school/materials/program/30993/> accessed 14 November 2012.

Prus, Edward, *SS-Galizien. Patrioci czy zbrodniarze?* (Wrocław: Nortom, 2001).

Pryshliak, Hryhorii, *Z kohorty nerozstrilianykh: Spohady, vystupy, poeziï* (Kolomyiia: Vik, 2000).

Purves, Grant, *War Criminals: The Deschênes Commission*, Political and Social Affairs Division, revised 16 October 1998, E. The Report of the Deschênes Commission, 1. General <http://dsp-psd.pwgsc.gc.ca/Collection-R/LoPBdP/CIR/873-e.htm> accessed 24 September 2010.

Redlich, Shimon, *Together and Apart in Brzezany: Poles, Jews, and Ukrainians 1919–1945* (Bloomington, IN: Indiana University Press, 2002).

——, 'Metropolitan Andrei Sheptyts'kyi, Ukrainians and Jews During and After the Holocaust', *Holocaust and Genocide Studies* 5/1 (1990), 39–51.

'Reklamy dywizji SS na ulicach Lwowa', *Gazeta.pl* (17 April 2009) <http://m.wiadomosci.gazeta.pl/wiadomosci/1,17915,6510598,Reklamy_dywizji_SS_na_ulicach_Lwowa.html> accessed 14 November 2012.

Rikmenspoel, Marc J., *Waffen-SS Encyclopaedia* (Bedford, PA: The Aberjona Press, 2004).

Roberts, Andrew, 'Blood on Our Hands; They Surrendered in Good Faith Only to Be Sent to Certain Torture and Death; the Betrayal of the Cossacks 60 Years Ago Was Not the Work of the Nazis or the Red Army, but of British Politicians', *The Daily Mail* (4 June 2005).

Rodal, Alti, 'How Perpetrators of Genocidal Crimes Evaded Justice: the Canadian Story', in John K. Roth and Elisabeth Maxwell, eds, *Remembering for the Future. The Holocaust in an Age of Genocide*, Vol 1, History (Basingstoke: Palgrave Macmillan, 2001), 702–25.

——, *Chapter XII – Part 3, The Ukrainian 'Halychyna' (Galician) Waffen-SS Division*, Commission of Inquiry on Nazi War Criminals in Canada (the Deschênes Commission, 1986).

Rolf, *Russen in der Waffen-SS: 29. Waffen-Grenadier-Division der SS 'RONA' (russische Nr. 1), 30. Waffen-Grenadier-Division der SS (russische Nr. 2), SS-Verband 'Drushina'* (Berlin: Michaelis, 2002).

——, Michaelis, *Esten in der Waffen-SS: die 20. Waffen-Grenadier-Division der SS (estnische Nr. 1)* (Berlin: Michaelis, 2000).

Rudling, Per Anders, '"They Defended Ukraine": The 14. Waffen-Grenadier-Division der SS (Galizische Nr. 1) Revisited', *The Journal of Slavic Military Studies* 25/3 (2012), 329–68.

——, 'Navuka zabivats'. 201-y batal'ion akhounai palitsyi i hauptman Raman Shukhevich u Belarusi u 1942 hodze', *ARCHEI* (7–8) (2012), 67– 87.

Schacter, Daniel L., *The Seven Sins of Memory Study: How the Mind Forgets and Remembers* (New York: Houghton Mifflin, 2001).

Schindler, Ella, 'Mynule – sudyty chy vyvchaty?', *Visti Kombatanta* 1 (2007), 34–7.

Shandruk, Pavlo, *Arms of Valor* (New York: Robert Speller, 1959).

——, *Faktychnyi stan i taktychne polozhennya 1 UD UNA pid Brodamy* (L'viv: 'Osnova', 1994).

Shankovs'kyi, Lev, *UPA i Dyviziia* in Mykhailo Slaboshpyts'kyi, ed., *Ukraïns'ka dyviziia 'Halychyna'. Istoryko-publitsystychnyi zbirnyk*, 3rd edn (Kyiv: Iaroslaviv Val, 2008), 66–77.

——, *Ukraïns'ka Armiia v borot'bi za derzhavnist'* (Munich: Dniprova Khvylia, 1958).

Sicher, Efraim, 'The Future of the Past: Countermemory and Postmemory in Contemporary American Post-Holocaust Narratives', *History and Memory* 12/2 (Fall/Winter 2000), 56–91.

Singh, Amritjit, Joseph T. Skerrett, and Robert E. Hogan, eds, *Memory Narrative and Identity. New Essays in Ethnic American Literatures* (Boston, MA: Northeastern University Press, 1994).

Sirs'kyi, Vasyl', *UPA i Dyviziia 'Halychyna' fakty i fantazia* (Canada: nakladom avtora, 2000).

Slaboshpyts'kyi, Mykhailo, ed., *Ukraïns'ka dyviziia 'Halychyna'. Istoryko-publitsystychnyi zbirnyk*, 3rd edn (Kyiv: Iaroslaviv Val, 2008).

——, and Valerii Stetsenko, eds, *Ukraïns'ka dyviziia 'Halychyna'. Istoryko-publitsystychnyi zbirnyk* (Kyiv and Toronto: Bratstvo kolyshnikh voiakiv 1-oï UD UNA, 1994).

Snyder, Timothy, *Bloodlands. Europe Between Hitler and Stalin* (London: Bodley Head, 2010).

——, 'Memory of Sovereignty and Sovereignty over Memory: Poland, Lithuania and Ukraine, 1939–1999', in Jan Werner Muller, ed., *Memory and Power in Post-War Europe. Studies in the Presence of the Past* (Cambridge: Cambridge University Press, 2002), 39–59.

Sodol, Petro, *UPA: They Fought Hitler and Stalin* (New York: Committee for the World Convention and Reunion of Soldiers in the Ukrainian Insurgent Army, 1987).

Stein, George, *The Waffen SS: Hitler's Elite Guard at War, 1939–1945* (Ithaca, NY: Cornell University Press, 1966 and 1984).

Stetkevych, Lev, *Iak z Berezhan do Kadry* (Ternopil': Dzhura, 1998).

Subtelny, Orest, *Ukraine: A History* (Toronto: University of Toronto Press, 1988).

Sych, Oleksandr, 'Natsiokratiia – politychnyi ideal natsionalizmu', *VO Svoboda. Ofitsiina storinka* (17 March 2009) <http://www.svoboda.org.ua/dopysy/dopysy/010221/> accessed 23 August 2012.

Sydorenko, Natalia, *Taborovi budni viis'kovopolonenykh na brytans'kykh ostrovakh (1947–1950)*, in *Persha ukraïns'ka Dyviziia ukraïns'koï natsional'noï armiï: istoriia stvorennia ta natsional'no-politychne znachennia. Materialy Naukovo-praktychnoï konferentsiï. Dopovidi ta povidomlennia* (L'viv: Novyi chas, 2002), 127–46.

Szijárto, István, 'Four Arguments for Microhistory', *Rethinking History* 6/2 (2002), 209–15.

Szkopliak, Zygmunt C., ed., *The Yalta Agreements. Documents prior to, during and after the Crimea Conference 1945* (London: Polish Government in Exile, 1986).

Taylor, Kate, 'Safe Haven in Britain', *The Searchlight Magazine* (February 2001) <http://www.searchlightmagazine.com/index.php?link=template&story=91> accessed 22 September 2010.

Tolstoy, Nikolai, *The Minister and the Massacres* (London: Century Hutchinson, 1986).

——, *The Victims of Yalta* (London: Corgi Book, 1986, original Hodder & Stoughton edn, 1977).

——, *Stalin's Secret War* (London: Jonathan Cape, 1981).

——, *The Secret Betrayal* (New York: Charles Scribner's Sons, 1978).

Topinka, Ievhen, *Tomáš Masaryk a Ukrajinci. Archiválie* (L'viv: Tsentr Ievropy, 2010).

Torke, Hans-Joachim and John-Paul Himka, eds, *German-Ukrainian Relations in Historical Perspective* (Edmonton: Canadian Institute of Ukrainian Studies Press, 1994).

Torzecki, Ryszard, *Polacy i Ukraińcy. Sprawa ukraińska w czasie II wojny światowej na terenie II Rzeczypospolitej* (Warszawa: Wydawnictwo Naukowe PWN, 1993).

Ts'olko, Roman, 'Heneral Pavlo Shandruk v Dyvizii', *Visti kombatanta*, 4 (2002), 65–71.

Tucker, Robert, *Stalin in Power. The Revolution from Above 1928–1941* (New York: W.W. Norton, 1990).

Turchenko, Fedir H., Petro P. Panchenko, and S.M. Tymchenko, eds, *Novitnia Istoriia Ukraïny. Chastyna druha 1939–2001. 11 klas* (Kyiv: Heneza, 2001).

Tys-Krokhmaliuk, Iurii, *Shchodennyk Natsional'noho heroia Selepka Lavochky* (Buenos Aires: YU. Serediak, 1954).

Ukrainian National Memory Institute <http://www.memory.gov.ua/> accessed 31 August 2009.

Ukraïns'ka Dyviziia 'Halychyna'. 14-ta strilets'ka dyviziia SS 'Halychyna'. 1-sha ukraïns'ka dyviziia Ukraïns'koï Natsional'noï Armiï, <http://www.galiciadivision.com/library/> accessed 17 January 2011.

'U L'vovi prezentuvaly posibnyk z istoriï Ukraïny dlia 5 klasiv', *20 khvylyn* (8 August 2012). <http://20minut.ua/Новини-Львова/news/У-Львові-презентували-посібник-з-історії-України-для-5-класів-10239321.html> accessed 15 November 2012.

'U L'vovi provely marsh vyshyvanok na chest' dyviziï "Halychyna"', *Vholos* (28 April 2012) < http://vgolos.com.ua/politic/news/46260.html> accessed 3 December 2012.

'U L'vovi z'iavylos' taksi SS "Halychyna"', *Ukraïns'ka Pravda* (12 October 2012) <http://life.pravda.com.ua/society/2011/10/12/87447/> accessed 3 December 2012.

Vehesh, Mykola, 'Velych i trahediia Karpats'koï Ukraïny', *Dzerkalo Tyzhnia*, 10 (485) (13–19 March 2004) <http://www.dt.ua/3000/3150/45817/> accessed 9 February 2010.

——, Karpats'ka Ukraïna. Dokumenty i fakty (Uzhhorod: Karpaty, 2004).

Veryha, Wasyl [Vasyl'], *Za Ridnyi Krai, za narid svii, abo Khto taki dyviziinyky?* (Kyiv: Vydavnytsvto imeni Oleny Telihy, 2006).

——, *Slidamy bat'kiv: narys istoriï 30 polku Dyviziï 'Halychyna'- 1-oï dyviziï Ukraïns'koï Natsional'noï Armiï* (L'viv: Bratstvo kol. Voiakiv 1-oï UD UNA, 2002).

——, *Pid sontsem Italiï: voiaky dyvizii 'Halychyna' – Pershoï ukraïns'koï dyvizii Ukraïns'koï natsional'noï armiï v brytiis'komu tabori polonenykh '5 TS' u Belliarii, Italiia, cherven'-zhovten' 1945* (Toronto: Vydavnytstvo Bratstva kolyshnikh voiakiv 1-oï UD UNA, 1984).

——, *Dorohamy Druhoï Svitovoï viiny: lehendy pro uchast' ukraïntsiv u zdushuvanni varshavs'koho povstannia 1944 r. ta pro Ukraïns'ku Dyviziiu 'Halychyna'* (Toronto: Nakladom Bratstva kol. voiakiv 1-oï UD UNA, 1981).

V'iatrovych, Volodymyr, *Stavlennia OUN do ievreïv. Formuvannia pozytsiï na tli katastrofy* (L'viv: Vydavnytstvo Ms., 2006).

Vidnians'kyi, S.V., 'Stan, problem ta perspektyvy doslidzhen' zi vsesvitn'oï istoriï v Ukraïni', *Ukraïns'kyi istorychnyi zhurnal*, 5 (2010), 166–79.

Virnyi, Mykola, *Nasha Dolia* (Kyiv: Iaroslaviv Val, 2007).

Visvaldis, Lācis, *The Latvian Legion According to Independent Observers* (Riga: Jumava, 2006).

Wiesel, Elie, 'For Some Measure of Humanity', *Sh'ma, A Journal of Jewish Responsibility* 5 (1975), 314–16.

Wilson, Andrew, *Ukrainian Nationalism in the 1990s: A Minority Faith* (London: Cambridge University Press, 1997).

——, 'The Donbas between Ukraine and Russia: The Use of History in Political Disputes', *Journal of Contemporary History* 30 (1995), 265–89.

Wolowyna, Oleh, and Natalia Levchuk, *Holodomor Losses in Ukraine within the Context of the 1932–1933 Famine in the Soviet Union*. Paper presented at the Association for the Study of Nationalities, New York, 2011.

'Written Answers. Column WA36', *Parliament.uk*, 5 February 2003 <http://www.parliament.the-stationery-office.co.uk/pa/ld200203/ldhansrd/vo030205/text/30205w01.htm#column_WA36> accessed 18 November 2012.

Wyman, Mark, *DPs: Europe's Displaced Persons, 1945–1950* (Ithaca, NY: Cornell University Press, 1998).

Yekelchyk, Serhy, *Ukraine. Birth of a Modern Nation* (Oxford: Oxford University Press, 2007).

——, 'Stalinist Patriotism as Imperial Discourse: Reconciling the Ukrainian and Russian "Heroic Pasts", 1939–45', *Kritika: Explorations in Russian and Eurasian History* 3/1 (Winter 2002), 51–80.

Yones, Eliyahu, *Smoke in the Sand: the Jews of Lvov in the War Years 1939–1944* (Jerusalem: Gefen Publishing House, 2004).

Yurkevich, Myroslav, 'Galician Ukrainians in German Military Formations and in the German Administration', in Yuri Boshyk, Roman Waschuk, and Andriy Wynnyckyj, eds, *Ukraine during World War II: History and its Aftermath: a Symposium* (Edmonton: University of Alberta, Canadian Institute of Ukrainian Studies Press, 1986).

Zahachevs'kyi, Ievstakhii, *Spohady frontovyka. Odiseia siroho 'koliaboranta'* (Munich: Vydannia Bratstva kol. Voiakiv 1-oï Ukraïns'koï Dyvizii UNA, 1952).

Zaitsev, Oleksandr, 'Natsionalizm iak relihiia: pryklad Dmytra Dontsova'. A paper presented at a seminar: 'Khrystyians'kyi universalizm ta natsionalizm: Hreko-Katolyts'ka tserkva ta ukraïns'kyi natsionalistychnyi rukh', Ukraïns'kyi Katolyts'kyi Universytet, L'viv (27 May 2009) <http://www.ucu.edu.ua/ukr/current/library/article;4215/> accessed 18 May 2010.

Zimmerman, Joshua D., ed., *Contested Memories: Poles and Jews during the Holocaust and its Aftermath* (New Brunswick, NJ: Rutgers University Press, 2003).

Archival Documents

UK National Archives (NA)

(NA) CAB 128/5, Conclusions of a Meeting of the Cabinet held at 10 Downing Street, SW1, 6 June 1946.

(NA) CAB 120/691, Russia. Threat to Western Civilisation. Operation 'Unthinkable', 22 May 1945.

(NA) CAB/129/10, Repatriation of Soviet Citizens, 20 May 1946.

(NA) CAB/129/33, Revision of Geneva Conventions on War Victims, 10 March 1949.

(NA) FO 371/66712, Felix Wirth to Tom Driberg, 7 June 1947.

(NA) FO 371/66712, M.L. Hyams to R.H.S. Crossman, 19 June 1947.

(NA) HO/213/1518, A.A. Stark of the Foreign Office to Mrs Hughes of the Aliens Department at the Home Office, London, 14 June 1948.

(NA) HO/213/1518. Minute sheet by the Under-Secretary of State for Foreign Affairs,10 June 1948.

(NA) HO/213/1851, 'Shelter for Brutes' written by Ex-Nr 3,399 (Addington, Surrey), *Evening News* (4 June 1947).

(NA) HO/213/1851, '8,000 Ukrainians to work in Britain', *Manchester Guardian* (26 May 1947).

(NA) HO/213/1851, 'Fought For Nazis – Coming Here', *The People* (25 May 1947).

(NA) HO/213/1851, Screening Commission Report, 21 February 1947. Original reference LACAB/18/RSC/RIC.

(NA) LAB 8/98 Foreign Office proposals regarding Ukrainian Prisoners of War in Italy to be brought to the UK. Ukrainian Surrendered Enemy Personnel and their Dependants, 10 July 1947.

(NA) LFWP/EAW, Secretariat and Statistics memo to SO I Secretariat, Subject: Ukrainians – Recording by Nationality, 11 March 1947.
(NA) PDWP/58378, PW & DP Technical Instruction, Subject: Displaced Persons Formerly Living in the Ukraine, 15 March 1947.
(NA) PWDP/58636/G, PW & DP Division, Zonal Executive Offices, Subject: Ukrainians – PWDP Technical Instruction, March 1947.
(NA) PWDP/59808/23, G.B. Vaughan-Hughes to F.R.C. Bray, Zonal Executive Offices, 18 March 1947.
(NA)WO/321/13190, Association of Ukrainians in Great Britain to War Office, 19 July 1948.

Government of Canada Files

File B53802, Admission of 'Surrendered Enemy Personnel', Government of Canada Files. G.R.B. Panchuk, MBE to the Office of the High Commission for Canada, London, 7 August 1947.
File B53802, Admission of 'Surrendered Enemy Personnel', Government of Canada Files. Appendix C, British House of Commons. Oral Answers to Questions. Wednesday, 18 June 1947.
File B53802, Admission of 'Surrendered Enemy Personnel', Government of Canada Files. J. Rudachek to R.N. Munroe, District Superintendent, Immigration Branch, Department of Mines & Resources, Winnipeg, Manitoba, Canada, 13 August 1947.
File B53802, Admission of 'Surrendered Enemy Personnel', Government of Canada Files. Letter from Theodore Danyliw, Secretary General to Hon. L.B. Pearson, Secretary of State for External Affairs, Ottawa, Canada, 23 March 1950.
File B53802, Admission of 'Surrendered Enemy Personnel', Government of Canada Files. Deputy Minister L. Fortier to the Minister of Citizenship and Immigration Walter Harris in Ottawa, Canada, 23 March 1950.
File B53802, Admission of 'Surrendered Enemy Personnel', Government of Canada Files. G.R.B. Panchuk to the Minister of Justice and Attorney General of Canada, Ottawa, Ontario, 23 November 1948.
File B53802, Admission of 'Surrendered Enemy Personnel', Government of Canada Files. Memorandum for the Cabinet Committee on Immigration Policy. Admission of Ukrainians (Surrendered Enemy Personnel) from the United Kingdom, 28 October 1948.
File B53802, Admission of 'Surrendered Enemy Personnel', Government of Canada Files. Letter to the Associate Commissioner in Ottawa, 19 November 1948.

File B53802, Admission of 'Surrendered Enemy Personnel', Government of Canada Files. A. Zaharychuk, Acting Secretary of the Ukrainian Canadian Committee, Winnipeg, Manitoba, Canada, 19 November 1948.

File B53802, Admission of 'Surrendered Enemy Personnel', Government of Canada Files. Letter to the Associate Commissioner in Ottawa, 19 November 1948.

File B53802, Admission of 'Surrendered Enemy Personnel', Government of Canada Files. William M. Toresio, President of the Association of United Ukrainian Canadians, Toronto, Ontario, 1 March 1949.

File B53802, Admission of 'Surrendered Enemy Personnel', Government of Canada Files. M.L. Keenleyside, Deputy Minister to M.H. Werahef, Esq. of the Office of the High Commissioner for Canada, London, 1 February 1949.

File B53802, Admission of 'Surrendered Enemy Personnel', Government of Canada Files. L.D. Wilgress, High Commissioner for Canada in the UK to the Secretary of State for External Affairs, Canada, 5 September 1950. From the Foreign Office letter dated 4 September 1950.

File B53802, Admission of 'Surrendered Enemy Personnel', Government of Canada Files. Samuel Bronfman, National President of the Canadian Jewish Congress to Hon. Walter Harris, the Minister of Citizenship and Immigration, Ottawa, Ontario, 4 July 1950.

File B53802, Admission of 'Surrendered Enemy Personnel', Government of Canada Files. Walter Harris, the Minister of Citizenship and Immigration, Ottawa, Ontario to Samuel Bronfman, National President of the Canadian Jewish Congress, Montreal, 5 July 1950.

File B53802, Admission of 'Surrendered Enemy Personnel', Government of Canada Files. Directive No. 26. HQ Files: 500–1 B-53802. Ukrainians (Surrendered Enemy Personnel) in the United Kingdom, 25 September 1950.

File B53802, Tracy Phillips to the editor of *Manchester Guardian*, 12 June 1947, Public Archives, Canada.

Foreign Affairs and International Trade Canada.

Documents on Canadian External Relations. Volume 16–966. Chapter IX. Western Europe. Part 1. General. Section E. Immigration. Memorandum from Minister of Citizenship and Immigration to Cabinet. Cabinet Document No 174 50 (Ottawa), 23 June 1950. Administration of Order in Council P.C. 2856. <http://www.international.gc.ca/department/history-histoire/dcer/details-fr.asp?intRefid=7987> accessed 19 August 2010.

Department of Justice, Canada

Crimes Against Humanity and War Crimes Programme Annual Reports <http://canada.justice.gc.ca/warcrimes-crimesdeguerre/researchreports-rechercherapports-eng.asp> accessed 24 January 2013.

Security Service of Ukraine, Kyiv

'Zvynuvachennia proty "Nakhtihaliu" – istorychna pravda chy politychni tekhnolohiï', Press Release of the Security Service of Ukraine, 6 February 2008 <http://www.sbu.gov.ua/sbu/control/uk/publish/article;jsessionid=B3B1A88145007156 36ED445C2F8EC0A0?art_id=74369&cat_id=74549> accessed 12 August 2012.

Author's Private Archive

'Complaint to O.A. Vasylenko, L'viv regional attorney, from 1st Secretary of the L'viv Regional Committee of the Communist party of Ukraine and deputy head of the Anti-Fascist Committee of Ukraine, Oleksandr Kalyniuk'. *Skarha v poriadku st. 12 Zakonu Ukraïny 'Pro prokuraturu' 2012.*

'L'vivs'ka oblasna rada XV sesiia VI sklykannia. Rishennia No 423 vid 16 bereznia 2012 roku', L'viv.

Ivan Muzyczka to Olesya Khromeychuk, Rome, 16 August 2009, 11 September 2009, 2 November 2009.

Michael James Melnyk to Olesya Khromeychuk (electronic correspondence) 3 December 2012.

Interviews

Interviewee S., 26 December 2006 (Ternopil').

Interviewee B., 27 December 2006 (L'viv).

Interviewee B., 20 May 2007, 9 September 2007, 2 December 2007 and 15 November 2009 (London).

Interviewee K., 14 April 2010 (Toronto).
Interviewee Oleksandr Khokhulin, 11 May 2009 (L'viv).
Interviewee Oleksandr Kalyniuk, 11 May 2009 (L'viv).
Interviewee Yurii Mykhal'chyshyn, 12 May 2009 (L'viv).
Interviewee Vladyslav Verstiuk, 15 May 2009 (Kyiv).

Index

NATIONALISMS ACROSS THE GLOBE

Although in the 1980s the widely shared belief was that nationalism had become a spent force, the fragmentation of the studiously non-national Soviet Union, Yugoslavia and Czechoslovakia in the 1990s into a multitude of successor nation-states reaffirmed its continuing significance. Today all extant polities (with the exception of the Vatican) are construed as nation-states, and hence nationalism is the sole universally accepted criterion of statehood legitimization. Similarly, human groups wishing to be recognized as fully fledged participants in international relations must define themselves as nations. This concept of world politics underscores the need for open-ended, broad-ranging, novel and interdisciplinary research into nationalism and ethnicity. It promotes better understanding of the phenomena relating to social, political and economic life, both past and present.

This peer-reviewed series publishes monographs, conference proceedings and collections of articles. It attracts well-researched, often interdisciplinary, studies which open new approaches to nationalism and ethnicity or focus on interesting case studies. The language of the series is usually English, with authors/editors of proposed volumes responsible for meeting the Peter Lang standards of copy-editing. Book proposals for *Nationalisms Across the Globe* and queries should be emailed to either, or both, of the series editors:

Dr Tomasz Kamusella (University of St Andrews, Scotland, UK), tomek672@gmail.com

Dr Krzysztof Jaskułowski (University of Social Sciences and Humanities, Poland), krzysztofja@interia.pl

Vol. 1 Tomasz Kamusella and Krzysztof Jaskułowski (eds):
Nationalisms Today. 334 pages, 2009.

Vol. 2 Cezary Obracht-Prondzyński and Tomasz Wicherkiewicz (eds):
The Kashubs: Past and Present. 307 pages, 2011.

Vol. 3 Sabelo J. Ndlovu-Gatsheni and James Muzondidya (eds):
Redemptive or Grotesque Nationalism? Rethinking Contemporary Politics in Zimbabwe. 446 pages, 2011.

Vol. 4 Blessing-Miles Tendi:
Making History in Mugabe's Zimbabwe. Politics, Intellectuals and the Media. 304 pages, 2010.

Vol. 5 Pavlos I. Koktsidis:
Strategic Rebellion. Ethnic Conflict in FYR Macedonia and the Balkans. 279 pages, 2012.

Vol. 6 Janusz Sawczuk:
Turbulentes 1989. Genese der deutschen Einheit. 327 pages, 2011.

Vol. 7 Chris Kostov:
Contested Ethnic Identity. The Case of Macedonian Immigrants in Toronto, 1900–1996. 330 pages, 2010.

Vol. 8 Alexander Maxwell (ed.):
The East–West Discourse. Symbolic Geography and its Consequences. 237 pages, 2011.

Vol. 9 Agnieszka Bielewska:
Changing Polish Identities. Post-War and Post-Accession Polish Migrants in Manchester. 208 pages, 2012.

Vol. 10 Anders E. B. Blomqvist, Constantin Iordachi and Balázs Trencsényi (eds):
Hungary and Romania Beyond National Narratives. Comparisons and Entanglements. 855 pages, 2013.

Vol. 11 Olesya Khromeychuk:
'Undetermined' Ukrainians. Post-War Narratives of the Waffen SS 'Galicia' Division. 217 pages. 2013.

Vol. 12 Michael Leach, James Scambary, Matthew Clarke, Simon Feeny and Heather Wallace:
Attitudes to National Identity in Melanesia and Timor-Leste. A Survey of Future Leaders in Papua New Guinea, Solomon Islands, Vanuatu and Timor-Leste. 232 pages. 2013.